India in a globalized world

Manchester University Press

India in a globalized world

Sagarika Dutt

Manchester University Press

Copyright © Sagarika Dutt 2006

The right of Sagarika Dutt to be identified as the author of this work has been asserted by her in accordance with the Copyright, Designs and Patents Act 1988.

Published by Manchester University Press
Altrincham Street, Manchester M1 7JA, UK
www.manchesteruniversitypress.co.uk

British Library Cataloguing-in-Publication Data is available

Library of Congress Cataloging-in-Publication Data is available

ISBN 978 0 7190 6901 7 paperback

First published by Manchester University Press in hardback 2006

This paperback edition first published 2014

The publisher has no responsibility for the persistence or accuracy of URLs for any external or third-party internet websites referred to in this book, and does not guarantee that any content on such websites is, or will remain, accurate or appropriate.

Printed by Lightning Source

Contents

	List of tables	*page* vi
	Preface	vii
	List of abbreviations	viii
	List of translations	xi
	Introduction: globalization theory and India	1
1	A brief history of India up to independence (1947)	16
2	The democratization of Indian politics	42
3	Identities and the Indian state	70
4	Economic development: from import-substitution industrialization to economic liberalization	98
5	India in the global (political) economy	124
6	Alternative approaches to 'development'	156
7	A nation on the move: the Indian diaspora	176
8	Indian foreign policy and global politics	194
	Conclusion: beyond globalization	215
	Index	220

List of tables and boxes

Tables

2.1	Indian prime ministers, 1947–	*page* 63
4.1	Selected health indicators	102
4.2	Sectors attracting the highest FDI approvals with inflows (January 1991–March 2004)	113
4.3	Shares of top five states attracting FDI approvals (January 1991–March 2004)	119
5.1	India's major trading partners, 2000–04	151

Boxes

2.1	Preamble to the constitution of India	48
6.1	The Bhopal Declaration	167

Preface

The idea of writing a book on India in a globalized world was conceived several years ago partly as a result of my personal interest in India and the process of economic liberalization that was taking place there, but also because of the enthusiasm of colleagues and students. India is a vast country and even though I am Indian and have lived, studied and worked in different parts of India, writing this book was a challenge.

My transnational experiences have shaped my perspective as has my academic background. My understanding of economic development and democracy in the Indian context has deepend over the years and the experience of living in other countries and my academic training have made me more critical. The primary sources used to write this book include the *Constitution of India, Economic Survey* published annually by the Indian government, statistics produced by the Central Statistical Organisation, the *Census of India 2001*, the *World Development Reports* published by the World Bank and *Human Development Reports* published by the United Nations Development Programme. A wide range of secondary sources has also been used, which has helped me to draw on research done by other scholars.

Each chapter has been written as a discrete unit and the reader can go straight to the topic that he/she is interested in. However, there are obvious links between all the chapters and they all contribute to the central arguments about how India has been affected by and has responded to globalization.

List of abbreviations

ABCDs	American-born confused *desis*
AGP	Asom Gana Parishad
AIADMK	All-India Anna-Dravida Munnetra Kazhagam
AICC	All-India Congress Committee
APEC	Asia-Pacific Economic Co-operation
ASEAN	Association of Southeast Asian Nations
ASEM	Asia-Europe Meeting
Assocham	Associated Chamber of Commerce and Industry
BHEL	Bharat Heavy Electricals Limited
BJD	Biju Janata Dal
BJP	Bharatiya Janata Party
BPO	business processing outsourcing
BSP	Bahujan Samaj Party
CENTO	Central Treaty Organization
CPI	Communist Party of India
CPI/M	Communist Party of India (Marxist)
DFID	Department for International Development
DMK	Dravida Munnetra Kazhagam
FDI	foreign direct investment
FERA	Foreign Exchange Regulation Act
FICCI	Federation of Indian Chambers of Commerce and Industry
FII	foreign institutional investors
GATT	General Agreement on Tariffs and Trade
GDP	gross domestic product
GNI	gross national income
GNP	gross national product
HDI	Human Development Index
HVP	Haryana Vikas Party
IAEA	International Atomic Energy Agency

IMF	International Monetary Fund
IMO	International Maritime Organization
IOC	Indian Oil Corporation
IR	International Relations
ISKCON	International Society for Krishna Consciousness
ITU	International Telecommunications Union
IVC	Indus Valley Civilization
MCWAS	Multicultural Women's Association of Slough
MDMK	Marumalarchi Dravida Munnetra Kazhagam
MNC	multinational corporation
MRTP	Monopolies and Restrictive Trade Practices Act
NAM	nonaligned movement
NCAER	National Council of Applied Economic Research
NCP	Nationalist Congress Party
NDA	National Democratic Alliance
NDTV	New Delhi Television
NGOs	non-governmental organizations
NHDR	National Human Development Report
NIC	National Integration Council
NRIs	non-resident Indians
NSSP	Next Steps in Strategic Partnership
OBCs	'other backward classes'
OECD	Organization for Economic Co-operation and Development
OFBJP	Overseas Friends of the Bharatiya Janata Party
ONGC	Oil and Natural Gas Corporation
PIO	person of Indian origin
PMK	Pattali Makkal Katchi
PSEs	public-sector enterprises
Rs	rupees
RCP	Revolutionary Communist Party of India
RHLCID	Report of the High Level Committee on the Indian Diaspora
RJD	Rashtriya Janata Dal
RSP	Revolutionary Socialist Party
SAARC	South Asian Association for Regional Co-operation
SAFTA	South Asian Free Trade Agreement
SAIL	Steel Authority of India Ltd
SCs	Scheduled Castes
SEBI	Securities and Exchange Board of India
SEATO	South East Asian Treaty Organization
SMEs	small and medium enterprises
SP	Samajwadi Party
STs	Scheduled Tribes
TMC	Tamil Maanila Congress

TRIMS	trade-related investment measures
TRIPS	trade-related intellectual property rights
UF	United Front
ULFA	United Liberation Front of Assom
UN	United Nations
UNCTAD	United Nations Conference on Trade and Development
UNDP	United Nations Development Programme
UNEP	United Nations Environment Programme
UNESCO	United Nations Educational, Scientific and Cultural Organization
UPA	United Progressive Alliance
UPU	Universal Postal Union
VHP	Vishwa Hindu Parishad
WEF	World Economic Forum
WTO	World Trade Organization

IMF	International Monetary Fund
IMO	International Maritime Organization
IOC	Indian Oil Corporation
IR	International Relations
ISKCON	International Society for Krishna Consciousness
ITU	International Telecommunications Union
IVC	Indus Valley Civilization
MCWAS	Multicultural Women's Association of Slough
MDMK	Marumalarchi Dravida Munnetra Kazhagam
MNC	multinational corporation
MRTP	Monopolies and Restrictive Trade Practices Act
NAM	nonaligned movement
NCAER	National Council of Applied Economic Research
NCP	Nationalist Congress Party
NDA	National Democratic Alliance
NDTV	New Delhi Television
NGOs	non-governmental organizations
NHDR	National Human Development Report
NIC	National Integration Council
NRIs	non-resident Indians
NSSP	Next Steps in Strategic Partnership
OBCs	'other backward classes'
OECD	Organization for Economic Co-operation and Development
OFBJP	Overseas Friends of the Bharatiya Janata Party
ONGC	Oil and Natural Gas Corporation
PIO	person of Indian origin
PMK	Pattali Makkal Katchi
PSEs	public-sector enterprises
Rs	rupees
RCP	Revolutionary Communist Party of India
RHLCID	Report of the High Level Committee on the Indian Diaspora
RJD	Rashtriya Janata Dal
RSP	Revolutionary Socialist Party
SAARC	South Asian Association for Regional Co-operation
SAFTA	South Asian Free Trade Agreement
SAIL	Steel Authority of India Ltd
SCs	Scheduled Castes
SEBI	Securities and Exchange Board of India
SEATO	South East Asian Treaty Organization
SMEs	small and medium enterprises
SP	Samajwadi Party
STs	Scheduled Tribes
TMC	Tamil Maanila Congress

TRIMS	trade-related investment measures
TRIPS	trade-related intellectual property rights
UF	United Front
ULFA	United Liberation Front of Assom
UN	United Nations
UNCTAD	United Nations Conference on Trade and Development
UNDP	United Nations Development Programme
UNEP	United Nations Environment Programme
UNESCO	United Nations Educational, Scientific and Cultural Organization
UPA	United Progressive Alliance
UPU	Universal Postal Union
VHP	Vishwa Hindu Parishad
WEF	World Economic Forum
WTO	World Trade Organization

List of translations

Adi Granth	the 'first book'; the Sikh scriptures
Adivasi	'original inhabitants', tribal groups, aboriginals
ahimsa	non-violence
andolan	movement
Arthashastra	'Science of Material Gain': written around 250 AD, dealing with the nature, politics and economy of the ancient Indian state
Bhagavadgita	religious and philosophical Sanskrit poem, dating from around 300 BC and forming an episode in the sixth book of the Mahabharata; it is one of the two great Hindu epics, and the supreme religious work of Hinduism
bhakti	devotion to God
Bharata	the foremost Aryan tribe
bharatnatyam	classical Indian dance form of south India
boxwallahs	urban salaried employees
Brahmins	the first, highest caste, the priests
buniya	a trading class
crore	10 million units, e.g of money/people
Dalit	the lowest castes/untouchables
dasas	slaves
devadasi	temple dancer-prostitute
dharma	religion, also duty, responsibility and law
dharma chakra	'wheel of the law'
dhimmis	protected peoples
dhoti-kurta	traditional Indian dress for men
dirigisme	economic control by the state
diwan	minister of revenue
diwani	revenue

List of translations

Doordarshan	Indian television channel
'garibi hatao'	'remove poverty'
Harijans	literally 'god's people'; name given to untouchables by Gandhi
homa	oblation; often of burnt ghee
jajmani	social system in which landlords look after locals in return for their services
Jana gana mana	the Indian national anthem
janambhoomi	birthplace
janapads	district, also an ancient Hindu popular assembly
jatis	subcastes
jihad	holy war
jiva	soul
jizya	a tax imposed on non-Muslims by Muslim rulers
kachcha	short cotton underwear (one of the Sikh five Ks)
kangha	comb (one of the Sikh five Ks)
kar sevaks	Hindu holy workers
kara	steel bracelet (one of the Sikh 5 Ks)
Kautilya	prime minister of Chandragupta Maurya and author of the *Arthashastra*
kes	long hair (one of the Sikh five Ks)
khadi	cloth woven by hand using handspun yarn
khalsa	pure
kirpan	sword (one of the Sikh five Ks)
Kshatriyas	the second caste, the warriors
lakh	100,000 units, e.g. of money/population
Lok Sabha	the lower house of the Indian parliament
lok sevak	servant of the people
Maharajadhiraja	Great King of Kings
malik	noble
mandala	circle
mansabdars	office holders ranked on the number of cavalry they maintained
maquiladoras	export processing zones
moksha	salvation, nirvana, freedom from the cycle of life and death
muhtasibs	censors of public morals
neem	the leaves and bitter bark of the Azadirachta Indica tree, used medicinally
nishka	an early measure of value, and later a gold coin
pahul	Sikh baptism ceremony
panchayat	village council

Panchsheel	five principles incorporated into a treaty between India and China over Tibet in 1954
paura	ancient Hindu popular assembly
pravasis	overseas Indians
puranas	old Hindu stories
raja	king
Rajput	Hindu warrior prince of Rajasthan
Rajya Sabha	the upper house of the Indian parliament
Rath Yatra	Hindu religious procession; a rath is a temple on wheels
Rig Veda	the earliest of the four Vedas, or sacred books of the Indo-Aryans, and the oldest scripture in the world
sangam	academy or college
sansad	parliament
Satavahana	an ancient Indian dynasty
satyagraha	a form of spiritual passive resistance (*satya* – truth; *agraha* – to hold)
shreni	artisan and merchant guilds
Shudras	the fourth caste, the labourers
Sri Guru Granth Sahib	Sikh sacred text
stupa	Buddhist monument
swadeshi	indigenous, e.g. goods made in India
swarajya	self-government
Vaishyas	the third caste, the commons, traders
varna	colour
varnashram	the Hindu caste system
vasudhaiva kutumbkum	the fundamental unity of all humanity
Veda/vedic	derived from *vid*, the holy books of the Aryans
vid	to know
videshi	foreign
zamindar	a landowner paying land tax

Introduction

In May 2004 the Indian National Congress won the fourteenth general elections in India. The party's fortunes had been in decline for many years and its return to power had not been predicted. It left the Bharatiya Janata Party (BJP) and its supporters crestfallen but they had to accept the nation's verdict. More than a decade earlier the leaders of the Indian National Congress, or the Congress (I) as it was then known,[1] had introduced economic reforms in India and thereby started the process of economic liberalization. Former prime minister P. V. Narasimha Rao and former finance minister Manmohan Singh had played a key role in this process. Following the 2004 election, Manmohan Singh became prime minister of India and at the time of writing it is his government's responsibility to take the process of economic liberalization forward. The Congress declared in its 2004 election manifesto that it is the only party 'whose philosophy on governance is rooted in combining sustainable economic growth with social justice, and marrying economic liberalism to social liberalism' (Indian National Congress, 2004). India is emerging as an important player in the global economy. However, what is equally important is that India is beginning to think 'global', and this thinking is not just limited to the economic realm but also extends to the political, social and cultural realms. Moreover, it is not just the government but also a large section of the citizenry that is enthusiastically embracing the new thinking, although left-wing parties and their supporters have their reservations about foreign investment.

We live in a globalized world. The phenomenon is acknowledged not only by the Indian government but also by the Indian people. Their core experience of globalization is double-edged; it leads to new opportunities but also new problems. At an India-EU business summit held in Lisbon on 27 June 2000, the former prime minister, Vajpayee, asserted

> We perceive globalization as an inevitable process that has both opportunities and risks.
> Opportunities to improve the competitive and productive efficiency of our system

by increasingly integrating our economy with global changes. And risks because given the vulnerability of most emerging economies, there can be serious human, cultural and social consequences if countries are not watchful.

We will pursue globalization in a manner that is calibrated. We will seek changes and sequence them in India's long-term interest … we will at all times ensure that the benefit accrues to the common man. (Vajpayee, 2000)

However, globalization is a contested concept. Held and McGrew (2000: 3) write that there is 'no single universally agreed definition of globalization. As with all core concepts in the social sciences its precise meaning remains contested.' For the purposes of this book, however, it is necessary to have a clear idea of the kind of phenomenon we are considering. Baylis and Smith (1997: 7) describe globalization as 'the process of increasing interconnectedness between societies'. In other words, we do not live in water-tight compartments; events taking place anywhere in the world often have an impact in other parts of the world. These events may be political, economic or social, and include wars and revolutions, recessions, financial crises and even environmental disasters or the birth of social movements. Held et al. (1999) argue that a satisfactory definition of globalization must also take into account its spatio-temporal dimensions. They highlight the growing extensity (stretching) and intensity of global interconnectedness, interactions and processes. There also is an increasing velocity of the global diffusion of ideas, goods, information, capital and people, partly due to the enmeshment of the local and the global. The clear implication of all this is that the boundaries between domestic affairs and global affairs are blurring. Furthermore, these connections across frontiers are not random but are regularized and patterns of interaction are discernable. Waters (1995: 3) defines globalization as 'a social process in which the constraints of geography on social and cultural arrangements recede and in which people become increasingly aware that they are receding'. Geography, territorial borders and geographical distance are becoming meaningless and increasingly irrelevant to the formation of social relations and networks.

But why does the growing irrelevance of territorial borders and geographical distance to social processes matter? The reason is that although the world remains divided into sovereign, territorial states, globalization does not respect the time-honoured principle of the sovereignty of the nation-state. Michael Mann (1997: 473–4) writes that there are four dimensions to the undermining of the nation-state. First, capitalism has become 'global, transnational, post-industrial, informational, consumerist, neoliberal and restructured', and undermined the state's control over macroeconomics, the welfare state and its citizens' sense of collective identity. Second, new global threats have emerged that the state cannot handle alone, such as global warming. Third, 'identity politics and new social movements, using new technology, increase the salience of diverse local and transnational identities at the expense of both national identities and those broad class identities which were traditionally handled by the nation-state'.

Global issues, new social movements and identity politics, it may be argued, are leading to the emergence of a new transnational 'civil society'. The evidence to support this argument is provided by social movements for peace, human rights, protection of the environment and social reform which are becoming truly global. Finally, post-nuclearism undermines state sovereignty and 'hard geopolitics', since war between nuclear powers is no longer an option and deterrence theory is based on the irrationality of a nuclear war. War begat the state but the power of the state in the early twenty-first century no longer depends on success in territorial wars alone. Armstrong (1998) too identifies seven factors that have contributed to the weakening of the authority of the state: global issues, (non-state) actors, markets, communication, culture, legitimacy and postmodernity. On the other hand, Anthony Giddens (1990: 67) argues that 'no state, however powerful, held as much sovereign control in practice as was enshrined in legal principle'. The history of the past two centuries is, therefore, not one of the progressive erosion of the sovereignty of the nation-state.

This book looks at India in the context of a globalized world. Chapter 1 deals with the history of the Indian civilization. It explores the roots of Indian identity and highlights processes such as foreign invasions, foreign trade, cultural imperialism, British colonial rule and the Indian national movement. Migration from the Indian subcontinent is discussed separately in Chapter 7. These processes have forged links between Indian and other societies. In the age of globalization these links are being emphasized by both the Indian government and the media as well as the Indian diaspora.

Chapter 2 examines the democratization of Indian politics. The process of constitutional development began in the nineteenth century and culminated in the drafting and adoption of a new constitution for independent India in 1949. The founding fathers wanted India to be a liberal democracy and drew on the constitutions of the United States of America, Britain, Canada, Australia and the Irish Republic. The constitution they adopted introduced a parliamentary system of government, universal adult suffrage, fundamental rights for all citizens and a Supreme Court to act as the guardian of the constitution. Most of these institutions have served India well for over half a century. However, centre-state relations continue to be an issue although access to foreign capital may signal the end of the dependence of the states on the centre but may also lead to greater indebtedness. Similarly greater integration with the global economy could lead to a more multicultural and cosmopolitan culture and a more egalitarian society. However, the revivalism of Hindu nationalism has not had a salutary effect on respect for human rights and secular values.

Chapter 3 discusses identity politics and the response of Indian governments to the demands of ethnic and linguistic groups. The federal framework enables the government to accommodate the demands of these groups for greater autonomy by conferring statehood on them. The States Reorganization Act of 1956 accepted the linguistic principle (that states should be formed on the basis of language). However, the problem of insurgency continues, often leading to state repression. Globalization has given an impetus to postmodern perspectives that focus on identity formation and question the basis of the state. In the Indian context it is not just ethnic difference but also economic problems and aspirations that have led to insurgency. Economic liberalization may solve or aggravate these problems.

India has a centrally planned economy. Chapter 4 examines the problems that have retarded economic development in India. It also discusses the priorities of the five-year plans. Fifty years of planning have achieved a great deal in India in terms of increasing industrial and agricultural production and reducing poverty. However, by the late 1980s it was clear that the policy of import substitution industrialization had outlived its usefulness. Moreover the 'license-permit' raj was hampering economic growth. International institutions such as the IMF and the World Bank were also putting pressure on the Indian government to introduce economic reforms. Thus the government cautiously began the process of economic liberalization in the early 1990s. Chapter 4 explains what this process has meant for India and highlights the controversies and debates to which it has given rise.

Chapter 5 examines the history of India's integration into the international/global economy. Foreign trade in pre-colonial times had increased the prosperity of many regions in India. The wealth of the Indian subcontinent had attracted European traders including the English East India Company to India's shores in the sixteenth, seventeenth and eighteenth centuries. However, British colonial rule in India did not give the Indians a voice in their country's economic development and foreign trade. The process of industrialization that was initiated benefited certain classes but its main objective was to increase export earnings. After India became independent the government had to determine the priorities of the new state. Restrictions were imposed on both foreign trade and foreign investment which were gradually reduced after the process of economic liberalization began in the 1990s. The chapter goes on to discuss emerging opportunities in the twenty-first century in the post-liberalization era.

Chapter 6 examines alternative approaches to development, especially Gandhian ideas. Gandhi put emphasis on rural development, self-sufficiency of villages and the empowerment of disadvantaged sections of Indian society whom he called Harijans (people of god). His ideas have inspired social reformers, social movements and political leaders and parties both in India and in other parts of the world.

Chapter 7 explains how migration from the Indian subcontinent has led to the formation of an Indian diaspora. There are large Indian communities in many different countries in Asia, Africa, North America, Europe and Australasia. Since the publication of the Report of the High Level Committee on the Indian Diaspora in 2002, the Indian government's policy regarding the Indian diaspora has become a lot clearer.

Chapter 8 examines the goals of India's foreign policy since independence. Jawaharlal Nehru, India's first prime minister, had a strong influence on India's foreign policy in the early years. Under his guidance India became a founder member of the nonaligned movement after the cold war started. However, since the late 1990s Indian foreign policy has been more focused on economic issues. The need to promote trade and investment is leading to more bilateral agreements between India and several Asian countries as well as the United States of America, the United Kingdom and many other countries.

Perspectives on globalization

Globalization has impacted on our lives to the extent that we feel that the world is shrinking and that we live in a borderless world. Modern technology has contributed to this feeling of proximity to those with whom we communicate regardless of their location. In all developed countries the telephone, telegraph, air travel, television, fax, e-mail and the mobile phone have become an essential part of life. The communications and internet revolution is an important aspect of globalization. Access to modern communication networks is important for individuals, firms and non-governmental organizations (NGOs). In India, as well as in many other developing countries, the use of mobile phones and e-mail is increasing rapidly. Within two years of its introduction in 1996 the number of mobile phones in India had reached a million and had become 'an integral part of the urban landscape' (*India Today*, 11 May 1998). However, the access to modern technology is determined by the quality of infrastructure in any society. Infrastructures (physical, regulative/legal, symbolic) may facilitate or constrain global interaction by having an impact on the extensity and intensity of global interconnectedness. This is because they mediate flows and connectivity: 'infrastructures influence the overall level of interaction capacity in every sector and thus the potential magnitude of global interconnectedness. Interaction capacity, understood as the potential scale of interaction defined by existing technical capabilities, is determined primarily, but not exclusively, by technological capacity and communications technology' (Held et al., 1999: 19). And that is what makes globalization a contemporary phenomenon. The capacity for interaction in the nineteenth century was considerably less than that of the contemporary era, in which satellites and the Internet facilitate instant and almost real-time global communication. But even in the nineteenth century there were differences between the Indians and the British. Infrastructural and technological innovations and advancements impacted on the growth of Britain's political power over its colonies. The Indian subcontinent had been prosperous in ancient and medieval times but struggled to compete with the British who had much greater capacity for global interaction. Investment in infrastructure can have important consequences for the development and evolution of global interaction capacity (Held et al., 1999). In contemporary times, this is an important factor that is affecting India's economic prospects, something that has been accepted by Indian governments for whom globalization is mainly about economic liberalization.

The economic dimension of globalization is one of the most important dimensions of this phenomenon. It relates to all aspects of global production, consumption, and exchange activities undertaken within national economies and the world market (Simai, 1997). Economic growth has become more interdependent internationally as a result of the growth of world trade and investment and the increasing role and transformation of capital and money markets. Cross-border investment is the engine promoting the global market. Global foreign direct investment inflows in 2004 were estimated to have risen by 6 per cent to US$612 billion, from $580 billion in 2003 (UNCTAD, 2005). Developing countries attracted $255 billion in 2004 compared with $173 billion in 2003. In addition to states, multinational corporations (MNCs) are important actors in the global economy. The value of the global sales of MNCs like Ford and IBM are greater than the gross national product (GNP) of many countries. The expansion of MNCs has been facilitated by transnational banks which also play an important role in maintaining global economic stability. The International Monetary Fund (IMF) defines globalization as 'the increasingly close integration of markets both for goods and services, and for capital' (IMF, cited in Kegley and Wittkopf, 1999: 207).

However, globalization is much more than a by-product of capitalism or technological advancements. It is also not synonymous with western modernity. Rather, globalization is a product of multiple forces, including economic, political and technological imperatives, as well as historical factors such as colonialism, the creation of the ancient silk route or the collapse of state socialism. It does not foster any fixed or given pattern of historical development and may impact societies in different ways simultaneously giving rise to co-operation as well as conflict, integration as well as fragmentation, exclusion and inclusion, convergence and divergence, order and disorder. Although this book does not promote binary divisions, some of these themes will be found in both the domestic and international politics of India, through the ages.

So when did globalization start? There are different views on this. Some writers argue that globalization began centuries ago and note the voyages of explorers and the first circumnavigation of the earth. Trade is another activity associated with globalization as are migration and colonization, and although these are modern day issues they started many centuries ago. Our discussion of India's history will therefore include these activities.

Another view is that globalization started in the nineteenth century with the setting up of regulatory bodies such as the International Telecommunications Union (ITU, 1865) and the Universal Postal Union (UPU, 1878). Or did it begin in the twentieth century? Two world wars, the establishment of universal intergovernmental organizations (League of Nations, United Nations (UN)) and the advent of nuclear weapons are some twentieth century developments that have led to thinking in terms of the global. In the late 1960s, Marshall McLuhan's idea of a 'global village' provided more food for thought. But the World Wide Web is proof of the virtual world we live in and since the 1990s it has completely revolutionized the way we live.

At the theoretical level there are many concepts related to globalization: interdependence/complex interdependence; transnationalism; world society; the cobweb model. There are, however, differences between the international and the global. International refers to cross-border relations and exchanges over distance, in other words, interterritorial relations. This approach assumes that the world is divided into territorial states. Clark (1998) provides an interesting discussion of globalization and the theory of international relations (IR). However, he is more interested in how the state shapes and is itself shaped by globalization rather than in whether globalization is making the state redundant. Global refers to transborder relations and exchanges without distance or supraterritorial relations. Baylis and Smith (1997: 15) put the difference in a nutshell: 'the international realm is a patchwork of bordered countries, while the global sphere is a web of transborder networks' and that is what the cobweb model of transnational relations depicts (Burton, 1972).

Some IR scholars such as Scholte do not equate globalization with internationalization, liberalization, universalization or westernization (Scholte, 2000). Rather, internationalization refers to the development of interterritorial relations and cross-border exchanges or activities; liberalization refers to the removal of barriers and government controls, especially in the economic sphere; universalization refers to the universalization of values and norms such as the Universal Declaration of Human Rights, common interests or the convergence of interests (in international relations liberals/idealists assumed that there was a harmony of interests in the world that would lead to world peace), and even homogenization or the emergence of a global culture; westernization refers to Europeanization/Americanization, cultural imperialism and colonization. Held and McGrew (2000: 4) too argue that globalization 'should not be read as prefiguring the emergence of a harmonious world society or as a universal process of global integration in which there is a growing convergence of cultures and civilizations. For not only does the awareness of growing interconnectedness create new animosities and conflicts, it can fuel reactionary politics and deep-seated xenophobia.' Similar views are expressed by Stuart Hall, who points out that there is often resistance to globalization (Open University video, *A Global Culture*).

Many people in the world have not been significantly affected by globalization and have not benefited from it, but more importantly there are people and communities that have been adversely affected by it such as women working in *maquiladoras,* or export processing zones, who are often exploited by their employers (Peterson and Runyan, 1993). It may be argued that only those who have capital, skills (including access to educational opportunities and training) and access to technology) can take advantage of the opportunities that globalization offers them (Pearson, 2000). Therefore, it has the potential to widen the gap between the haves and have-nots and should not be seen as a universal process experienced uniformly across the entire planet. Moreover, where globalization threatens communities, their traditional values or livelihoods, there is resistance to it.

For Scholte (2000), globalization is the rise of supraterritoriality, a deterritorialization of social life, which leads to issues of global governance. Governance has been defined by the Commission on Global Governance (1995: 2) as the sum of the many ways that individuals and institutions, public and private, manage their common affairs. Global governance may be defined as the identification and management of global issues (Groom and Powell, 1994: 81). Global issues include the environment, disease (e.g. HIV/Aids), terrorism and global finance. Supraterritorial institutions such as the World Trade Organization (WTO), IMF, UN and a host of specialized agencies such as the ITU, UPU, the International Maritime Organization (IMO) and the International Atomic Energy Agency (IAEA) have been set up to perform regulatory functions. Of course, one should not confuse global governance with the UN system or the WTO. Global governance involves a range of actors operating at different levels, the global, international, regional, national and local. Local agendas are linked to global agendas, for example, the Rio Summit (1992) adopted Agenda 21 that stresses the importance of local authorities as the level of governance closest to the people. This distinction is extremely significant for developing countries even if it is only conceptual. However, as Higgott points out, the emergence of an agenda for global governance should not simply be a response to the process of economic liberalization but must also take into account global ethics (Higgott, 2000).

Globalization may also be seen as something sinister. The reason is 'the discourse of globalization is understood as a primarily ideological construction; a convenient myth which, in part, helps justify and legitimize the neoliberal global project, that is, the creation of a global free market and the consolidation of Anglo-American capitalism within the world's major economic regions' (Held and McGrew, 2000: 5). Globalization became an issue 'just at that juncture when the neoliberal project – the Washington consensus of deregulation, privatization, structural adjustment programmes (SAPs) and limited government – consolidated its hold within key Western capitals and global institutions such as the IMF' (Held and McGrew, 2000: 5). It is this aspect of a perspective on globalization that the Indian government is concerned about. Arun (2002), an Indian academic, writes: 'globalization has led to polarization among and within nations, among economic entities and among individuals.' According to Arun, there is a distinct pattern in this polarization. Rich countries have gained much more than poor countries. Among the developing countries, 'the more developed ones have gained over the least developed ones. Among the entities, big business has gained over small business, and transnational companies have squeezed out the smaller

producers and entrepreneurs'. Globalization often creates winners and losers, and a Marxist or structuralist (in IR) perspective would consider it to be a new mode of western imperialism dominated by the needs and requirements of finance capital within the world's major capitalist states.

However, those who argue that globalization is 'real' rather than a convenient myth point out that we should think in terms of a global rather than an international economy. The activities of MNCs and the growth of global financial markets are defining features of the global economy together with interdependence between states as well as transnationalism. Global communications, as mentioned above, is another aspect of globalization. Giddens (1990: 77) comments that 'mechanized technologies of communication have dramatically influenced all aspects of globalization since the first introduction of mechanical printing into Europe. They form an essential element of the reflexivity of modernity and of the discontinuities which have torn the modern away from the traditional'. He argues that modernity is inherently globalizing.

Giddens also recognizes that one of the dimensions of globalization concerns industrial development. It has led to a global division of labour and different levels of industrial development. He argues that 'modern industry is intrinsically based on divisions of labour, not only on the level of job tasks but on that of regional specialization in terms of type of industry, skills, and the production of raw materials' (Giddens, 1990: 76). It has also led to global interdependence, global sourcing and relocation of industries (and in recent years even services), including the deindustrialization of some regions in the developed countries and the emergence of the 'newly industrializing countries' in the Third World. India and many other developing countries are aware of this and often compete for foreign direct investment. However, clearly industrialization does not lead to homogenization or the emergence of a global culture and neither do the media or global cultural products. Global products often have to be adapted to local markets, for example, McDonald's burgers in India cannot contain beef as Hindus are forbidden to eat it. Appadurai argues that globalization produces indigenization and not homogenization. He writes that 'as forces from various metropolises are brought into new societies, they tend to become indigenized in one or another way: this is true of music and housing styles as much as it is true of science and terrorism, spectacles and constitutions'(Appadurai, 1990). Moreover, smaller communities fear cultural absorption by larger polities, especially those that are nearby, rather than Americanization. Stuart Hall argues that globalization leads to hybridization and creolization by moving culture around the world and bringing people and ideas into contact with one another. Something new is created through this process (Open University video, *A Global Culture*).

What industrialization does lead to are 'threats', such as global warming, that nation-states are not able to deal with on their own. Countries such as India and China are not prepared to let environmental concerns slow down their economic growth by voluntarily agreeing to reduce CO^2 emissions, although they have expressed an interest in the transfer of 'clean' technologies. Similarly, urbanization is taking place rapidly in developing countries and giving rise to environmental problems (Dutt, 2000). At the launch of a new atlas called *One Planet Many People* in Geneva on 3 June 2005, Klaus Toepfer, the chief of the United Nations Environment Programme (UNEP), warned that urban dwellers and lifestyles are mainly responsible for global warming (UN Wire, 6 June 2005). The emergence of global issues is therefore an important aspect, even consequence, of globalization.

With regard to culture, Held and McGrew write that the movement of cultures is linked with the movement of people across regions and continents and has been going on for centuries. The history of India not only bears testimony to their argument but also proves that cultural changes are not a special feature of globalization or even the modern age. The rich cultural heritage and cultural diversity of India are not considered to be products of modern-day globalization, primarily driven by western agencies and entrepreneurs and more often than not associated with the modern age. Indian culture may, however, be packaged in modern times for consumers by western agents or contribute to the emergence of hybrid cultures. For example, the combination of disco and Indian music has produced Bhangra beat. However, information about other cultures is also flooding into India. Globalists argue that at both the domestic and the international level, cultures, societies and economies are becoming more information dense and it is becoming increasingly difficult for people to live in any place culturally isolated from the wider world (Held and McGrew, 2000). In other words, even less developed regions are exposed to external influences.

But that does not mean that 'national' cultures are in terminal decline. Agents of cultural globalization – Coca-Cola, McDonald's, Microsoft and so on – are primarily interested in business, commerce and profits and not in creating alternative centres of political identity and legitimacy. On the whole, 'the world remains a place of competing cultures, all investing in their own symbolic resources, and seeking to enlarge their spheres of influence' (Held and McGrew, 2000: 191). Like the territorial states, national cultures too are resilient. In fact, the resilience of national cultures partly explains why territorial states persist and continue to play such an important role in determining the shape of international order. Anthony D. Smith strongly argues that the idea of a 'global culture' is a practical impossibility, except in interplanetary terms. Thinking in terms of humanity may help us to promote certain norms and values such as human rights but thinking in terms of the human species does not help us to conceive of a global culture as the men and women who inhabit this planet have diverse lifestyles and beliefs (Smith, 1990; 1991).

The identification of global issues has already been noted above and they are matched by transnational social and political movements that are diverse and include human rights and environmental movements. Some of these movements are opposed to globalization. The demonstrations in Seattle in 1999 and in many other cities of the world where meetings of the WTO, IMF, World Bank or World Economic Forum (WEF) were taking place show that globalization is by no means a phenomenon that is accepted by all. The views of the Indian government and certain groups in India show that although Indians have now accepted globalization as inevitable and perhaps beneficial, they are also cautious and do not endorse it unreservedly. However, social movements also highlight the issue of relations between the state and civil society and related themes that are often global. It is an issue that will also be explored in this book.

On the other hand, globalization is often considered to be more relevant to the developed world, as modern technology is expensive and has not reached the remoter areas of the developing world, nor do the people living there have the knowledge and skills required to use it. Moreover, MNCs have their headquarters in developed countries which have a lion's share of world trade and write the rules. Even regulatory bodies such as the WTO are controlled by them. Transnational economic relations are concentrated in the developed world and are more 'trilateral' than global. Europe, North America and East Asia are the world's three main capitalist centres. Over 85 per cent of world trade takes place among them, over 90 per cent of production in advanced sectors like electronics is dominated by them, plus the headquarters of all but a handful of the top 100 multinationals (including banks) are located in these areas (Kiely and Marfleet, 1998). This does not necessarily mean capitalism is not global. As most countries of the world are opening up their economies capitalism is replacing socialism and communism. However, capitalism is associated with cores and peripheries that are locked together in a global network of interaction. As suggested by world system theory it leads to wealth and poverty at the same time – wealth in the core areas and poverty in the periphery. According to this theory, the world capitalist economy has its origins in the sixteenth and seventeenth centuries and is integrated through economic connections and not by a political centre such as a nation-state. The modern world system consists of a core, a semi-periphery and a periphery, all defined in terms of their level of economic development and the kind of function they perform for the system as a whole, for example, exporting cheap agricultural products and raw materials to be processed and consumed in more economically developed areas. The physical, geographical and regional location of these areas changes over time. Nevertheless, as Dicken argues, capitalism retains a geo-economic order, dominated by the economies of the advanced nation-states (Dicken, 1998).

Since the advanced nation-states are mainly the western states, globalization may also be seen as westernization and even western imperialism, an important aspect of which is cultural imperialism. It may be perceived as a way of spreading western values and maintaining the dominance of the west; often it is associated with Americanization. However, globalization does not necessarily discriminate against non-white and non-western peoples. It creates winners and losers in both the developed and developing world and may lead to exploitation because of the capitalist methods that it employs. In other words it is just another name for capitalism. Although this may appear to be based on a narrow definition, economic globalization is closely associated with capitalism. Differentiating the different aspects of globalization is therefore important as it helps us to understand the forces that promote it. It is also important to realize that globalization has no normative content. For example, it may promote organized crime, while on the other hand, global interconnectedness may be used by social movements and non-governmental organizations to promote human rights, democratic norms and respect for the environment. Higgott writes that in the 1980s and 1990s globalization was understood to be a process of economic liberalization. By the end of the 1990s, it was recognized that globalization cannot be simply driven by the neoliberal economic agenda. He argues that 'even leading globalizers – that is, proponents of the continued liberalization of the global economic order occupying positions of influence in either the public or private domain – now concede that in its failure to deliver a more just global economic order, globalization may hold within it the seeds of its own demise' (Higgott, 2000: 131). Globalization has to be politically legitimized, democratized and socialized if the gains of the economic liberalization process are not to be lost to its major beneficiaries.

This book argues that India is much more than a state (created in 1947). It has a long history that has had a tremendous impact on the society, culture, politics and economy of this vast country and our perceptions of it. Yet various phases of globalization have forced changes on India that have not been endogenous. The superimposition of change on traditional Indian communities, ranging from modernization in the colonial age to economic liberalization in the late twentieth century, has led to anomalies in Indian society that are reflected in its politics. Democracy is not the dominance of the Congress Party, and industrialization does not eradicate poverty in the absence of economic and social reforms that tackle it from the grassroots.

Therefore it is necessary to consider how globalization has brought about change in India. It may be argued that, on the whole, globalization has promoted and not challenged modernity (as defined in the west). However, there have been some reactions to it in the form of religious revivalism: Islamic and Hindu fundamentalism, ecocentrism personified by the views of ecofeminists like Vandana Shiva, and postmodern perspectives that question the basis of political identity. Armstrong (1998: 465) writes that postmodernists assert that 'globalization is undermining the dominant "discourse" of modernity and the Enlightenment, a discourse that links positivist approach to knowledge … with the constitution of specific dichotomies … since the state, and the categories of identity and difference that it incorporates, are centrally involved in such dichotomies, the state also becomes problematical, if not meaningless'. It may be argued that, since the day India was created, although the goal of the revolutionaries had been achieved and the imperial order had been overthrown, India was under pressure to integrate into the international system and the global economy, to adopt the norms of the international system of states and maintain a facade of legitimacy.

The infrastructure inherited from the British enabled Indians to unify the country and introduce some reforms designed to bring about a more democratic society as well as economic growth. The role of the Congress Party as well as its ideology was fundamental to the construction of a modern nation-state. But with a decline in the dominance of the Congress Party since the mid-1990s and the rise of pluralism in Indian politics, more space has become available for other movements and Indian politics has finally come of age. Global interconnectedness as defined in this chapter has made it impossible for India and the Indians to isolate themselves from the rest of the world and neither do they want to, as certain sections of the society are keen to take advantage of the opportunities that globalization is offering them (business, employment, education, consumption, lifestyles) – interdependence, a key concept in western societies, is becoming increasingly important for the Indians.

Globalization is not only opening up economies but also creating greater awareness as social movements in India become linked to global movements and draw inspiration (and even resources) from them. And the flow of ideas is not in one direction only – just as Mahatma Gandhi's ideas had inspired nationalist movements in the early twentieth century and the civil rights movement in the United States, traditional Indian knowledge, cultural products as well as modern manufactured goods are becoming popular the world over. Indian migrants, companies/multinationals and the tourist industry are exporting India and Indian cultural products all the time (a good example is entrepreneur Karan Bilimoria and his product, Cobra beer; also Bollywood films and Indian cuisine). Unfortunately, however, because of the size of the country, its growing population and the extent of poverty in India and in South Asia, India is also contributing to the creation of global problems such as global warming, but equally importantly it needs to be involved in the politics of solving these problems. The Indian diaspora, although only numbering twenty million, as well as the millions of Indians who travel abroad to study and work as well as for leisure, take back ideas with them and erode the boundaries that previously existed between the Indian and the non-Indian, although globalization is also creating a transnational Indian community. A new India is emerging, one that does not want to be marginalized in the international system (India wants a permanent seat in the UN Security Council) or peripheralized in the global economy (India wants a larger share of world trade and is proactive in the negotiations of the WTO). With a population of more than 1 billion and 260 million living below the poverty line (NDTV, 31 December 2003) social and economic reforms are needed, although not necessarily of the neo-liberal kind. This book will explore all these issues in detail to ascertain the kind of India that is emerging in the twenty-first century.

Notes

1   The Congress Party was originally called the Indian National Congress when it was established in 1885. Under Indira Gandhi's leadership it was renamed Congress (I) and became closely associated with her as a political leader as well as with the Nehru-Gandhi dynasty. In recent years the party has reverted to the original name.

References

Appadurai, A., 1990, 'Disjuncture and difference in the global cultural economy', *Public Culture*, 2: 2, Spring.
Armstrong, D., 1998, 'Globalization and the social state', *Review of International Studies*, 24: 4.
Arun, R., 2002, 'Situating India in the dynamics of globalisation', available at www.ipcs.org/issues/articles/486-ifp-rahul.html.
Baylis, J. and Smith, S., 1997 and 2001 (second edition), *The Globalization of World Politics*, Oxford University Press, Oxford.
Burton, J., 1972, *World Society*, Cambridge University Press, Cambridge.
Clark, I., 1998, 'Beyond the great divide: globalization and the theory of International Relations', *Review of International Studies*, 24:4.
Commission on Global Governance, 1995, *Our Global Neighbourhood: the Report of the Commission on Global Governance*, Oxford University Press, Oxford.
Corbridge, S. and Harriss, J., 2000, *Reinventing India: Liberalization, Hindu Nationalism and Popular Democracy*, Polity Press, Cambridge.
Dicken, P., 1998, *Global Shift: Transforming the World Economy*, third edition, Paul Chapman, London.
Dutt, S., 2000, 'Megacities of joy: the environmental problems of Calcutta in the age of globalization', *Australian Journal of International Affairs*, 54:3.
Giddens, A., 1990, *The Consequences of Modernity*, Polity Press, Cambridge.
Groom, A. J. R. and Powell, D., 1994, 'From world politics to global governance – a theme in need of a focus', in Groom, A. J. R. and Light, M. (eds), *Contemporary International Relations: A Guide to Theory*, Pinter, London and New York.
Held, D., McGrew, A., Goldblatt, D. and Perraton, J., 1999, *Global Transformations: Politics, Economics and Culture*, Polity Press, Cambridge and Stanford University Press, Stanford.
Held, D. and McGrew, A. (eds), 2000, *The Global Transformation Reader*, Polity Press, Cambridge.
Higgott, R., 2000, 'Contested globalization', *Review of International Studies*, 26, special issue, December.
Holm, Hans-Henrik and Sorensen, G., 1995, *Whose World Order? Uneven Globalization and the End of the Cold War*, Westview Press, Boulder, San Francisco and Oxford.
India Today, 1998, 'Enter the Cellerati', 11 May.
Indian National Congress, Election Manifesto 2004, available at www.aicc.org.in/manifesto-2004.html.
Kegley, C. W. and Wittkopf, E. R., 1999, *World Politics: Trend and Transformation*, seventh edition, St. Martin's Press, New York.
Kiely, R. and Marfleet, P. (eds), 1998, *Globalisation and the Third World*, Routledge, London and New York.
Mahbub ul Haq Human Development Centre, 2002, *Human Development in South Asia, 2001*, Oxford University Press, Oxford.

Malhoutra, J., 'Globalization and interdependence', available at www.indianembassy.org/policy/trade/eco_fin_oct_26(1)_99.html.
Mann, M., 1997, 'Has globalisation ended the rise and rise of the nation-state?', *Review of International Political Economy*, 4: 3.
Mittelman, J. H., 1996, *Globalization, Critical Reflections*, Lynne Rienner Publishers, London.
Open University, *A Global Culture*, video.
Pearson, R., 2000, 'Moving the goalposts: gender and globalisation in the twenty-first century', *Gender and Development*, March.
Peterson, V. Spike and Runyan, Anne Sisson, 1993, second edition 1999, *Global Gender Issues*, Westview, Boulder, CO.
Scholte, Jan Aart, 2000, *Globalization: A Critical Introduction*, Palgrave, Basingstoke.
Simai, M., 1997, 'A globalizing world', in Kirdar, U. (ed.), *Cities Fit for People*, United Nations, New York.
Smith, A. D., 1990, 'Towards a global culture?', *Theory, Culture and Society*, 7.
Smith, A. D., 1991, *National Identity*, Penguin, London.
UNCTAD, 2005, 'World FDI flows grew an estimated 6% in 2004, ending downturn', press release UNCTAD/PRESS/PR/2005/02, available at www.unctad.org.
Vajpayee, A. B., Speech at India-EU Business Summit, 27 June 2000, in Ministry of External Affairs, Government of India, *Foreign Relations of India, Select Statements, January 2000–March 2001*, New Dehli.
Waters, M., 1995, *Globalisation*, Routledge, London and New York.

1 A brief history of India up to independence (1947)

Introduction: history without borders?

Contemporary Indians believe they are the descendents of the Aryans and the Dravidians. The languages spoken in the Indian subcontinent lend credence to this belief. The Indo-Aryan languages of northern India such as Punjabi, Gujarati, Bengali, Hindi and so on have their roots in Sanskrit, while the languages spoken in south India, including Tamil, Telegu, Kannada and Malayalam, are Dravidian. The identity of modern India and Indians draws heavily on the Aryan/Hindu identity, notwithstanding the commitment to secularism, the presence of other religious communities and the 'inevitability' of globalization. One of the reasons the Aryan/Hindu identity is becoming more important to the Indian people is because they are able to relate to it. Both colonialism and secularism had taught that traditional identities were 'backward'. However, the history of the Indian subcontinent shows that notwithstanding the '(economic) backwardness' that may be found in the more remote corners of the region as well as in most rural areas, Indian culture and identity has not remained static over the centuries; on the contrary, it has evolved. Invasions, migration, trade and colonization have all left their mark, and also resulted in cultural syncretism that make it possible for us to speak of global India, not just simply in terms of the most recent phase of globalization but also in terms of the historical processes that cannot and should not be restricted to the policies and institutions of the Indian state post 1947. The existence of mass poverty does not mean that India is and has always been 'backward', but that there is a gap between the rich and the poor; the 'haves' and the 'have-nots' in Indian society. Many factors are responsible for poverty in India and they will be explored in Chapter 4 on economic development.

Even India's first prime minister, Jawaharlal Nehru, acknowledged that Indian culture/civilization was a synthesis of many religions, languages and customs. This culture was dominated by Hinduism in many parts of India. However, Hinduism in premodern times was 'vague, amorphous, many sided, all things to all men' and embraced many beliefs and practices (Nehru, 1969: 75). It was difficult to define it and it was a way of life rather than a religion. In his opinion, Indian culture was inclusive rather than exclusive and marked by a flexibility and tolerance that enabled it to synthesize the many cultures of the invaders of India into the one culture; one dominated not by any specific set of beliefs and practices but by the principle of tolerance (Seth, 1993). Nehru attempted to present Hinduism in a good light, however, Hinduism is the dominant religion in modern India and despite the cultural diversity there is tremendous cultural affinity in the Indian subcontinent, a common history (notwithstanding local histories) and a common identity, or an Indianness, that does not depend entirely on legal citizenship and other artefacts of modernity. A globalist will consider Indian history to encompass all influences and processes that have moulded Indian society regardless of national boundaries.

The Bharatiya Janata Party's (BJP) approach to Hinduism is different but more potent, as it is a right-wing political party that is based on the ideology of Hindu nationalism. Brass comments that the BJP's 'leading slogans are that India is a Hindu country and that Hindus have a right to be proud of their history and culture and to draw the central symbols of national identity from them' (Brass, 1994: 87). Its success in recent years supports the argument that Hindu identity is popular because people can relate to it. However, that does not mean that it is inevitable that India is destined to be a Hindu fundamentalist state (Hewitt, 1997: 189–90; also Chapter 3). Former prime minister Vajpayee states that

> India is a blend of many strains, a tapestry of many strands which have evolved over centuries. We are a multi-ethnic, multi-lingual and multi-cultural society. This magnificent diversity is not only our heritage. It is also our future because it has by now become a way of life ... The story of our civilization has been one of constant reconciliation and accommodation. A creative assimilation, rather than intolerant rejection, a spirit of openness and philosophical enquiry, rather than an arbitrary uniformity have been the essential elements of our heritage. (Vajpayee, 11 March 2000)

Another reason that makes the history of India so important, even in modern times is that it gives a fillip to the tourist industry. The cultural diversity that is found in India, including art, architecture and philosophy, attracts tourists from all over the world and also inspires Indians to travel and enjoy and learn about their cultural heritage. Before the Taliban attempted to destroy the gigantic statues of Buddha in Bamiyan in Afghanistan, not many Indians even knew that Buddhism had once flourished in what is now an Islamic country. Some of the historical sites such as the Taj Mahal are United Nations Educational, Scientific and Cultural Organization (UNESCO) designated world heritage sites. The country has around twenty-six such sites and many protected monuments,[1] and in recent years the Indian government requested UNESCO to give the same status to the endangered Red Fort (Lal Qila) in Delhi built by emperor Shah Jahan in the seventeenth century. The global tourist industry thrives on the cultural heritage of different countries. In 2003, around 2.8 million foreign tourists visited India and India's travel and tourism industry was expected to generate 2 per cent of GDP and 11 million jobs (*Business India*, 8–21 December 2003).

Indus Valley Civilization

The recorded history of India begins with the Indus Valley Civilization (IVC) which was a pre-Aryan, possibly Dravidian, civilization.[2] Archaeological excavations at Harappa on the east bank of the river Ravi in the Punjab and Mohenjo-daro further south have revealed that this civilization existed between 2500–1600 BC (Wolpert, 1993: 14). Since the boundary between India and Pakistan came into existence only in 1947, the IVC can be considered to be a common heritage. From west to east it covered an area of approximately 1,600 kilometres and from north to south an area of around 1,100 kilometres. Cities have been excavated which prove that the pre-Aryans were more advanced and sophisticated than the semi-barbaric hoards of Aryan invaders from the west, and had made more technological progress. There are clear evidences of town-planning in Mohenjo-daro, Harappa, Kalibangan, Ropar and Lothal. The average residential house consisted of a courtyard and four to six living rooms, a bathroom and a kitchen. There were both private and public wells for the supply of water and a drainage system. The citadel at Mohenjo-daro contained many imposing buildings including a great bath, a college, a granary and an assembly hall, all of which were made of kiln-burnt bricks.

Lal (1975) comments that the IVC represented 'a perfect Bronze Age', though cert blades continued to be used for certain specific purposes. Bronze objects for domestic use included knife blades, saws, sickles, chisels, celts, razors, pins, tweezers and fish hooks. Weapons included spears, arrow heads and short swords. Agriculture was the backbone of the Indus economy and the people cultivated wheat, barley and cotton. They also domesticated animals. Their diet included cereals, vegetables and fruits, fish, fowl, mutton, beef and pork.

As regards the people of the Indus Valley, they were a racial mix. The population included Mediterraneans, proto-Australoids, Alpines and Mongoloids. Inscriptions on seals prove that they were literate, although as yet their script has not been deciphered. From seals and statuettes found, historians have deduced that they worshipped Shiva or his prototype. Mother-goddess worship was an important element in the religious life of Harappan civilization. Historians had earlier believed that the Aryan invaders destroyed this civilization, however, it is now thought that a series of floods and earthquakes destroyed it.

Aryan age

The first wave of Aryan immigration into India began around 1500 BC. The Aryans lived in tribal villages with their herds and were not as civilized as the people of the Indus Valley. But they were superior warriors, had better weaponry and horses and succeeded in subjugating and enslaving the pre-Aryans who came to be known as *dasas*, or slaves. The main source of information regarding the political, social, religious and economic life of the Aryans is the *Rig Veda*, one of the four *Vedas*, or sacred books of the Indo-Aryans, and the oldest scripture in the world.

The Aryans settled in the Punjab, and it was during this period that the *Rig Veda* was composed. They brought with them a new language, Sanskrit,[3] their religious practices, gods and goddesses, as well as a patriarchal, patrilineal family and a three-class social structure. The three classes were the priestly class, the warrior class and the commons, known as the Brahmins, Kshatriyas and Vaishyas respectively. The Hindu caste system started as a class system called *varnashram dharma* (*varna* actually means colour). The fourth caste or class, the Shudras, were the *dasas* and those of mixed Aryan-*dasa* origin. They were excluded from participating in Vedic ritual and worshipped their own gods. The foremost Aryan tribe was called Bharata, from which independent India or Bharat possibly gets its name. The Aryan tribes gradually expanded eastwards over a period of about five centuries. It is worth noting that the name Bharatvarsha has a resonance for the people of India and is of Indo-Aryan origin. The BJP, for example, refers to 'our ancient nation' as Bharatvarsha (BJP, 2004).

Political and social organization

The Aryan tribes were composed of families and were ruled by a king whose position was usually hereditary. There was also a Council of Elders, composed of the heads of families. Monogamy was the norm. The father was the head of the family and the mother had a subordinate, although honourable, position. Slavery was not uncommon. The slaves were usually prisoners of war, although a tribesman who was in debt could also become the slave of his creditor.

While kingship and priesthood were commonly hereditary, all the tribesmen fought in wars. As mentioned above, a class system did exist, but in the beginning it was not very rigid. The main social division appears to have been between Aryans and non-Aryans. According to the *Rig Veda*, the fair-skinned Aryans hated the dark-skinned Dravidians. However, the Aryans had Dravidian slaves and intermarriage was not forbidden. The Aryans also began to use words from Dravidian languages and diverge from the written language of the learned. This process of conflict, co-operation and assimilation between the Aryans and non-Aryans affected the nature of Hindu religion and society and is significant even in contemporary times.

The economy

When the semi-nomadic Aryan tribes first arrived in the Indian subcontinent, they were primarily cattle-rearers. Animal husbandry was, therefore, more important than agriculture and the cow was a valued animal. The Aryans also had horses to draw chariots, sheep, goats, donkeys and dogs. Tanning, weaving and metal work were common occupations. Weaving was mainly a woman's work.

As the Aryan tribes began to settle down, they took to agriculture. In the beginning land was owned in common by the village. With the decline of tribal units land was divided among the families in the village and private property came into being. The main crops they raised were wheat, barley, rice, millets, pulses, sugarcane and oilseeds, the main staples of the Indian subcontinent even today. Agriculture led to trade, which in the beginning was restricted to local areas. The river Ganges became a natural highway of trade and the numerous settlements on its banks acted as markets. Barter was the common practice. The cow was the unit of value in large-scale transactions. The *nishka*, which in later periods was the name of a gold coin, was also a measure of value. Wealthy landowners, who employed others to cultivate their land, started trading and in this way, trading communities arose from the landowning sections of the society.

Hinduism

The basis of Hinduism, which is one of the oldest religions in the world, lies in the four *Vedas* of the Aryans. The word *Veda* is derived from *vid*, which means 'to know'. The *Vedas* are known as *sruti*, that is 'heard or revealed knowledge'.

The *Rig Veda* is the earliest and the most important *Veda*. It is the oldest scripture in the world and was composed between 1500 and 1000 BC. It consists of over 1,000 hymns, prayers to gods like Agni (fire), Vayu (wind), Indra (thunder), Mitra (friendship), Soma (a sacred potion), Usha (dawn) which were deifications of natural forces. It was a form of nature worship. They were worshipped with sacrifice and offerings. This was the vedic rite of homa. There were no temples or images. The other three *Vedas* are the *Yajur Veda,* dealing with sacrificial invocations; the *Sama Veda*, which contains melodic invocations; and the *Atharva Veda*, which deals with medicines and magical incantations.

However, popular Hinduism is based on the later Vedic literature, the *puranas* (old stories). Some of the *puranas* date back to the pre-Christian era but others are believed to have been written between the third and seventh centuries AD. The epics Ramayana, written by Valmiki, and Mahabharat, by Vyasa, were written in this period and are also considered to be religious texts. The puranic gods of Hinduism are Brahma, the creator, Vishnu, the preserver and Shiva the destructor. They are the holy trinity. The *puja* rite which replaced the Aryan *homa* was adopted from the Dravidians. *Puja* involves the offering of flowers, fruits, leaves, water and so on to an image or symbol of divinity. Romila Thapar (1975: 48) points out that by the fourth century AD Hinduism had become significantly different from the religion of the early Vedic period. There were two fundamental changes. One was a tendency towards monotheism, which was stressed by the increasing worship of either of the two deities, Vishnu and Shiva. The other was the changing nature of worship. More emphasis began to be put on *bhakti* (devotion to god) rather than on sacrifice.

There are six schools of classical Hindu philosophy. *Nyaya* is the Hindu system of logic and is closely related to the *Vaisesika* school which develops the atomic theory of the universe; the basic premise of the *Vaisesika* school is the unique character of each element of nature. The *Samkhya* (numbers) school is purely philosophical and metaphysical. The universe according to this school is not created by a god but through constant evolution, the product of interaction between spirits and matter defined in terms of energy. The *Yoga* system is the third school and is a method for training the body and the mind. The fourth school is Purva-mimansa or 'early inquiry'. It is based on the study of *Rig Vedic* ritual and sacred texts. This school gave great importance to the performance of rituals. It was an extreme form of Brahmin orthodoxy which became less and less popular over the centuries. *Vedanta* (end of the *Vedas*) derives its inspiration from the Upanishads and is also called *Uttara-mimansa* ('later inquiry'). *Vedanta* philosophy seeks a reconciliation of all seeming differences and conflicts in Hindu scripture through the monistic principle of *Brahman* (the Supreme Being). The greatest *Vedanta* teacher was Shankara (780–820 AD), a South Indian Brahmin. According to him the world was an illusion (*maya*) and the only reality was *Brahman*, whose name was also *Atman* (soul). There were other schools of *Vedanta* which, however, were not so strictly monistic. A great *Vaishnava* (devotee of Vishnu) teacher, Ramanuja, for example, rejected the notion of *maya* and stressed the importance of *bhakti*, by which he meant intense and loving meditation and devotion to god, as the surest path to *moksha* or salvation.

Hinduism emerged as a synthesis of Aryan and non-Aryan ideas. However, it must be noted that the word 'Hindu' originally was the Persian rendering of the Indian word 'Sindhu', the sanskrit name of the river Indus. At that time, however, the word 'Hindu' simply meant Indian and had no religious connotation. With the passage of time, evils crept into Hindu religion and perversions occurred. But from time to time religious reformers attempted to purge the religion of evil practices and cults.

Moreland and Chatterjee (1957: 16) argue that Hinduism is more than just a religion. It is a way of life. Arising from a distinctive outlook on the universe, the term covers not merely creed and worship, but also public and private law and practically the whole of social and economic life. It is a complete rule of life.

The caste system

The caste system has evolved over time. In Aryan society intermarriage among the four classes, the Brahmins, Kshatriyas, Vaishyas and Shudras, was not absolutely barred. Offspring of mixed marriages tended to form distinct classes. Some scholars hold that caste divisions existed among the pre-Aryans or Dravidians. The system gradually became more and more rigid, however, and intermarriage between people of different castes was barred. Each caste or subcaste thus became an endogamous group. Moreover, social intercourse between the different castes was also restricted.

Other religions

Buddhism and Jainism

Buddha, the founder of Buddhism was born a Kshatriya prince in Kapilavastu around 563 BC. He was troubled by suffering and became an ascetic. He advocated the noble eightfold path to the elimination of suffering: to hold, practice and follow right views, right appreciations, right speech, right conduct, right livelihood, right effort, right mindfulness and right meditation. The ultimate goal was the attainment of *nirvana*, what the Hindus called *moksha*, which means freedom from the cycle of birth and death. Yet another order of monks was formed by Vardhaman Mahavira (540–468 BC). He too was a Kshatriya prince who became an ascetic. His followers are known as Jains, 'followers of *jina* [conquerors]'. The two most important Jain doctrines are *jiva* (soul) and *ahimsa* (non-violence).

The first imperial unification of India

By the sixth century BC, Magadha had emerged as the most powerful kingdom of the Gangetic plain. The dynasty which succeeded in unifying almost the whole of the Indian subcontinent was the Maurya dynasty. The first king was Chandragupta Maurya. At about this time Alexander invaded the subcontinent but did not get beyond the river Beas.

Chandragupta's able Brahmin prime minister and mentor, Kautilya (also known as Chanakya), is believed to have written the *Arthashastra* (Science of Material Gain) which is similar to Machiavelli's *Prince*. It deals with the nature, politics and economy of the ancient Indian state. However, on the basis of his analysis of the *Arthashastra*, Thomas Trautmann comes to the conclusion that it was probably completed around 250 AD, and Kautilya, therefore, could not have written the whole text. Other Brahmin ministers and bureaucrats also contributed to it (Trautmann cited in Wolpert, 1993: 57). The duties of the king were one of their main preoccupations. The raja or king is advised to be 'energetic' and 'ever wakeful' and never to keep his petitioners waiting at the door. At the close of the day he should observe the evening prayer. The king is told that 'in the happiness of his subjects lies his happiness; in their welfare his welfare'. The *Arthashastra* also urges the king to be 'ever active and discharge his duties' and argues that 'by activity he can achieve both his desired ends and abundance of wealth'. He must also learn to control his senses, especially lust, anger, greed, vanity, haughtiness and exuberance, and also his subjects. Another one of their preoccupations appears to have been the selection and supervision of government servants. Megasthenes[4] observed seven 'classes' in Mauryan India. The royal councillors were the highest class, followed by the Brahmins. The other classes were agriculturists, herdsmen, soldiers, artisans and spies. The Mauryan empire was divided into *janapadas* or districts, which reflected earlier tribal boundaries and were administered by the emperor's trusted relatives or generals.

India's classical *mandala* (circle) theory of foreign policy is also explained in the *Arthashastra*. According to this theory every kingdom is at the centre of twelve concentric rings. The kingdom or state adjacent to the one in the centre is its 'enemy' and the one beyond the 'enemy' is its 'friend'. Every alternate ring in the arena represents the friend of a friend or the enemy of an enemy. The eleventh ring represents the 'intermediate king' and the king in the centre must try to prevent him from allying with his enemies. Kautilya writes that 'the conqueror shall think of the circle of states as a wheel – himself at the hub and his allies, drawn to him by the spokes though separated by intervening territory, as its rim' (Kautilya, 1992: 541). Former minister of external affairs, Yashwant Sinha, argues that the *Arthashastra* provides evidence of a tradition of strategic thought in India (Sinha, 2002).

The economy

A mixed economy existed for more than two thousand years in India. In theory the king owned all land and wealth, including mines and vital industries such as shipbuilding and armament factories and large centres of spinning and weaving. Agriculturists, traders and artisans were all taxed. However, land revenue became and remained the most important source of revenue right up to British rule. There were also many artisan and merchant guilds (*shreni*), which were privately owned corporate bodies and exercized judicial autonomy over their members.

Chandragupta's grandson Ashoka (269–232 BC) was the greatest of the Mauryan kings. In the beginning he was an imperialist like all the other Mauryan kings, but after the Kalinga (modern Orissa) war he converted to *ahimsa* or non-violence He patronized Buddhism and popularized the concept of *dharma*, which means 'religion' but can also mean duty, responsibility and law. He sent emissaries to Ceylon, Burma and Southeast Asia to convert people to Buddhism and through Buddhism to Mauryan pacification and Indian civilization. Between 250 and 240 BC Ashoka hosted the Third Great Council of Buddhism at Pataliputra, his capital, which had by then become Asia's foremost centre of art and culture.

During Ashoka's reign pillars were built (usually called the Ashokan pillars) which were surmounted by capitals decorated with animal sculpture, the most famous of which are the four lions of Sarnath, near Varanasi in the state of Uttar Pradesh. The lions supported an enormous stone 'wheel of the law' (*dharma chakra*), commemorating the Buddha's first sermon at Sarnath. Three of these lions have become the national emblem of modern India while the *dharma chakra* has been placed at the centre of the Indian flag. The lion emblem is a symbol of contemporary India's reaffirmation of its commitment to world peace and goodwill. It is worth noting that modern India has chosen a symbol associated with Buddhism and not Hinduism.

By the end of Ashoka's reign, the Mauryan empire covered almost the whole of the Indian subcontinent, extending from Kashmir in the north to Mysore in the south and from Bangladesh to the heart of Afghanistan. Only three Dravidian kingdoms, Kerala, Chola and Pandya, as well as Ceylon, were independent of Mauryan rule. India's first great unification lasted 140 years. Following the collapse of the Mauryan dynasty, for five centuries India was politically fragmented. North India was later reunified under the imperial Guptas between 320–550 AD. However, the Indian kingdoms continued to expand their trade with countries overseas. There was a demand for Indian products in both the Roman and Chinese empires and many Indian merchants and artisan *jati* (subcaste) and *shreni* (guilds) benefited from it and prospered.

The Indo-Greeks

As mentioned above, Alexander had invaded the Punjab in 326 BC and defeated king Porus. By 180 BC the whole of the Punjab was under the control or rule of the Greco-Bactrians. A Buddhist monk, Nagasena, converted King Menander to Buddhism. The Gandhara region in the upper Indus famous for its distinctive classical Buddhist art was dominated by the Indo-Greeks for more than a century. Medicine, astronomy, astrology and religion were all influenced by the process of Indo-Greek syncretism.

The Shakas and Kushans

The Indian subcontinent was also invaded by the Scythians or Shakas and the Kushans from around 50 BC. The Shakas had been driven from their original homeland in Central Asia by the Kushans. The Punjab was dominated by the Shakas for about a century. The Shakas were joined by the Persian Pahlavas or Parthians. The rule of the Shakas and Pahlavas lasted till about 50 AD, when they were defeated by the more powerful Central Asian nomads, the Kushans. The Shakas were driven south and settled in the region of Malwa around Ujjain. The Shaka power was finally crushed by Chandragupta Vikramaditya about four centuries later.

The Shaka or Scythian warriors were assimilated and Indianized. They adopted Kshatriya names and had their horoscopes cast by Brahmins in keeping with Vedic tradition. Wolpert (1993: 73–4) comments that the 'periodic infusions of Central Asian blood helped generate a particularly vital, romantic and variegated regional culture in Rajasthan and Central India's "Middle Province", Madhya Pradesh. Many of the Hindu warriors of Rajasthan (Rajputs), who were among the fiercest opponents of the Muslim invasions a thousand years later, were descendants of these Shakas, Kushans, and later Huns'.

The Kushans

The greatest of the Kushan monarchs was Kanishka, who reigned for more than two decades around 100 AD. His empire extended from Bactria to Benaras and included Kashmir, the Punjab, Sind, Delhi, Mathura and Sanchi. His capital was Purushapura (modern Peshawar). Kanishka converted to Buddhism and hosted the Fourth Great Council of Buddhism in Kashmir. The authoritative texts of the Hinayana canon were engraved on copper plates at this council and apparently deposited in a *stupa* (a Buddhist monument shaped like a solid dome) especially built to protect them. The Council also gave impetus to the development of Mahayana Buddhism and its emigration to China. It was during Kanishka's reign that Buddha's statues began to be carved in stone and bronze throughout Gandhara (modern Afghanistan) and in Mathura. However, in Mathura the artistic style was distinctly Indian while in Gandhara it was Hellenistic Roman.

It was a period of economic prosperity and cultural and literary advancement. Trade flourished between South Asia, China and the west. Gold coins struck by Kushan monarchs matched the weight of the Roman *denarius*. Monks and merchants from all parts of Asia were attracted to Kanishka's court, as were artists, poets and musicians. Ashvaghosha, the famous Buddhist poet-dramatist, wrote *Buddha Charita* (Life of the Buddha) which is one of the earliest examples of classical Sanskrit poetic literature. The Kushan dynasty lasted for more than a century after the death of Kanishka and was overthrown around 240 AD by the expanding power of the Sassanians from the west.

Other Indian dynasties

While the Central Asian invaders ruled mainly over the north-west parts of the Indian subcontinent, Magadha (which is now modern Bihar) remained under Shunga rule till 72 BC and included Bengal, Bhopal and Malwa within its boundaries. The first Shunga ruler was an orthodox Brahmin but later Shunga monarchs patronized Buddhism and built elaborate *stupas* in Sanchi and Bharhut. The Sanchi *stupas* are now UNESCO world heritage sites, as is Bodh Gaya where Buddha attained enlightenment. They are also important pilgrimage centres. The Shunga dynasty was followed by the Kanvayana dynasty, which lasted almost half a century. In 27 BC Magadha was conquered by the Andhra or Satavahana dynasty of South India. Their descendants now live in the Indian state of Andhra Pradesh and are Dravidian Telegu-speaking people. Their rule extended over much of south and central India from the second century BC until the second century AD. The Andhras were apparently a powerful race and although they were Dravidians, they had been Aryanized. The Sanskrit word *satavahana* most probably meant 'seven mounts' and referred to the seven-horse chariot of Vishnu, whose mounts each represent one day of the week.

In the south there were three kingdoms, the Cheras (or Keralas) in the west, the Pandyas in the centre, and the Cholas on the east coast (Coromandal literally means Chola circle). The name Pandya may have been derived from Pandu, the royal family of the epic Mahabharat and gives an indication of the earliest source of the Aryanization of Tamilnad. The three kingdoms were constantly at war with one another.

Society and culture in south India

Tamil society was matriarchal and matrilineal. Cross-cousin marriage was the norm and in this respect the Dravidians sharply differed from the Indo-Aryans who were exogamous and did not marry their blood relations. The Tamils were divided into castes based on where they lived. Thus, there were hills people, plains people and castes which identified with their habitat; forests, coastal areas and deserts. Within these five main groups there were occupational subdivisions such as the pearl divers, fishermen, boatmen and boat makers.

Madura (modern Madurai), which was the capital of the Pandyan kingdom and is renowned for its beautiful temples such as the famous Meenakshi temple, was the centre of Tamil literary culture. Several *sangams* (academies or colleges) flourished there from the second century AD. Wolpert (1993) writes that over 2,000 *sangam* poems have survived, collected in nine anthologies, and a Tamil grammar, the *Tolkappiyam*, which is also a source of information about the social life of the early Tamils. Song and dance were important aspects of their culture. There were troops of peripatetic actors and actresses who sang and danced in the royal court. Temple dances developed in the south; the *bharatnatyam*, a famous classical dance form, developed in south India, where the *devadasi* system also probably originated. The *devadasis* were temple dancer-prostitutes, however, the practice is now a legal offence.

The prosperity of the Tamil kingdoms can be attributed to overseas trade and the discovery of gold and precious jewels. According to some sources, the Chola monarchs traded mainly with Southeast Asia. However, hoards of Roman coins have been found in south Indian ports, which not only indicates that the Tamils traded with the Romans but that the balance of trade favoured India. Ivory, onyx, cotton goods, silks, pepper and other spices and jewels were shipped from peninsular India's ports. The most prosperous ones were Broach on the river Narmada, Surparaka near Bombay and Arikamedu near Pondicherry.

The growth of trade and commerce led to the emergence of Indian bankers and financiers, new cities and the patronage of religious orders and the arts throughout the country. Prosperous *shrenis* donated fortunes to religious orders, especially Buddhist and Jain. This gave an impetus to the building of magnificently carved caves, the most famous of which are at the world heritage sites at Ajanta and Ellora. However, village and rural economies remained non-monetary and based on the *jajmani* system whereby the landlords who were the patrons looked after the local people, especially in times of need, in return for their services as and when required.

The Guptas

The Gupta empire in north India lasted for more than two hundred years, from 320 to 550 AD. The Gupta empire, as well as the reign of Harsha Vardhana (606–47 AD) of Kanauj may be studied as classical prototypes of the Hindu state and comprize India's classical age. The Gupta kings patronized Hinduism, Buddhism and Jainism. They also patronized art and architecture and Sanskrit literature.

Chandragupta I was crowned king at Pataliputra in 320 AD and assumed the exalted Sanskrit title *Maharajadhiraja* (Great King of Kings). His son Samudragupta was a great imperialist and expanded the frontiers of his empire to the Punjab on the west and Bengal on the east, Kashmir in the north and the Deccan in the south. He even crushed the power of the mighty Kushans and Shakas. His son, in turn, Chandra Gupta II (also known as Chandragupta Vikramaditya), was also a great imperialist and patron of art and literature. Kalidasa, the 'Shakespeare of India', was his court poet-playwright. Seven of Kalidasa's brilliant Sanskrit classics have survived, one of which is the popular drama, *Shakuntala*.

Fa-hsien, a Chinese Buddhist monk, who visited Chandragupta's court, reports that Pataliputra was an affluent city of palaces. There were free hospitals for the poor and destitute. However, he notes that there were untouchables in Hindu society. Fa-hsien's account is an important source of information regarding the reign of Chandragupta II (see Legge, 1986).

During the Gupta era, the Hindu temple emerged as India's classic architectural form. Each temple was built for a particular deity, and this continues to be the practice in contemporary India. An image of the deity was and still is kept inside the temple and devotees go in to pray and offer gifts to it. The early Hindu temples were usually quite small; it was only after the eighth century that temples became extravagantly ornate structures, especially in south India.

Foreign trade and cultural imperialism

The Indians continued to trade with China and Southeast Asia. Indian exports included cotton, ivory, brassware, monkeys, parrots and elephants, while China's exports to India consisted primarily of musk, raw and woven silk, tung oil and amber. Indian and Chinese traders used the famous silk routes of Central Asia as well as the sea route. However, neither tea nor opium had become major exports. Incidentally, India's trade with Rome declined after the third century as the Roman economy became weak and the empire began to crumble.

The proselytizing zeal of Buddhism was another factor which promoted intercourse between India and Southeast Asia, as was Indian cultural imperialism. In Indo-China, the kingdom of Fu-nan was ruled by a Hindu Brahmin king, Kaundinya, who introduced Sanskritic culture to most of the peninsula, as well as the archipelago. Remnants of ancient Indian culture may still be found in the island of Bali. The kingdoms of Sri-Vijaya in Sumatra and Cho-po in Java were ruled by Hindu and then Buddhist kings. By the fifth century AD there were many Hindu and Buddhist states in Burma, Thailand, Indo-China, Malaysia and Indonesia which were modelled on ancient Indian states. Lamb (1975: 442) writes that 'the cultures of modern South-East Asia all provide evidence of a long period of contact with India'. Many Southeast Asian languages, such as Malay and Javanese contain words of Sanskrit or Dravidian origin. The scripts of some of these languages are clearly derived from Indian models, for example, Thai. Southeast Asian concepts of kingship and authority owe much to ancient Hindu political theory. Lamb writes that 'the Thai monarchy, though following Hinayana Buddhism of the Sinhalese type, still requires the presence of Court Brahmans (who by now have become Thai in all but name) for the proper performance of its ceremonials' (1975: 442). The traditional dance and shadow-puppet theatres, which are so popular, enact the adventures of Rama and Sita and Hanuman.

Harsha Vardhan

Harsha Vardhan reigned in North India from 606 to 647 AD. The chief sources of information regarding Harsha's reign are the *Harsha Charita* (Life of Harsha) written by Bana, his Brahmin courtier, and the account written by Hsuan Tsang, a brilliant Buddhist pilgrim from China. Harsha's empire extended from Kathiawar to Bengal.

Turko-Afghan invasion of the Indian subcontinent

Although Arabs conquered Sindh in the eighth century, Turko-Afghan invasion of the Indian subcontinent began towards the end of the tenth century AD. In 997 AD Mahmud of Ghazni began his raids or *jihad* (holy war) against India and destroyed temples and looted cities. However, Muslim rule was established in India for the first time in 1206 AD by Qutb-ud-din Aibak, the slave lieutenant of Mohammed of Ghur, a Turko-Afghan. The story of how Mohammed of Ghur defeated the famous Rajput prince and ruler of Delhi, Prithviraj Chauhan, is folklore in India. Aibak founded the slave dynasty at Delhi and the Delhi Sultanate thus came into existence. However, the Hindu kings or Rajputs who ruled mainly in the north-western parts of the Indian subcontinent and who were great warriors themselves, put up a spirited resistance. Throughout the history of Muslim rule in India they continued to oppose Muslim rule. The four major Rajput dynasties were the Pratihara, Parmara, Chauhan and Chalukya. They were themselves descendants of Central Asian tribes which had invaded the subcontinent in the first century and this partly explains their fierce, fighting spirit. The Turko-Afghans also persecuted the Buddhists, killing thousands, and sacked the renowned Nalanda University and other major Buddhist centres. As a result, thousands of Buddhists fled to Nepal and Tibet. However, Nehru argues that it is wrong and misleading to talk of a Muslim invasion of India or of a Muslim period in India. Islam did not invade India. India was invaded by Turks, Afghans and Turko-Mongols. He also asserts that they became completely Indianized and looked upon India as their homeland (Nehru, 1969: 241).

Qutb-ud-din was succeeded by his son-in-law Iltutmish. He consolidated his rule around Delhi and over the Gangetic plain and won the support of most of the Turkish military bureaucrats. As regards the Hindus, he practised religious toleration although they had to pay a tax. They became *dhimmis* or 'protected peoples'.

Iltutmish was succeeded by his daughter Raziya, the only Muslim woman to rule in India. After only three years, however, she was murdered by her courtiers. Her palace guards ruled conjointly for a few years after which Balban, who had been Sultana Raziya's chief huntsman, seized power and ruled for forty years and also assumed the title of sultan.

A few years after Balban's death, in 1290, his Turkish army general, Jalal-ud-din Firuz Khalji became sultan and started the Khalji dynasty. By this time the Turkish sultans had began to recruit Indians, i.e. people who were not of Turko-Afghan descent. They had also begun to rely on their support. Jalal-ud-din was succeeded by his nephew Ala-ud-din who was an able but cruel ruler. He was also an imperialist and defeated many Rajput chiefs and penetrated the Deccan right up to the Pandyan territory in Tamilnad. Ala-ud-din died in 1316. His sons and successors were weak and in 1320, Ghiyas-ud-din Tughluq, the son of a court Turkish slave and a Hindu Jat woman, founded a new dynasty, the Tughluq dynasty. However, he died five years later and was succeeded by his son Muhammad. His lack of concern for the welfare of his subjects, economic mismanagement and severe and prolonged periods of drought and famine during which the sultan did nothing to alleviate the suffering of the people led to widespread economic discontent and rebellions throughout the sultanate which were most effective in the south.

In 1336 Harihara I founded the kingdom of Vijayanagar, south of the Tungabhadra river. In 1347 Hasan Gangu proclaimed himself sultan of the

Deccan. He assumed the name of Ala-ud-din Bahman Shah and founded the Bahmani dynasty which survived for more than two centuries. Both the Vijayanagar and Bahmani kingdoms were powerful states and constantly at war with one another.

Bengal declared its independence from Delhi in 1338 and remained so until the sixteenth century. One of Bengal's leading *maliks* (nobles), Malik Haji Ilyas, assumed the title of Sultan Shams-ud-din in 1339 and founded the Ilyas Shahi dynasty.

Muhammad Tughluq was killed fighting a rebellion in Sind in 1351. He was succeeded by his cousin, Firuz, who reigned for thirty-seven years (1351-88). He is known for his passion for building. He built many new mosques, colleges, hospitals and towns and also supported the construction of dams and reservoirs. He is reputed to have been an intelligent and enlightened monarch who in addition to his other constructive and humanitarian projects, also abolished torture. However, he was an orthodox Muslim and like his predecessors continued to discriminate against the Hindus who had to pay the *jizya* (a tax imposed on non-Muslims by Muslim rulers). He did not exempt even the Brahmins. After his death, the sultanate began to break up and the Indian subcontinent was invaded by Timur the Lame's armies several times. They plundered the Punjab and Delhi and took away with them thousands of slaves.

The next dynasty to rule from Delhi was the Sayyid. The founder of this dynasty was a Turk, Khizr Khan who reigned from 1414 to 1450. The Sayyids were deposed by the Lodhis, a clan of Afghans. Buhlul Lodhi, the founder of the dynasty reigned over Delhi and the Punjab from 1451–89. He was succeeded by his son Sikander. The last Lodhi ruler was Ibrahim Lodhi, who had to face a number of rebellions and also the Hindu Rajput confederacy, led by Rana Sanga of Mewar. His rule came to an end when Babur, the king of Kabul and the founder of the Mughal dynasty, invaded the Indian subcontinent.

The birth of Sikhism

Sikhism was founded by Guru Nanak who lived in the Punjab between 1469 and 1539. He preached that there was only one God for Hindus and Muslims and all human beings are equal. On his death he was succeeded by his disciples who also became gurus. Sikhism teaches that Sikhs should remember God at all times and lead a virtuous and truthful life while maintaining a balance between their spiritual obligations and temporal obligations.

The Gurus have built up the modern Sikh community. The fifth guru, Arjan Dev, compiled the Adi Granth, the first sacred book of the Sikhs. The most famous Guru is Guru Govind Singh. He organized the Sikhs into a militant community, instituting *pahul* or baptism in water stirred by a dagger. Those who were baptized were known as the *Khalsa* (pure) with the designation Singh (lion). All members of the *Khalsa* had to wear the five Ks – *kes* (long hair), *kangha* (comb), *kirpan* (sword), *kachcha* (short cotton underwear) and *kara* (steel bracelet). Guru Govind Singh was the tenth and last guru and died in 1708. He declared that the Sikhs no longer needed a living guru and that the Sri Guru Granth Sahib (sacred text) should henceforth be their spiritual head and provide spiritual guidance.

The *Khalsa* soon emerged as a valorous fighting unit. It enabled the Sikhs to form a state of their own under Maharaja Ranjit Singh in 1799. However, the British annexed Punjab in 1849, so their success was short-lived.

The Mughals

Babur, a Chagatai Turk, was a descendant of Timur and Ghengiz Khan. In April 1526, Babur defeated Sultan Ibrahim Lodhi in the battle of Panipat. In March of the following year he defeated the Rajput confederacy led by Rana Sanga of Mewar in the battle of Khanua. In 1529, in another battle, he defeated Mahmud Lodhi, the son and successor of Ibrahim Lodhi. Nehru (1969) argues that Babur's success was probably due not only to the weakness of the Delhi Sultanate but to his possessing a new and improved type of artillery. However, Bose and Jalal (1998: 36) contest this idea and claim that the Mughals were more reliant on cavalry in making their conquests.

Babur died in Agra in 1530 and was succeeded by his son Humayun. However, he was not a strong ruler and was more interested in opium and astrology than in power. He was challenged by his younger brothers and Babur's Afghan generals and soon lost his father's empire. In the battle of Chausa, in 1539, and the battle of Kanauj in 1540, Humayun was defeated by Sher Khan Sur, one of the most powerful Afghan generals. Sher Khan had himself crowned Shah and was thereafter known as Sher Shah Suri. He was an able ruler and administrator. His reorganization of the revenue system was commendable. India's minister of external affairs, Natwar Singh, comments that 'Sher Shah Suri, is recalled today not because of his success on the battle field, but because he envisaged and established, 400 years ago, the Grand Trunk Road that stretched over hundreds of kilometres, from Patna in the East to Peshawar in the West, linking millions of people who used this facility to exchange goods and ideas, move comfortably on pilgrimages, and, when the need arose, to migrate to new towns' (Singh, 2005). He was killed in battle in May 1545. In 1555 Humayun recaptured the Punjab, Delhi and Agra, but died in January 1556.

The earlier Muslim rulers discriminated against and even persecuted the Hindus. They had to pay *jizya* and a pilgrimage tax. Akbar, Humayun's son and successor, was only thirteen when his father died. He was the third and greatest Mughal emperor who recognized the importance of winning the friendship of the Hindu kings and embarked on a policy of making alliances with them, even marrying the daughter of Raja Bharmal of Amber in 1562. He also abolished the hated *jizya* and pilgrimage tax; however, he did not hesitate to use force against the Rajput princes if they were not prepared to swear allegiance to him. The Rana of Mewar was defeated in a battle in 1567.

Akbar's empire extended from Bengal to Kabul and included a part of the Deccan up to the Godavari river. Wolpert (1993: 129) comments that Akbar's 'control over northern and central India was, in fact, greater than that of either the Mauryas or the British, and after conquering those regions he established stable administrations within them, creating a pattern followed by his Mughal descendants as well as by early British administrators'.

Akbar introduced the *mansabdari* system of administration. The *mansabdars* were office-holders who were ranked on the basis of the number of cavalry they maintained for imperial service. There were thirty-three ranks. The princes of royal blood were given the highest *mansabs*, ranging from five to ten thousand. All of the higher ranks were hand-picked officials and about 70 per cent of them were Muslim soldiers born outside India. About 15 per cent were Hindus, mainly Rajputs, some of whom held higher *mansabs*. Raja Todar Mal, a Hindu, was appointed *diwan* (minister of revenue), which was a very senior appointment.

Akbar was obviously a benevolent ruler. Peasants were given assistance during droughts and crop failures. Revenue collectors were ordered to remit taxes in afflicted districts. In general, less coercion or brutality was used in the collection of revenue. Francis Watson comments that Raja Todar Mal was the 'chief and able agent' of this system which was somewhat fairer to the peasants (Watson, 1979: 114).

Akbar considered himself to be a divine Indian emperor and not a Muslim monarch. In 1581 he founded a 'Divine Faith' (Din-i-Ilahi). This court religion was influenced by Sufism and other religions, such as Hinduism, Jainism, Sikhism, Zoroastrianism and Christianity. It was eclectic and reflected Akbar's interest in different faiths. In 1570 he undertook the building of a new city, Fatehpur Sikri (now a UNESCO world heritage site), in honour of a Sufi saint, Shaikh Salim Chisti, whose blessings had enabled him to produce a son and heir. Akbar even forbade cow-slaughter by imperial decree. Akbar had by then ceased to be an orthodox Muslim.

He reintroduced Persian as the official language. However, in addition to Persian and Urdu languages and literature, he also patronized Hindi literature. He even appointed a poet laureate for Hindi, Raja Birbal. The most famous and popular Hindi work written during Akbar's reign was the translation of the epic *Ramayana* by Tulsi Das. A distinctive Mughal culture was also taking shape.

Wolpert argues that although 'the elegant decadence of Mughal dress, decor, manners and morals all reflected Persian court life and custom' (1993: 133), Mughal culture had, by the time Akbar became emperor, become more than an imported culture. In architecture as well as painting a blend of Perso-Islamic and Rajput-Hindu styles and motifs was evident. The buildings at Fatehpur Sikri are a good example of the unique synthesis of Indian craftsmanship and design employed in the service of one of Islam's most liberal monarchs.

Akbar was poisoned by his eldest son and heir, Salim, and died in October 1605. Salim then assumed his Persian title name, Jahangir. The history of Jahangir's reign is characterized by political intrigues. In 1611 he married a Persian widow, Mehr-ul-Nisa whom he renamed Nur Jahan (Light of the World). She was very beautiful, intelligent and ambitious. She virtually usurped her husband's throne. Under her influence Persian became the dominant language and culture. The Mughal rulers, their elite courtiers and senior officials continued to live in great luxury. Jahangir was aesthetically inclined and prided himself on his Persian poetry and artistic skill. He even wrote his memoirs, *Tuzuk-i-Jahangiri*. He patronized art and architecture and had a penchant for beautiful gardens; he designed the famous Shalimar gardens in Srinagar, Kashmir. Jahangir started the practice of moving to hill stations during the summer months, a practice which the British continued.

Jahangir died in October 1627 and was succeeded by one of his sons, Shah Jahan, who had rebelled against him during his lifetime and eliminated his rivals with his father-in-law's help. His father-in-law, Asaf Khan, Nur Jahan's brother, had been appointed premier by her. However, she was unable to manipulate him after Jahangir's death and when Shah Jahan became emperor, she was pensioned off and went to live in Lahore till she died in 1645.

The reign of Shah Jahan from 1628 to 1658 was the golden age of Mughal architecture (Briggs, 1975: 322). The most magnificent building he built was, of course, the Taj Mahal in Agra, the mausoleum of his beloved wife, Mumtaz Mahal. Shah Jahan had to subdue rebellion in the Deccan and Bundelkhand and like his predecessors continued to wage costly wars. His eldest son Dara Shikoh, a philosopher and intellectual who believed in religious toleration, was his heir to the throne. However, his most ambitious son was Aurangzeb. He eliminated his brothers, ascended the throne in July 1658 and reigned till his death in March 1707. Aurangzeb the Alamgir (World Conqueror) 'was at once the most pious and the most ruthless of the Great Mughals, a single-minded leader of brilliant administrative capacity and as cunning a statesman as ever mounted an Indian throne' (Wolpert, 1993: 157).

Aurangzeb was a religious zealot who reversed his predecessors' policy of religious toleration and thus alienated the Hindus. Aurangzeb even appointed 'censors of public morals' (*muhtasibs*) to enforce Islamic law and the performance of prayers. He outlawed Hindu religious fairs and did not give permission to build Hindu temples or even repair old ones. He re-imposed the *jizya* in 1679 and raised taxes on land and agricultural produce, enraging the landlords and peasants, especially the Hindus, who rebelled against him and his policies. He spent the latter part of his reign battling against the Marathas under their illustrious leader Shivaji. However, Aurangzeb's successors were weak rulers and this soon led to the downfall of the Mughal dynasty and the break up of the Mughal empire. The last Mughal ruler, Bahadur Shah, was taken prisoner by the British in 1857 and exiled to Burma where he died in 1858.

Arrival of the Europeans

The first Europeans to arrive in India were the Portuguese. With Vasco da Gama's historic arrival in India in 1498 began an era of Western European conquest that lasted four and a half centuries. Dutch, English and French traders followed the Portuguese route and laid the foundations of British rule in India.

When the Europeans arrived in India in the 16th century, northern India was under Mughal rule but several independent kingdoms existed in South India. European traders competed with each other to establish a base in India. They quickly learnt how best to exploit the communal conflicts and social divisions within India's fragmented, pluralistic society. In 1510 the Portuguese seized control of Goa which became a Portuguese colony. The Portuguese later occupied Diu (1534) and Daman (1559). Panaji became the capital of Goa in 1843. The Portuguese territory of Goa, Daman and Diu became a part of independent India in December 1961.

The English East India Company

In 1600, a royal charter granted the English East India Company the right to trade with the Indies. In 1608 the company arrived in India and in 1619 built a factory in Surat. In 1639 Francis Day purchased land in Mandarez (modern Madras) and built an English fort there (St George). In 1658, the company was based at Hughli in Bengal, and in 1668, it acquired Bombay from the British government for an annual rent of £10. Bombay had been given to Charles II as part of Catherine of Braganza's dowry in 1661. In 1691, Job Charnock, a merchant of the Bengal Council, founded Calcutta on the banks of the river Hughli, which later became the British empire's first capital in India.

How did the East India Company establish its rule in Bengal? First of all, the gradual disintegration of the Mughal empire after the death of Aurangzeb led to political fragmentation. Bengal became independent under Alivardi Khan and his successor Nawab Siraj-ud-dowlah had to deal with the company when it began to fortify its settlements, even though he had forbidden it from doing so. This situation led to the Battle of Plassey in 1757. The Nawab was betrayed by one of his generals, Mir Jafar, with whom the company had made a secret agreement, and the company won the battle. Its military superiority also helped it to win this as well as subsequent wars. Mir Jafar was installed as the new Nawab of Bengal and Siraj-ud-Daulah was beheaded by Mir Jafar's son. However, Mir Jafar soon fell out with the company and was deposed. He was replaced by Mir Qasim who also resented the interference of the company in his affairs and joined forces with the Nawab Wazir Shuja-ud-Daulah of Oudh and the Mughal Emperor Shah Alam to challenge the company in the battle of Buxar in October 1764. The company won the battle and emerged as the masters of Bengal, Bihar and Oudh. It succeeded in eliminating French competition: its forces defeated the French forces in the battle of Wandewash in January 1760 and ended the French dream of establishing a dominion in India. Thereafter, French control was restricted to only Chandra Nagar in Bengal, Pondicherry, Yenam and Mahi.

In 1765, the company got *diwani* rights in Bengal, Bihar and Orissa, i.e. they got the permanent right to collect revenue in these provinces. This right was given to them by Shah Alam, the Mughal emperor. In return, the company agreed to cede Allahabad and Kara to the Mughal emperor and also pay him a sum of Rupees (Rs) 26 *lakhs* annually.[5] Robert Clive became the first English governor of Bengal. However, the Company shared responsibility for governing Bengal with the Nawab in Murshidabad. This dual government led to 'confusion, bribery, corruption and extortion' (Sir J. Malcolm cited in Wolpert, 1993: 187) and Bengal was soon stripped of its wealth and became an impoverished province. Employees of the company robbed the peasants and the company alike and with equal impunity. In 1767, the company declared that it was unable to pay the annual tax of £400,000 to the treasury; this led to a parliamentary inquiry and the Regulating Act of 1773 which was the first step towards parliamentary supervision of the Company's affairs.

In 1772, Warren Hastings took over as governor. In 1784 Pitt's India Act was passed by the British parliament which increased the British government's control over the company's affairs. Hastings was succeeded by Cornwallis, whose Permanent Settlement in 1793 created a class of permanent landlords. Previously, landlords only collected tax and maintained law and order. Cornwallis thought that this would create a class of loyal Indian supporters for the British Raj. However, they often lost their lands to Calcutta bankers and moneylenders; and in this way many of the old Mughal aristocrats of Bengal were displaced by Hindu families – Roys, Sens and Tagores – whose descendants became the 'new elites', promoting cultural syncretism and westernization in Calcutta society.

British rule not only affected Indian politics but also its economy, as Chapter 5 argues. The effects of cultural imperialism neither should be underestimated. English education was introduced in India in the early nineteenth century, with Thomas Babington Macaulay, the first law member of the Bengal Council appointed in 1835, its strongest advocate. Macaulay categorically stated in his famous minute on education that the aim of English education in India was to form a class who would be interpreters between the British rulers and the Indians, 'a class of persons, Indian in blood and colour, but English in taste, in opinions, in morals, and in intellect' (Macaulay cited in Wolpert, 1993: 215). However, orientalists like Sir William Jones thought that Indians would benefit more from learning more about Indian civilization. In 1784 William Jones founded the Asiatic Society of Bengal in Calcutta. However, the main reason why Indians were encouraged to learn English was so that they could be recruited as administrators and clerks. The alternative would have been to expect British officers to learn Indian languages which would have been both an expensive and unpopular proposition and less effective. Western education introduced the Indians to western political ideas and ideology, principally western liberalism, and shaped the thought of some of the leaders of the Indian national movement.

The effect of *laissez-faire* economics was, however, disastrous. Indian weavers had to compete with Lancashire textile industries. Not only did Indian cotton exports decline, the Indian market was flooded with cheaper machine-made cotton from England. This led to the collapse of Bengal's home-spun cotton industry and high unemployment (Parthasarathi, 2001). Wolpert (1993: 214) comments that 'this quiet revolution from economic self-sufficiency to foreign dependence was to prove a far more powerful factor than the English language in first binding India to Britain and later impelling her to seek independence'.

British rule affected all aspects of Indian life. The Englishmen who went to India were not just merchants and officials in the service of the East India Company or the Crown but also Christian missionaries who wanted to convert the Indians. The desire to reform or 'civilize' the Indians was also expressed by the British rulers. In 1828, Lord William Bentinck was appointed governor-general of British India. He passed a law against the Hindu custom of *sati* (the immolation of Hindu widows on the funeral pyres of their dead husbands) and *thugi* (ritual murder by strangling and highway robbery in the service of the Mother-Goddess Kali) on humanitarian grounds. This was seen by orthodox Hindus as undue interference in their religious life. However, progressive Hindu social and religious reformers such as Raja Ram Mohun Roy supported him. Ram Mohun Roy is considered to be the father of the Hindu Renaissance and founded the Brahmo Samaj in Calcutta in 1828.

Thus, while orientalist education led to the regeneration and revival of Hinduism, a new synthesis of Anglo-Indian culture also began to emerge. It was a combination of these two factors that helped in the growth of Indian nationalism and nationalist ideas.

The Indian mutiny

By 1850, British rule extended from Bengal to the Indus and from Kashmir to Cape Comorin in the south. Military success played a major role in the expansion of British rule. The East India Company's forces defeated Hyder Ali in the Second Mysore war (1780–84), Tipu Sultan in the Fourth Mysore war (1799), the Marathas in the Second Anglo-Maratha war (1803–05), and the Sikhs in the First and Second Anglo-Sikh wars in 1845–46 and 1848–49 respectively. The Punjab was annexed to British India after the Second Anglo-Sikh war. However, the policy of annexing the kingdoms of princes who did not have a natural heir to the throne, pursued by Lord Dalhousie in accordance with the Doctrine of Lapse, enraged the local rulers. His successor, Lord Canning, enacted several unpopular measures which further alienated the Indian soldiers and the Indian people. The General Services Enlistment Act required Indian soldiers to serve anywhere, even abroad. Another Act permitted Hindu widow remarriage. The Hindus thought that this Act was an undue interference in their social and religious life. However, the last straw was the introduction of the Enfield rifle. The cartridges were smeared with animal fat and lard. The soldiers had to bite the tip off the cartridges before using them which angered them. This led to what became known as the Great Mutiny of 1857, starting in Meerut on 9 May and spreading to other parts of the country. Indian rulers who had been alienated by the British joined the mutineers. Delhi, Lucknow and Cawnpore were the centres of revolt. Indian nationalists consider it to be India's first war of independence. However, by 20 September 1857, Delhi was firmly under British control and the Indian rulers who led the mutiny were all taken prisoner or died in the battlefield. On 2 August 1858 the British parliament passed the Government of India Act transferring 'all rights' that the East India Company had hitherto enjoyed in India directly to the Crown.

Birth of the Indian National Congress

The Indian national movement began in the nineteenth century. Many factors contributed to the growth of Indian nationalism. Social and religious movements led by Raja Ram Mohan Roy, Swami Dayanand Saraswati, Sri Rama Krishna and the Rama Krishna Mission, Swami Vivekanand and also the Prarthana Samaj and the Theosophical Society, revived pride in India's ancient culture and heritage. These leaders wanted to reform Hindu society and bring about its rejuvenation. Raja Ram Mohan Roy has been described as the Father of Indian Renaissance. Swami Dayananda inspired love for *swarajya* (self-government) and promoted *swadeshi* (indigenous as opposed to foreign). At the same time, the spread of western education enabled Indians to study the political theories of western philosophers such as John Milton, Edmund Burke, John Stuart Mill and Herbert Spencer and led to aspirations for self-government and for representative institutions.

Communication between leaders and the masses was facilitated by the modern infrastructure built by the British, such as the network of railways and telegraphs. However, British rule also enraged Indians. Many educated, middle-class Indians who wished to serve their country believed that they were being systematically discriminated against and kept out of the Indian civil service. They were also concerned about the economic exploitation of the country. Traditional industries and agriculture were being neglected and peasants were being exploited. Famines were a frequent occurrence. Newspapers in Indian languages came into existence and began to criticize the policies of the government. The government responded by passing the Vernacular Press Act in 1878 which imposed restrictions on the press. The growing political unrest in India and the poverty of the masses prompted a retired civil servant, Allan Octavian Hume, to initiate the establishment of the Indian National Congress. He felt that the Indians needed an organization that would enable them to come together to discuss issues and social matters and offer constructive criticism to the government.

On the advice of Hume, the Indian National Congress was established in 1885. Its first meeting was held the same year in Bombay under the presidency of Womesh Chandra Bannerjee, a Calcutta barrister. Most of its members were high-caste Hindu and Parsi intellectuals, lawyers and businessman. For about twenty years it was dominated by the moderates such as Gopal Krishna Gokhale, Phirozshah Mehta, Surendranath Banerjee and Madan Mohan Malviya, who believed in constitutional methods and asked for piecemeal reform. The demands of the Congress centred on representative government and an expansion of the number and functions of legislative councils both in the provinces and at the centre; Indianization of higher services; and poverty in India.

However, the younger elements – or the radicals and extremists – soon lost patience with the moderates and their methods and declared that their goal was *swarajya*. The extremists were led by Balgangadhar Tilak, Bipin Chandra Pal and Lala Lajpat Rai, and hailed from different parts of the country. Leaders like Tilak were rooted in their culture and the masses strongly identified with them. The national movement was by no means dominated by a homogenous elite.

The formation of the Muslim League

In October 1906, a Muslim delegation approached Lord Minto with their demand for greater representation of Muslims on official councils. Lord Minto gave them his full support. The same year, thirty-five Muslim delegates from every province of India and Burma met at Dacca to found the All-India Muslim League. It is worth noting that they were all upper-class Muslims, *zamindars* (landowners paying land tax) and ex-bureaucrats and included personages like the Aga Khan, the Nawab of Dacca and Nawab Mohsin-ul-Mulk. Bipin Chandra comments that the Muslim League was founded as 'a loyalist, communal and conservative political organization'. The League supported the partition of Bengal, which was proposed by the government in 1905 for administrative convenience as it was a very large province, but opposed by the Hindu community. It 'raised the slogan of separate Muslim interests, demanded separate electorates and safeguards for Muslims in government services, and reiterated all the major themes of communal politics and ideology enunciated earlier by Syed Ahmad and his followers' (Chandra, 1989: 417).

The Morley-Minto reforms

The Morley-Minto reforms of 1909 drawn up by John Morley, the secretary of state for India and Lord Minto, the viceroy, were embodied in the Indian

Councils Act of 1909. It provided for greater association of qualified Indians with the government in deciding public questions. One seat on the governor general's council was reserved for an Indian. Satyendra Sinha (later Lord Sinha of Raipur) was the first Indian to be appointed to the council as Law Member. In the provincial councils, the Muslim community got representation. However, the reforms did not pacify or satisfy the Indians.

The freedom struggle

Meanwhile, the national movement led by the Indian National Congress had gathered momentum. In 1915 Mohundas Karamchand Gandhi joined the Congress on his return from South Africa and soon became the undisputed leader of the national movement. Gandhi's ideas are discussed in Chapter 6. He had developed his technique of *satyagraha*, a non-violent method of non-co-operation and civil disobedience, in South Africa in his struggle against apartheid. In 1920, he launched the non-co-operation movement and was arrested. In 1922, he launched the civil disobedience movement. However, the movement turned violent and he suspended it on this account. In 1930, it was relaunched.

In March 1940, at its annual session in Ramgarh, the Congress demanded complete independence and a constituent assembly to draft a constitution for free India. The British, on the other hand, wanted to introduce representative and responsible government in India, gradually and by instalments. In March 1942, the British government sent Sir Stafford Cripps to India with proposals for a new constitution. The Cripps proposals were found unsatisfactory and were rejected both by the Congress and the Muslim League. In May 1942, Gandhi called on Britain to 'leave India to God. If this is too much, then leave her to anarchy'. In August 1942, the Congress working committee passed the Quit India resolution. Gandhi's confidence partly stemmed from his attack on the 'colonization of the mind'. Nandy argues that 'the main threat to the colonizers is ... the latent fear that the colonized will reject the consensus and, instead of trying to redeem their "masculinity" by becoming the counter players of the rulers according to the established rules, will discover an alternative frame of reference within which the oppressed do not seem weak, degraded and distorted men trying to break the monopoly of the rulers on a fixed quantity of machismo' (Nandy, 2001: 175–6). Gandhi successfully played on these fears.

In the meantime, the Muslims in India were becoming more insecure and feared Hindu majority rule in an independent India. The Muslim League, under its leader Mohammed Ali Jinnah, began to agitate for a separate state for the Muslims, namely Pakistan. A parliamentary commission, known as the Cabinet Mission, was sent to India to negotiate the question of Indian independence. It announced a constitutional scheme that implicitly recognized the right of the Muslims to have a state of their own. The scheme was accepted by the Muslim

League but rejected by the Indian National Congress. Communal riots began, the first of which was the Great Calcutta Killings of August 1946. The rioting made the partition of the country inevitable. Lord Mountbatten, India's last viceroy, announced the partition of India in March 1947. The provinces where the Muslims formed the majority were to be constituted into a separate state, Pakistan. In August 1947 India was granted independence.

Notes

1 See http://whc.unesco.org/en/list/; www.cultural-heritage-india.com/india-world-heritage-sites/.
2 Ethnological studies have revealed that there were six main races in the Indian subcontinent. The earliest was the Negrito, followed by the Proto-Australoid, the Mongoloid, the Mediterranean, the western Brachycephals and the Nordic. The Mediterranean race is generally associated with Dravidian culture, while the Aryans belonged to the Nordic race. However, Aryan does not refer to race or ethnie, but a speech group of Indo-European origin.
   Dutt and Noble have written that both Dravidians and Aryans belong to the same Caucasoid stock. The Dravidians probably came to India from Asia Minor and the eastern Mediterranean coasts. But they were driven south by the Aryan invaders. The Dravidian languages which are spoken in south India include Tamil, Telegu, Malayalam and Kannada and form a language family of their own. Only the ancient language of Brahui still exists in the middle Indus Valley. (Allen G. Noble and Ashok K. Dutt, 1982, 'The culture of India in spatial perspective: an introduction' in Allen G. Noble and Ashok K. Dutt (eds), 1982, *India, Cultural Patterns and Processes*, Westview Press, Boulder, CO, p.4.)
3 When Europeans first came to India they thought Sanskrit was an obscure language. However, in the late eighteenth century, Sir William Jones, a scholar and also a judge of the Supreme Court in Calcutta, put forward the view that Sanskrit belongs to a large family of languages. Like Greek and Latin, with which it had similarities, as well as Gothic, Celtic and Old Persian, it had sprung from a common source.
4 Megasthenes was a Greek ambassador sent to Chandragupta's court.
5 1 *lakh* is equal to 100,000 units (e.g. of money/people).

References

Basham, A. L. (ed.), 1975, *A Cultural History of India*, Clarendon Press, Oxford.
Bose, S. and Jalal, A., 1998, *Modern South Asia*, Routledge, London and New York.
Brass, P., 1994, *The Politics of India Since Independence*, Cambridge University Press, Cambridge.
Briggs, M. S., 1975, 'Muslim architecture in India' in Basham, A. L. (ed.), *A Cultural History of India*, Clarendon Press, Oxford.
Chandra, B., 1989, *India's Struggle for Independence*, Penguin Books, New Delhi and London.
Channel Four, 2001, *Untold India, Rogue Trader*, 7 October.
Hewitt, V., 1997, *The New International Politics of South Asia*, Manchester University Press, Manchester.

Kautilya, *Arthashastra*, edited, rearranged, translated and introduced by L. N. Rangarajan, 1992, Penguin Books, New Delhi and New York.
Lal, B. B., 1975, 'The Indus civilization' in Basham, A. L. (ed.), *A Cultural History of India*, Clarendon Press, Oxford.
Lamb, A., 1975, 'Indian influence in ancient South-East Asia' in Basham, A. L. (ed.), *A Cultural History of India*, Clarendon Press, Oxford.
Legge, J. (trans.), 1986, *Record of the Buddhistic Kingdoms*, Clarendon Press, Oxford.
Malcolm, Sir J., 1993, *Life of Clive*, Vol. 2 cited in Wolpert, S., *A New History of India*, Oxford University Press, Oxford.
Moreland, W. H. and Atul Chandra Chatterjee, 1957, *A Short History of India*, fourth edition, Longman, London.
Nandy, A., 2001, 'Colonization of the mind' in Rahnema, M. and Bawtree, V. (eds), *The Post-Development Reader*, Zed Books, London and New Jersey.
Nehru, J., 1969, *The Discovery of India*, Asia Publishing House, Bombay, New Delhi, London and New York.
Noble, A. G. and Dutt, Ashok K., 1982, *India, Cultural Patterns and Processes*, Westview Press, Boulder, CO.
Parthasarathi, P., 2001, *The Transition to a Colonial Economy: Weavers, Merchants and Kings in South India, 1720–1800*, Cambridge University Press, Cambridge.
Seth, S., 1993, '"Nehruvian socialism", 1927–1937: Nationalism, Marxism, and the pursuit of modernity', *Alternatives*, 18.
Natwar Singh, K., 2005, Minister of External Affairs, valedictory address at Petrotech Vigyan Bhawan, New Delhi, 19 January, available at http://meaindia.nic.in/speech/2005/1/19ss01.htm.
Sinha, Y., 2002, 'Future directions of Indian foreign policy', *International Institute for Strategic Studies*, 30 October.
Thapar, R., 1966, *A History of India*, Vol. I, Penguin, Harmondsworth.
Thapar, R., 1975, 'Asokan India and the Gupta Age' in Basham, A. L. (ed.), *A Cultural History of India*, Clarendon Press, Oxford.
Trautmann, T. R., 1993, *Kautilya and the Arthashastra: A Statistical Investigation of the Authorship and Evolution of the Text*, E. J. Brill, Leiden, 1971, cited in Wolpert, S., *A New History of India*, fourth edition, Oxford University Press, Oxford.
Vajpayee, A. B., Speech at the University of Mauritius, 11 March 2000 in Ministry of External Affairs, Government of India, *Foreign Relations of India, Select Statements, January 2000–March 2001*, New Delhi.
Watson, F., 1979, *India, A Concise History*, Thames and Hudson, London.
Wolpert, S., 1993, *A New History of India*, Oxford University Press, Oxford.

2 The democratization of Indian politics

In the opening chapter, we saw how modern India emerged as an independent state. Today, India is hailed as the world's largest democracy. The Indian constitution and political system is meant to demonstrate progress towards modernity characterized by 'democratic' institutions. Fukuyama argues that, 'if we looked beyond liberal democracy and markets, there was nothing else towards which we could expect to evolve; hence the end of history. While there were retrograde areas that resisted that process, it was hard to find a viable alternative civilization that people actually wanted to live in after the discrediting of socialism, monarchy, fascism and other types of authoritarianism' (Fukuyama, 2001: 21). He believes that democracy and free markets will continue to expand as the dominant organizing principles for much of the world. He asserts that liberal democracy and free markets work best in societies with certain values, however, the institutions of modernity will work outside the western world and the proof lies in the progress that democracy and free markets have made in regions such as East Asia, Latin America, orthodox Europe, South Asia and even Africa. Furthermore, millions of people have migrated and continue to migrate from the developing world to the west. Migration from the Indian subcontinent is discussed in Chapter 7, although the focus is not on migration to the west but on the dispersal of Indians on a global scale. This chapter argues that the adoption of a new constitution for independent India was indeed an attempt to transform India into a liberal democracy.

However, the experience of the last fifty or so years has shown that a distinction is not always made between liberal democracy and its trappings, such as the holding of elections. The core principle on which the concept of democracy is based is accountability. Liberal democracy calls for public influence on government through such institutions as political parties, regular elections, and an alternation in power. Most states accept that democracy requires an institutional framework and embodies certain processes. However, in practice, liberal democracies often exclude some groups from both meaningful participation in politics and the distribution of economic benefits (Mittelman, 1997: 8). Some critics have also argued that the Indian state is based on some foundational mythologies. However, globalization has exposed the Indian populace to global ideas and experiences and stimulated the development of Indian ideas. It has also enabled Indians to participate in global networks, thus shaking them out of the 'fatalistic' attitude that often characterizes developing societies and countries. These new social movements will be considered in Chapter 6. The Indian national movement discussed in Chapter 1 was also an important movement that challenged the colonial state and helped to bring about its demise. Former minister of external affairs, Jaswant Singh, asserts that the 'values of democracy, human rights, pluralism and respect for rule of law, all civilizational influences, have acquired almost universal validity'. For him, civilizations are not based only on narrow religious affinities. It is 'what is common, what is shared and that which enriches all'. The Indian civilization is based on belief in the fundamental unity of all humanity, *vasudhaiva kutumbkum*, which means that the entire world is a family. Singh argues that 'the central question that we have to grapple with is how to forge societies that are truly liberal and multicultural, but which retain a sense of unity and a corpus of common values: how they can best contribute to the emergence of a truly shared and liberal "human civilization"' (Singh, 5 September 2000).

The creation of India (and Pakistan)

The creation of the two states of India and Pakistan was not a straightforward task. The principle on the basis of which the two states were created was simply that the Muslim majority states, mainly in the north-west and Bengal, would go to Pakistan and the rest of the subcontinent to India, although the princely states (under the semi-autonomous rule of princes) were given the right to remain independent if they so desired. However, this meant that borders had to be drawn, a task performed by the Radcliffe Commission. In the event, partition caused much human suffering as a result of the tensions and hostilities which had flared up between the Hindus and the Muslims due to the communal politics of the Muslim League and Muslim political elites and certain Hindu organizations. People who suddenly found themselves on the wrong side of the border and who were victimized by communal forces left their homes and tried to cross the border. Millions of people were killed or became homeless. The partition created around 1.25 million refugees (*India Today*, 18 August 2003).

Apart from this, even uniting India was not an easy task. Before the dawn of independence, British India comprised a number of provinces and around 562 princely states under the suzerainty of the British Crown but ruled by semi-autonomous rulers. Some of these princely states posed a problem as their rulers were not from the majority community and therefore did not represent its views. For example Hyderabad, with a Hindu majority, had a Muslim ruler, while

Kashmir, with a Muslim majority, had a Hindu maharaja. It was Sardar Vallabhbhai Patel, a great Indian statesman and a close colleague of Gandhi, who persuaded the rulers of these states to join the Indian Union and accept the Indian constitution (Mehta, 1993). However, the state of Kashmir has a unique status in the Indian federation conferred on it by Article 370 of the constitution. Basically, it has more autonomy than the other states. Initially, the maharaja of Kashmir had tried to remain independent but in October 1947, following attacks on the state by armed tribesmen and other elements from across the border with the intention of forcing it to join Pakistan, the maharaja acceded to the Indian Union.

After independence was achieved, it was recognized that a reorganization of India's states had to be undertaken. Due to the demand for the creation of states on the basis of language, some were formed on the basis of the linguistic principle. In 1956 the States Re-Organization Act was passed, creating fourteen states and five union territories. Four years later the Bombay Re-organization Act was passed which divided the province into Maharashtra and Gujarat. Agitation in the Punjab finally led in 1966 to the creation of the state of Haryana out of the Hindi-speaking areas of the Punjab. Linguistic identities in India are discussed in Chapter 3. Other states created after independence include Nagaland, Meghalaya, Manipur and Tripura and, in the twenty-first century, Chhattisgarh, Jharkhand and Uttaranchal. At present the Indian Union has twenty-eight states and six union territories and the national capital region, Delhi. The British had never accepted language as the sole basis for any territorial or provincial reorganization of the country; the Indian National Congress too had accepted the idea only after a lot of hesitation. They were acutely aware of the danger of 'Balkanization'.

Constitutional development

The constitution and political system of independent India are considerably influenced by western models and the process of constitutional development started well before independence was achieved in 1947. However, some Indian nationalist writers and historians believed that India was destined to be a republic. K. P. Jayaswal, in his book *Hindu Polity*, tried to prove that the ancient Hindu political system consisted partly of republics of the Athenian type, and partly of constitutional monarchies such as that of Great Britain. There were popular assemblies such as the *paura* and the *janapada* acting as checks on the powers of the king. Jayaswal argued that 'the constitutional progress made by the Hindus has probably not been equalled much less surpassed by any polity of antiquity'. He also expressed the hope that the 'Golden Age of this polity lies not only in the past but in the future' (cited in Sharma, 1996: 5).

However, the main landmarks in the constitutional development of modern India were the Regulating Act, 1773; Bengal Judicature Act, 1781; Pitt's India

Act, 1784; Charter Act, 1793; Charter Act, 1813; Charter Act, 1833; Charter Act, 1853; Government of India Act, 1858; Indian Councils Acts, 1861, 1892 and 1909; Government of India Act, 1919 and 1935. Agarwal (1981: 15–16) writes that the Regulating Act of 1773 'was undoubtedly a landmark in the constitutional development of India ... Through this Act, the Parliament made a bold attempt to establish Parliamentary control over the [East India] Company'. He argues that this Act 'laid the foundation of the future constitution of India' and 'was first in the series of those Acts which moulded the structure of the Government of India'. The greatest achievement of Pitt's India Act of 1784 was that it firmly established Crown's control over all the civil, political and military affairs of India. The Charter Act of 1833 was, according to Lord Morley, 'the most important Act passed by the Parliament till 1909'. The Act accomplished a strong centralized government for the whole of British India; such legislative centralization ensured uniformity of laws in the country. It was also supposed to ensure the fair and impartial treatment of Indians in the matter of selection for state service. Agarwal (1981: 31) remarks that 'no other Act passed in the 19th century contained such lofty principles as this one. It accorded the subject race equality of status with the ruling community'. Race and religion would not debar a person seeking employment from the higher services. Macaulay described this provision as the most 'wise, benevolent and noble clause of the Act'. The Charter Act of 1853 was 'a step forward in the constitutional development of India'. It further reduced the powers of the directors of the company and enlarged the governor-general's executive council for legislative purposes. The legislative wing began to function as a miniature parliament. Every bill passed through three readings and scrutiny by an expert committee before it was adopted. The Act also took away the power of the directors to make nominations for the Indian civil services. Henceforth candidates were to be selected through competitive examinations, open to all British subjects.

The Government of India Act of 1858 closed one great period of Indian history and ushered in another – the direct rule of the Crown. The Act provided that India henceforth was to be governed by and in the name of Her Majesty, changed the designation of the governor-general to the 'Viceroy of India' and also provided for the transfer of the military and naval forces of the company to the Crown. The Indian Councils Act of 1861, is important in the constitutional history of India for different reasons, first, because it enabled the governor-general to associate Indians with the work of legislation, and furthermore by restoring legislative powers to the governments of Bombay and Madras. In addition, by making provision for the institution of similar legislative councils in other provinces it laid the foundation of the policy of legislative devolution which resulted in the grant of almost complete internal autonomy to the provinces in 1937.

The Act of 1892 is yet another landmark in the constitutional development of India and a definite advance on the Act of 1861. For the first time, the Act introduced the elective principle. Elected Indians were to share the privilege of law-making for their country with the viceroy. However, members of the legislature were elected through restricted and indirect elections. The Act also authorized the members to ask questions and discuss the budget. The right of the members to discuss and criticize the financial policies of the executive, laid the foundation of parliamentary government. The new Act gave effect to the official policy stated in the Act of 1861 which gave Indians a larger share in the administration of the affairs of their country. However, as Pattabhai Sitaramayya points out, 'the so-called right to election to the legislatures enjoyed by local bodies and by other electorates amounted merely to nominations by those bodies, but it was up to the Government to accept them or reject them' (cited in Agarwal, 1981: 79). Therefore, the persons who got into the legislatures through indirect elections did not represent the people in the real sense of the word.

The Indian Councils Act of 1909 (also known as the Morley-Minto reforms) marked an important stage in the growth of representative institutions in India. For the first time, recognition was given to the elective principle as the basis of the composition of legislative councils, although an official majority was retained in the imperial legislative council and the combined strength of official and nominated non-official members still outnumbered the elected members of the provincial legislative councils. The Act was a subtle attempt to combine the two elements of autocracy and constitutionalism, thus creating a constitutional autocracy. The father of the Act, Secretary of State Morley, stated in the British House of Lords in 1908 that 'if I were attempting to set up a parliamentary system in India, or if it could be said that this chapter of reforms led directly or necessarily up to the establishment of a parliamentary system in India, I, for one would have nothing to do with it' (cited in Agarwal, 1981: 139). In his opinion, the conditions in India were not suitable for the introduction of a parliamentary form of government. However, his statement disappointed the Indians. The Indian nationalists were also displeased with another feature of the Act, namely the introduction of communal electorates, which marked the beginning of communal politics in India. Highlighting this Gandhi later wrote that 'the Morley-Minto reforms have been our undoing. Had it not been for separate electorates then established, we (Hindus and Mohammadans) should have settled our differences by now' (cited in Agarwal, 1981: 140). Nehru too was against the introduction of separate electorates and considered them to be divisive.

The preamble to the Government of India Act of 1919, which was based on reforms proposed by a new secretary of state, Montagu, in consultation with the viceroy, Mr Chelmsford, and a committee of four members stated that 'it is the declared policy of the Parliament to provide for the increasing association of Indians in every branch of Indian administration, and for the gradual development of self-governing institutions, with a view to the progressive realization of responsible Government in India as an integral part of the British Empire' (Agarwal 1981: 158).[1] The Act introduced dyarchy, which literally means government by two rulers, and was introduced in the provinces; responsive autocracy was retained at the centre. The administrative subjects were divided under the headings 'Central' and 'Provincial'. The provincial subjects were further divided into 'Reserved' and 'Transferred'. The reserved subjects were to be administered by the governor while the transferred subjects were placed in the charge of Indian ministers responsible to the legislature. Dyarchy facilitated gradual transition from irresponsible to responsive government. However, the government of India remained responsible to the secretary of state for India and the British parliament. Nevertheless it was deemed desirable that the Indian legislative council should be enlarged and made more representative, and its opportunities of influencing government increased.

The Government of India Act of 1935 marked the second milestone on the road to full responsible government. The Act provided for an All-India Federation comprising the British Indian provinces and the Indian states. However, the states were not forced to join the federation. Commenting on the elections that were held under this act, Nehru (1969: 5) wrote that 'the general elections in 1937 for the provincial assemblies were based on a restricted franchise affecting about twelve per cent of the population. But even this was a great improvement on the previous franchise, and nearly thirty millions all over India, apart from the Indian States, were now entitled to vote'.

It is interesting to note that many of the provisions of the Government of India Act of 1935 are reproduced in the Indian constitution almost verbatim. However, Ambedkar, the chairman of the drafting committee, argued that it was not plagiarism. The provisions taken from the Act relate mostly to the details of administration. As democratic traditions were at a formative stage in India, it was felt that it would be unwise to leave the constitution in general terms. It is worth noting that Ambedkar was initially against the creation of a constituent assembly. For this reason, as well as the fact that many of his proposals were not accepted by the assembly, Arun Shourie (1998) argues that he should not be regarded as the 'father' of the Indian constitution. However, Shourie is a staunch supporter of the BJP and Ambedkar was a leader of the depressed classes and Scheduled Castes (SCs) whose interests he sought to protect.[2] He had misgivings about majority rule and was not as enthusiastic about independence and the ending of British rule as the Indian National Congress was. On the other hand, the Nehru report of 1928 was also rejected by the Indian nationalists in 1929, although the main reason appears to be that it favoured dominion status as the immediate goal rather than complete independence.

The constituent assembly

A constituent assembly was set up in 1946 to draw up the new constitution for India. The members of the constituent assembly were indirectly elected by the elected legislative assemblies of the provinces and the total membership was 385.

> **Box 2.1 Preamble to the constitution of India**
>
> We, THE PEOPLE OF INDIA,
> having solemnly resolved to constitute India into a
> SOVEREIGN, SOCIALIST, SECULAR DEMOCRATIC REPUBLIC,
> and to secure to all its citizens:
> JUSTICE, social economic and political;
> LIBERTY of thought, expression, belief, faith and worship;
> EQUALITY of status and of opportunity;
> and to promote among them all
> FRATERNITY assuring the dignity of the individual and the unity and integrity of the nation;
> IN OUT CONSTITUENT ASSEMBLY this twenty-sixth day of November 1949 do HEREBY ADOPT, ENACT AND GIVE TO OURSELVES THIS CONSTITUTION.
>
> *Note*: The Preamble as originally adopted in 1949 did not contain the terms 'socialist', 'secular' and 'integrity'. These were added by the Forty-second Amendment of the Constitution in 1976.

Its president was Dr Rajendra Prasad. It took Ambedkar's drafting committee almost three years to draft and finalize the constitution, and it was passed and adopted by the assembly on 26 November 1949. The values on which the constitution was based are clearly enunciated in the preamble. However, as these are not traditional Indian values they should be considered to be the basis of a reform movement, although some scholars argue that they are foundational mythologies.

The Indian Union

The constituent assembly created a federal state, although it did not use the word 'federal'. India was to be a union of states. By 2000 there were twenty-eight constituent states: Andhra Pradesh, Arunachal Pradesh, Assam, Bihar, Chhattisgarh, Goa, Gujarat, Haryana, Himachal Pradesh, Jammu and Kashmir, Jharkhand, Karnataka, Kerala, Madhya Pradesh, Maharashtra, Manipur, Meghalaya, Mizoram, Nagaland, Orissa, Punjab, Rajasthan, Sikkim, Tamil Nadu, Tripura, Uttar Pradesh, Uttaranchal and West Bengal. In addition there were six centrally administered union territories: Andaman and Nicobar Islands, Chandigarh, Daman and Diu, Dadra and Nagar Haveli, Lakshadweep, and Pondicherry. The national capital, Delhi, has its own legislature and head of government but it is still not considered to be a fully fledged state.

Federalism

A federal state is normally expected to have three features: a written constitution, a constitutional division of power between the central and state (provincial) governments, and a Supreme Court or independent judiciary to act as the guardian of the constitution and settle disputes between the central government and the state governments that arise from conflicting interpretations of constitutional provisions. The Indian state has all three.

There are two ways in which a federal state can come into existence. It may be created on the basis of an agreement between a number of independent countries with shared attributes and goals, as in Australia and the United States of America. Autonomous governments cede a defined part of their sovereignty or autonomy to a new central authority. A federation may also be the product of a devolution of power from a previously centralized system of government, as in Canada and India. In these two countries the provinces did not have an existence independent of the colonial government; in both cases, a federal arrangement was imposed by British statute (Thakur, 1995). A unitary system of government, on the other hand, concentrates all legal power in a central government. Subordinate units of government are the creation of and subject to the will of that central government, for example the United Kingdom before the devolution of power to Scotland and Wales.

Distribution of powers

India is a federal state and there is a clear division of power between the central and state governments. The constitution contains three lists of legislative powers, the union list, the state list and the concurrent list. The union list consists of ninety-nine items, including defence, armed forces, atomic energy, foreign affairs, citizenship, railways, shipping and navigation, post and telegraphs and currency. Uniformity of legislation throughout the union is essential in these areas. The parliament has exclusive powers of legislation with regard to these items.

The state list consists of sixty-one items, including public order, police, prisons, local government, public health and sanitation, agriculture, irrigation and fisheries. The state legislatures have exclusive powers of legislation with regard to these items. However, there are three exceptions to this general rule:

1 If the Rajya Sabha (the council of states or the upper house of parliament) declares by a resolution supported by two-thirds of the members present and voting, that it is necessary or expedient in the national interest that parliament should make laws with respect to any matter enumerated in the state list (for the whole or any part of India). Such a resolution remains valid for a year.

2   While a proclamation of emergency is in operation
3   If the legislatures of two or more states pass resolutions to the effect that it is desirable to have a parliamentary law regulating any of the matters included in the state list.

The concurrent list consists of fifty-one items. The parliament of India and the state legislatures have concurrent power of legislation over these items. However, if a state law conflicts with a union law, the union law prevails over the state law. The residuary powers of legislation are vested in the union. The distribution of powers has led to some controversy over the nature of the Indian federation that will be discussed in a subsequent section.

The union government

The president of India

India is a republic and has a parliamentary form of government. The president of India is the constitutional head of the state. His position and powers are more or less the same as those of the British monarch. He has to act in accordance with the advice of the council of ministers.

The president is elected indirectly by the people, that is by an electoral college, which is composed of (a) the elected members of parliament and (b) the elected members of the state legislative assemblies, for a period of five years. The president can be impeached only for the violation of the constitution. The charge may be preferred by either house of parliament and is investigated by the other house.

Powers of the president

Executive powers

The president is the commander-in-chief of the defence forces. He has vast powers of appointment. He appoints the prime minister and other ministers, the chief justice and other judges, ambassadors etc. He also has the power to grant pardons.

Legislative powers

The president summons the houses of parliament and prorogues them. He can dissolve the Lok Sabha (the house of the people, or the lower house of parliament). Every bill passed by parliament must be presented to the president for his assent. He can promulgate ordinances, except when both the houses of parliament are in session.

Emergency powers

The president can declare an emergency either in any part or the whole of India if he is satisfied that there is:

1   a threat of war or external aggression or internal disturbance
2   a breakdown of the constitutional machinery in any state
3   a financial breakdown.

In reality, the emergency powers are exercised on the advice of the prime pinister and the council of ministers and can potentially lead to the suspension of the democratic process, for which the Indian government has been criticized several times. On the other hand, hung parliaments have in recent years increased the authority of the president especially to summon and dissolve the Lok Sabha.

The prime minister

The prime minister is the leader of the party that commands the majority in parliament and the head of the council of ministers. They are collectively responsible to the Lok Sabha. If they lose the confidence of the Lok Sabha they go out of office. The council of ministers headed by the prime minister is the real executive. The long list of powers vested in the President are in reality exercised by the prime minister. Table 2.1 gives a list of Indian prime ministers, their terms of office and their political affiliations.

Parliament (Sansad)

Lok Sabha

The Lok Sabha is directly elected by the people on the basis of universal adult suffrage. Each state is allotted a certain number of seats on the basis of its population in proportion to the total population of all the states. It has a maximum of 550 members, who represent constituencies in both states and union territories. The Lok Sabha is elected for a term of five years and is presided over by the speaker who is elected by the house from among its own members.

Rajya Sabha

The Rajya Sabha or council of states is an indirectly elected body consisting of not more than 250 members. Of these 232 are elected by the elected members of state legislative assemblies and twelve are nominated by the president of India. The nominated members should be persons with special knowledge of certain subjects or practical experience in certain areas, such as 'literature, science, art and social service'. The Rajya Sabha is a permanent body like the American senate. Its members are elected for six years. At the end of every second year, one-third of the members are re-elected.

Both the houses have co-equal powers. However, in financial matters, the Rajya Sabha has only an advisory role and the Lok Sabha has the final say. The Rajya Sabha is presided over by the vice-president of India.

The Supreme Court

India has a single integrated hierarchical system of judiciary at the apex of which stands the Supreme Court. It is the guardian of the constitution and its highest interpreter. *It is the protector of the fundamental rights of the people guaranteed under the constitution.* In the exercise of this power it can declare union or state laws invalid or issue writs or orders to any administrative authority in any part of India with a view to preventing the infringement of any fundamental rights guaranteed under the constitution.

The Supreme Court consists of the chief justice and twenty-five other judges, all appointed by the president of India. The constitution envisages an independent court. A judge retires at sixty-five, and can otherwise be removed only on the grounds of proved misbehaviour or incapacity. A resolution has to be passed by both houses of parliament supported by two-thirds of the members present and voting and a majority of the total membership of the house.

The Supreme Court has both original and appellate jurisdiction. It has original exclusive jurisdiction in most disputes (a) between the government of India and one or more states; or (b) between the government of India and any state or states on one side and one or more other states on the other; or (c) between two or more states.

The original jurisdiction of the Supreme Court also extends to cases of violation of the fundamental rights of individuals and the court can issue writs for the enforcement of these rights. The appellate jurisdiction of the court extends to constitutional, civil, criminal and special matters if an interpretation of the constitution is involved. The Supreme Court may in its discretion, grant special leave to appeal from any judgement, decree, determination, sentence or order passed or made by any court or tribunal in the territory of India.

The Supreme Court also plays the role of adviser to the president of India. The president can refer to the court either a question of law or a question of fact provided that it is of public importance.

State government

The state governments consist of the governor, the chief minister and the council of ministers, the state legislature and the state judiciary.

The governor

The governor is the constitutional head of the state as the president is for the whole of India. Essentially an agent of the union government, he is appointed by the president for a period of five years and holds office at his/her discretion.

The governor appoints the chief minister and other ministers, convenes the state legislature and can prorogue or dissolve it. Every bill that is passed by the state legislature has to be presented to the governor for his assent. He can also promulgate ordinances during the recess of the Legislature. Finally, he also has the power to grant pardons for the violation of a state law.

The chief minister

The chief minister is the leader of the majority party in the state legislative assembly and the head of the council of ministers. The council of ministers is the real executive and is collectively responsible to the assembly.

State legislatures

Only six states (Bihar, Jammu and Kashmir, Maharashtra, Madhya Pradesh, Karnataka and Uttar Pradesh) have a bicameral legislature, i.e. both a legislative assembly and a legislative council. The rest of the states have a unicameral legislature i.e. only a legislative assembly.

The legislative assembly is elected by the people of the state on the basis of universal adult suffrage. It is elected for five years but may be dissolved earlier by the governor. The legislative council is elected by local government bodies, University graduates and teachers. Some members are elected by the members of the legislative assembly and some are nominated by the governor. One-third of its membership retires every two years.

State judiciary

Every state has a high court operating within its territorial jurisdiction. These operate directly under the Supreme Court as parts of a single, integrated, hierarchical, all-India judicial system. However, the Supreme Court does not have any direct administrative control over the high courts. They are independent judicial institutions. Neither the state executive nor the state legislature has any power to control the high court, or to alter the constitution or organization of the high court. Every high court judge is appointed by the president of India and retires at the age of sixty-two. He can be removed from office only for proved misbehaviour or incapacity.

The high courts have original and appellate jurisdiction. The constitution also vests in them four additional powers: (1) the power to issue writs or orders for the enforcement of the fundamental rights or for any other specified purpose; (2) the power of superintendence over all courts in the state; (3) the power to transfer cases to themselves from subordinate courts concerning the interpretation of the constitution; and (4) the power to appoint officers and servants of the high court.

Judges of the district courts are also appointed by the governor in consultation with the high court. Subordinate courts have been placed under the superintendence of the high court in order to secure the independence of the judiciary from the executive. In fact, the independence of the judiciary is an important issue in many developing countries.

Fundamental rights and directive principles of state policy

The constitution of India guarantees a list of six fundamental rights which are justiciable, i.e., they can be enforced by a court of law: *the right to equality, the right to freedom, the right against exploitation, the right to freedom of religion, cultural and educational rights and the right to constitutional remedies.* A seventh right, namely the right to property, was also guaranteed by the constitution when it was first adopted, however, the Forty-Fourth Amendment (1979) to the constitution removed this from the list of fundamental rights.

Baxter notes that 'the constitution, with its impressive list of rights, seeks to alter the traditional Indian system of social stratification based on ascriptive assignment of status' (1998: 56). The constitution abolishes untouchability and introduces the equality of all individuals in the eyes of the law. To assuage the fears of Muslims and other minorities, it provides for freedom of religion and worship and prohibits discrimination in administrative, political and social life on the basis of religion, caste, creed, gender or social origins. Having said this, however, it must also be noted that the government's reservation policy has given rise to much controversy. The reservation policy refers to the reservation of seats for Scheduled Castes, Scheduled Tribes (STs) and 'other backward classes' (OBCs) in the parliament, state legislatures, educational institutions and public services. In 2003 *India Today* pointed out that 'ideally, when a nation progresses, catches up with the world, the idea of affirmative action becomes redundant'. Unfortunately in India many castes aspire to be 'backward' and political parties continue to be in favour of reservations (*India Today*, 25 August 2003).

To an extent the Indian constitution enshrines fundamental global/universal values. The issue of rights had been given some thought even before the creation of the constituent assembly and before the adoption of the 1948 Universal Declaration of Human Rights, although the influence of western liberal thought on these ideas and proposals was unmistakable.

The suspension of the fundamental rights enshrined in the constitution during the emergency years imposed by Indira Gandhi between 1975 and 1977 led to a reign of terror. The nation heaved a sigh of relief when she lost the 1977 elections. A few years later Nani Palkhivala wrote that 'no period in the history of our Republic is of more educative value than 1975–1977. [Writer and philosopher], George Santayana said "progress far from consisting in change depends on retentiveness. Those who cannot remember the past are condemned to repeat it." If our basic freedoms are to survive it is of vital importance that we remember the happenings during the emergency when the freedoms were suspended, what has happened before can happen again' (Palkhivala, 1984: p. xiii).

The constitution is an eclectic document that draws on various sources of ideas. As Thakur writes, the simultaneous attraction of western democracy and

Soviet socialism is particularly apparent in the chapters on fundamental rights and directive principles of state policy. Part IV of the constitution, for example, entitled 'The Directive Principles of State Policy', contains non-justiciable rights such as the right to employment and education. The citizen has no judicial remedy if he is denied the enjoyment of these rights, so what is their value? Taken together, these principles form a charter of economic and social democracy in India and aim to create a welfare state. It is the duty of the state to apply these principles in making laws; they lay down a code of conduct for administrators. The framers of the constitution were influenced by the constitution of the Irish Republic which embodies a chapter on 'Directive Principles of Social Policy'. However, the Irish themselves had drawn on the constitution of Republican Spain. Indeed, the idea of such principles can be traced to the Declaration of the Rights of Man and Citizen proclaimed by revolutionary France and the Declaration of Independence proclaimed by the American colonies, and also to the ideas of Jeremy Bentham, the political and social stand of the liberal and radical parties of western Europe, the principles of Fabian socialism (and to some extent guild socialism), The Government of India Act of 1935 and the Charter of the United Nations. The Universal Declaration of Human Rights was drafted at the same time as the constitution of India. However, Pylee stresses that a number of these principles are entirely Indian in character, particularly those dealing with village *panchayats* (councils), cottage industries, prohibition, protection against cow-slaughter, SCs, STs and other socially and educationally 'backward' classes. Some of these principles are associated with Gandhi (Pylee, 1994). Ambedkar also stressed the importance of economic rights. In fact he argued that political rights were not worth much unless they were accompanied by economic ones and, moreover, that these should be enshrined in the constitution. He also held that these economic rights could only be secured through state socialism (Shourie, 1998: 428).

The directive principles of state policy include the following provisions: (1) the state shall secure a social order for the promotion of the welfare of the people; (2) the state shall organize village *panchayats* as units of self-government; (3) the state shall strive to secure the right to work, to education, an adequate means of livelihood, just and humane conditions of work, a living wage, a decent standard of life, leisure, social and cultural opportunities and public assistance in cases of undeserved want, such as unemployment, old age, sickness and so on; (4) the state shall endeavour to secure a uniform civil code applicable to the entire country.

Other principles relate to the participation of workers in the management of industries, free and compulsory education for children up to the age of fourteen years, the educational and economic interests of the weaker sections of the society, especially the SCs and the STs, improvement of public health and the prohibition of intoxicating drinks and drugs, organization of agriculture and animal husbandry, protection of the environment, protection of monuments of historic interest and national importance, and the separation of the judiciary from the executive.

Article 51 of the constitution deals with international relations and states that the state will endeavour to promote international peace and security, maintain just and honourable relations between nations, foster respect for international law and treaty obligations and encourage the settlement of international disputes by arbitration.

However, even after more than fifty years of independence India is not a welfare state, notwithstanding the good intentions of the Indian leaders, government and the efforts of the planning commission. Moreover, for many Indians the fundamental rights are meaningless; they do not have even the basic necessities of life. A rapidly growing population has no doubt diluted the achievements of these years and traditional societies based on inequality are not easy to change by legal means alone. The Indian government claims that they have succeeded in bringing the percentage of people living below the Indian poverty line down but also acknowledges that more public action is necessary to achieve the goals that the Indians have set for themselves. The Common Minimum Programme adopted by the Congress-led United Progressive Alliance (UPA) government in May 2004 is a step in that direction.[3] It pledges to raise public spending in education to at least 6 per cent of GDP; at least half of this amount will be spent on primary and secondary sectors. It also pledges to raise public spending on health to at least 2-3 per cent of the GDP by 2009, with a focus on primary health care. The UPA government has affirmed its commitment to 'ensure the welfare and well-being of all workers, particularly those in the unorganized sector who constitute 93 per cent' of India's workforce. It has also made a commitment to deal with the exploitation of vulnerable groups and the environment: 'Eviction of tribal communities and other forest-dwelling communities from forest areas will be discontinued. Co-operation of these communities will be sought for protecting forests and for undertaking social afforestation. The rights of tribal communities over mineral resources, water sources, etc. as laid down by law will be fully safeguarded'. Moreover, international targets such as the Millennium Development Goals that are very similar to the directive principles enshrined in India's constitution are now as relevant to India as they are to other developing countries, and India will have to make renewed efforts to achieve them.

The future of secularism

Secularism can mean equal and due respect for all religions and faiths or the separation of the state from the church. The preamble to the constitution of India says that India is a 'secular democratic republic'. One of the fundamental rights guaranteed to the people of India by the constitution is the right to freedom of religion. There are three restrictions on the exercise of this right: it should not adversely affect public order, morality or health.

However, communal riots (between Hindus and Muslims) are not uncommon and there are traditional restrictions on social intercourse between the two communities. Also the rise of the BJP (a Hindu nationalist party) is often seen as a threat to secular principles. In recent years, Hindu right-wing organizations have engineered attacks on minorities and their institutions and this has led to a public debate on the future of secularism in India.

In 1984, the assassination of Indira Gandhi by two of her Sikh bodyguards led to communal attacks on Sikhs in the capital, New Delhi. It is estimated that around 2,000 Sikhs, including women and children, were killed by Hindu extremists. The Gujarat riots of February 2002 are reminiscent of the attacks on the Sikh community. *India Today* estimates that twelve *lakhs* people participated in the riots, which were sparked off by an allegation that on 26 February 2002 the Sabarmati Express carrying pilgrims returning from Ayodhya was set alight by a Muslim mob in the town of Godhra in the Indian state of Gujarat. Around fifty-nine people, mainly Hindus, were burnt to death. The victims of the riots were mainly Muslims. The Gujarat government was criticized by several welfare groups for failing to prevent the spread of violence in the state. Human Rights Watch even accused the BJP state government of playing a role in the rioting.

However, chief minister Narendra Modi and his BJP party won the Gujarat state elections in December 2002. The Indian media described the election results as 'extremely ominous for the country's future as a truly secular and pluralist polity' (*The Hindu* cited on *BBC News*, 16 December 2002). The BJP's arch rival, the Congress, declared in its 2004 election manifesto that it was 'deeply concerned that secularism has come under the most severe assault in the past few years' and that 'the misuse of any religion to spread hate and discord in our society is communalism'. It also accused the BJP of deliberately inciting and sponsoring a communal carnage in Gujarat, glorifying violence against missionaries and encouraging viciously communal and fascist organizations like the Vishwa Hindu Parishad (VHP) and the Bajrang Dal to spread hate (Indian National Congress, 2004). A commission has been set up by the central government to investigate the cause of the fire that burnt a coach of the Sabarmati Express; initial forensic investigations suggest that the fire was started inside a carriage and not by a mob outside. Meanwhile, the British government and other European nations have taken a clear stand that they would have nothing to do with Mr Modi after the Gujarat killings (*The Hindu*, 24 March 2005).

The demolition of the 400-year-old Babri Masjid mosque by *kar sevaks* (Hindu holy workers) on 6 December 1992 is yet another incident that cast a shadow on secularism in India. Certain Hindu fundamentalist organizations wanted to build a Ram *janambhoomi* (birthplace) temple in Ayodhya, believed to be Lord Rama's birthplace. Unfortunately, the Babri Masjid already stands at the site they have chosen for building the temple and which they claim is the exact spot where Rama was born. The Hindu groups also claim that a temple had once existed there but was torn down by Babur, the Mughal ruler, in the sixteenth century and the mosque built in its place. The incident took the country by surprise and as news of the demolition spread, communal riots broke out all over the country and the army had to be deployed in many areas to maintain law and order. The Indian government complained that the coverage given to the incident by the foreign media, especially the BBC and the CNN, had aggravated the situation and led to more violence in the country and abroad (Dutt, 1993). However, this does not mean that the Indian government does not respect the principle of freedom of information or the role of the media in a democracy. A free press has always striven to ensure accountability, and India's traditions in this field are quite well established. Even in 1878 when Lord Lytton had attempted to gag the press by passing the Vernacular Press Act, and in 1919 when the infamous Rowlatt Acts were passed, the country had revolted against them. Despite the fact that for many years the Indian TV channel Doordarshan has been controlled by the Indian government, since the early 1990s the popularity of cable and satellite TV has increased. The 1991 Gulf War had made CNN a household name and in 1993 Rupert Murdoch acquired a 63.6 per cent stake in Star TV. The Cable Television Networks (Regulation) Act was passed in 1995 and by 2003 there were 30,000 cable operators in India providing access to 40 million households, with the number of satellite channels rising to seventy (*India Today*, 18 August 2003). As regards the Ayodhya dispute, to this day the Ram temple has not been constructed although the BJP has made it abundantly clear that it is in favour of building this temple.

The nature of the Indian federation

India is a federal state. It has a written constitution, a clear division of power between the central and state governments, a double set of governments and an independent judiciary to settle disputes between the union and the states.

However, there is a tendency towards a high degree of centralization. As a result, India is sometimes described by political scientists as a quasi-federal state or a unitary state with subsidiary federal features, and not a federal state with subsidiary unitary features. Unlike most other federal states, the division of powers between the union and the states favours the union. In addition, the states do not have constitutions of their own, and further the territorial jurisdiction of each of the states can be changed, and states created, without amending the constitution. Furthermore, the state governors are appointed by the president of India and are essentially agents of the union government. However, the federal system established under the constitution aimed to achieve the fundamental objective of unity in diversity. Conditions in India at the time of the transfer of power and immediately thereafter were such that those in authority feared that a federal set-up without adequate special safeguards to preserve unity would dissipate the century-old effort at national unity.

Thus, the states have not been given the right to secede from the union and the framers of the constitution preferred to use the term 'union' and not 'federal' to emphasize that it is 'indestructible'. Some analysts point out, however, that the Indians inherited a centralized state from the British and merely consolidated the system that they inherited. Therefore, the institutions of government as well as the organizing principles remained more or less unchanged even after independence. Thakur writes that 'indeed the legacy that brought the greatest satisfaction to the British themselves is that of the bureaucracy' (Thakur, 1995: 3–5). The Indian Civil Service, the 'steel frame' of British administration, was inherited by independent India. Although it was rather elitist, the loyalties of the ICS officers were pan-Indian rather than regional, communal or provincial, and they helped to foster a sense of centralized governance. As Thakur (1995: 44) comments, in comparison with other Third World countries, for example the Belgium Congo, India 'had cause to be grateful for the legacy of a centralized, cohesive, dedicated and efficient administration which had been opened up significantly to "the natives" by the time of independence'. However, according to a different view, Nehru felt that the administrative machinery was 'fossilized' and his successors set up the Administrative Reforms Commission. On 24 June 2004 the prime minister, Manmohan Singh, asserted in his address to the nation that 'the government at every level is today not adequately equipped and attuned to deal with the economic and social challenges facing the nation'. The setting up of an Administrative Reforms Commission 'to prepare a detailed blueprint for revamping the public administrative system' is very much on the agenda (Khosla, 2004). Moreover, the high degree of centralization has affected relations between the central government and state governments and will be discussed next.

Centre–state relations

Centre-state relations are asymmetrical and therefore often strained. There has also been a persistent demand from the states for greater autonomy. Some regional political parties, such as the Akali Dal in the Punjab are in favour of curtailing the powers of the union government. It should only control foreign affairs, defence, communications and railways and currency.

The states have also complained that while the centre is entrusted with considerable financial resources, they, with many vital functions to perform, are financially starved. This inadequacy was sought to be made up by the use of central grants-in-aid, which were also meant to help backward states. Besides grants, the states approach the centre for loans and advances; the resources transferred from the centre have accounted for over 45 per cent of the states' total expenditure. But the states do not like being financially dependent on the centre. The twelfth Finance Commission on sharing of taxes between the centre and states for 2005–10 is in favour of grants rather than the devolution of taxes. The panel chair, Mr Rangarajan, has argued that this would benefit the poorer states whose share of tax revenue is lower (*The Statesman*, 18 December 2004). However, economic liberalization has created more opportunities for states also to obtain loans from private sources. This could lead to indebtedness and the central government has urged state governments to deal with fiscal deficits and introduce reforms. India is already a nation in debt: the total debt of its central and state governments is around 66 per cent of GDP and the central government spends almost half of its total revenues on interest payments (Mukherjee, 2002; *Economic Survey 2003–2004*: 29). Furthermore some state governments, such as those of Gujarat and Andhra Pradesh, are enthusiastically promoting private investment and economic growth and have shown greater keenness than the central government to privatize state enterprises (Mukherjee, 2002).

A serious complaint of other states like Kerala is about the regional imbalances in industrial development. The complaint is that the centre has not used its fiscal dominance over the states to correct regional imbalances. Nor has the centre used other instruments at its disposal to promote balanced regional development. However, the states themselves have not fully exploited the resources they command. They are reluctant to tax agricultural incomes and have been abolishing land levies despite the gaping deficits in their budgets. They lack political courage. The state tax administrations are also often hopelessly corrupt and inefficient.

In 1983 the Sarkaria Commission was set up by the government of India (under Indira Gandhi) to review existing arrangements between the centre and the states. Its report, released in 1987/88, recognized that 'the central theme of the criticism levelled against the working of union-state legislative relations is "over-centralization"' (cited in Saez, 1999). However, this issue was emphasized mainly by the non-Congress state governments of Andhra Pradesh, Karnataka, Tamil Nadu, Punjab and West Bengal. The commission proposed some moderate changes relating to legislative relations between the central and state governments, the role of the governor, emergency powers and financial relations between the central and state governments, but many of its recommendations were never implemented. For example, it had recommended that Article 356 'should be used very sparingly, in extreme cases, as a measure of last resort, when all available alternatives fail to prevent or rectify a break-down of constitutional machinery in the State' and suggested that 'the State Legislative Assembly should not be dissolved either by the Governor or the President before the Proclamation issued under Article 356 (1) has been laid before Parliament and it has had an opportunity to consider it' (cited in Saez, 1999: 51). Article 356 of the Indian constitution empowers the governor of any state to dissolve the state legislative assembly whenever there is a breakdown of the constitutional machinery of a state. According to former deputy prime minister, L. K. Advani, this article 'has dominated the [Inter-State] Council's deliberations since its inception in 1990' (*The Hindu*, 29 August 2003) and continues to give rise to

controversy. Governors are often accused of misusing this power. For example, the dismissal of Goa's Manohar Parrikar-led BJP government by the state governor, S. C. Jamir, in February 2005, hours after the government won a confidence vote in the legislative assembly was condemned in many quarters.[4] In the Common Minimum Programme, the UPA government has promised to revisit the issue of centre-state relations: 'The Sarkaria Commission had last looked at the issue of Centre-State relations over two decades ago. The UPA government will set up a new Commission for this purpose keeping in view the sea-changes that have taken place in the polity and economy of India since then'. However, the BJP-led National Democratic Alliance government had appointed a National Commission to Review the Working of the Constitution in 2000 whose remit included the examination of centre-state relations. It submitted its report in March 2002 which, while endorsing the recommendations of the Sarkaria Commission, recommended that in resolving problems and co-ordinating policy and action, the union as well as the states should more effectively utilize the forum of inter-state council. This would lead to mutual confidence and also the resolution of issues expeditiously.[5]

Political culture

Democratic institutions were introduced in India not because there was a demand for them from the masses but because the western-educated elites believed that through the introduction of universal suffrage and consequent mass political participation, a traditional society based upon an ascriptive and hierarchical structure would transform itself into an egalitarian and open society. They also hoped that modernization would promote democratic values. The social transformation that they were hoping for has not happened but citizens, even in the villages, have developed political awareness and are becoming more politicized and are learning to use their political power. The lower castes and Dalits are beginning to challenge the domination of the land-owning upper castes.[6] This is discussed further in Chapter 6. Although loyalties are often based upon subgroup identity (as discussed in Chapter 3) which leads to voting *en bloc* along communal lines, the electorate also express an interest in electing competent national leaders and in good governance. Moreover, turnout rates at elections tend to be quite high (Baxter, 1998: 47).

Social conflict is inherent in the Indian system and is often brought to a head by the politics of value allocation. Fortunately, Indians have inherited from their past a tradition of consensus building, conciliation, compromise and accommodation that has enabled the political system to meet internal challenges successfully.

There is, however, a dark side to Indian politics. Unfortunately, with the passage of time, electoral politics have become 'amoral'. Politicians and political parties give and accept bribes[7] and are often in league with criminals and other anti-social elements. Some politicians are more interested in furthering their personal ambitions rather than national goals. The acquisition of political power has become an end in itself.

Political parties

Political parties form the link between the state and civil society. In theory, there are three kinds of political parties in India – national, regional and communal. All-India political parties have been officially defined as national parties that have broad-based national support and are able to win a minimum of 4 per cent of the votes or more than 3 per cent of the seats in at least four state legislative assemblies, or 4 per cent of the votes or 4 per cent of seats in the Lok Sabha. These parties present national platforms and emphasize national issues in the parliamentary elections (Baxter, 1998: 94). Based on the results of the 1984 and 1985 elections the following parties were classified as All-India parties: the Congress (I), the Bharatiya Janata Party (BJP), the Janata Dal, the Communist Party of India (CPI) and the Communist Party of India (Marxist) (CPI/M). These parties continue to enjoy this status in the twenty-first century.

The regional parties represent regional nationalism based on common language, culture and history. They try to aggregate regional interests regardless of the caste and religious affiliations of their members. The best-known regional parties are: Dravida Munnetra Kazhagam (DMK) and All-India Anna-DMK (AIADMK) of Tamil Nadu, the Telegu Desum of Andhra Pradesh, the National Conference of Jammu and Kashmir and the Asom Gana Parishad (AGP) of Assam. The communal parties represent only the members of a particular religious or ethnic community, e.g. the Akali Dal (representing the Sikh community of the Punjab), the Muslim League and the Shiv Sena (a pro-Hindu, pro-Marathi party in Maharashtra).

However, the Indian National Congress, the party founded in 1885 and which had led the nationalist movement, dominated Indian politics until the mid-1990s. Table 2.1 gives a list of prime ministers and their political affiliations from 1947 until 2004. It may be noted that a majority were from the Congress. The party claims that it is a broad national movement that enables people from diverse social backgrounds to come together in the service of the country.[8] But there is also a strong reliance upon a multiethnic, multilingual and middle-class elite to manage national politics. The members of this elite are committed to secularism and do not favour any religion or religious order over others in the performance of their public duties; they are also committed to political democracy. But behind the scenes the Congress relies upon a complex set of patron-client relations that reaches right down to the district level. The party's electoral strategy depends on the formation of alliances with dominant caste groups in each state and the accommodation of minorities and regional diversities (Hewitt, 1997: 176; Baxter, 1998: 95–9). Baxter writes that the party was

Table 2.1 *Indian prime ministers, 1947–*

Name	Term of office	Political party
Jawaharlal Nehru	Aug. 1947–May 1964	Congress
Lal Bahadur Shastri	June 1964–Jan. 1966	Congress
Indira Gandhi	Jan. 1966–Mar. 1977	Congress
Morarji Desai	Mar. 1977–July 1979	Janata
Charan Singh	July 1979–Jan. 1980	Janata (Secular)
Indira Gandhi	Jan. 1980–Oct.1984	Congress (I)
Rajiv Gandhi	Nov. 1984–Dec.1989	Congress (I)
V. P. Singh	Dec. 1989–Nov.1990	Janata Dal
Chandra Shekhar	Nov. 1990–June 1991	Janata Dal (S)
P. V. Narasimha Rao	June 1991–May 1996	Congress (I)
Atal Bihari Vajpayee	May 1996–June 1996	BJP
H. D. Deve Gowda	June 1996–Apr. 1997	Janata Dal
I. K. Gujral	Apr. 1997–Apr. 1998	Janata Dal
Atal Bihar Vajpayee	Apr. 1998–May 2004	BJP
Manmohan Singh	May 2004–	Congress (I)

originally based on a broad consensus, however, after the death of Nehru and a split within the party in 1969, Indira Gandhi became the dominant force within the party and it became dependent on her charismatic personality and populist policies for electoral victories. In 1977, there was another split in the party due to its defeat in the elections following the termination of Indira Gandhi's emergency rule, and many old leaders left. It then became even more closely identified with Indira Gandhi and was renamed the Congress (I). After the assassination of Rajiv Gandhi in 1991 the Congress (I) lost its popularity but returned to power more than a decade later in May 2004.

However, since the start of the era of coalition governments in the mid-1990s, many regional parties have began to participate in national politics. The main political parties since the 1990s include the following: Akali Dal; AIADMK; All-India Forward Bloc; Asom Gana Parishad; Bahujan Samaj Party (BSP); BJP; Bihar Peoples Party; Biju Janta Dal; CPI/M; Congress (I); DMK; Indian National League; Janata Dal; Janata Dal United Party; Kerala Congress (Mani faction); Muslim League; National Conference; Rashtriya Janata Dal (RJD); Revolutionary Socialist Party (RSP); Samajwadi Party (SP); Samata Party; Shiv Sena; Tamil Maanila Congress (TMC); Telegu Desum; and the Trinamool Congress. Brass (1994: 67) writes that 'the diversities and social fragmentation of Indian society have produced a proliferation of regional and other political parties which often give to each state in the Indian Union a unique party system imperfectly integrated into the "national party system"'. Moreover, although there are ideological differences among the parties, there is no ideological cleavage in the party system. Most Indian political parties also exhibit certain characteristics such as factionalism and dynastic succession to leadership.

Another factor that has become significant in more recent years is the support that some of these parties receive from the Indian diaspora. For example, both the Congress (I) Party and the BJP have supporters in foreign countries like the UK and the US. Members of groups such as the Overseas Friends of the BJP (OFBJP) have campaigned in Indian elections, raised funds for the party and even supported controversial programmes such as the proposed construction of a temple at the disputed site occupied by the Babri Masjid mosque in Ayodhya (Dhume, 2002).

Since the BJP has now become a dominant party in Indian politics, it is necessary to explain what it stands for. Brass (1994: 87) writes that 'between 1989 and 1992, the BJP became the most dynamic political force in the Indian party system'. In the 1989 elections, it emerged as the third largest party in the Lok Sabha after the Janata Dal and the Congress (I). It also performed well in the state legislative assembly elections of 1990 in several states such as Madhya Pradesh, Himachal Pradesh and Rajasthan. It became the ruling party in the first two states and the leader of the ruling coalition in the third. It continued to perform well (notwithstanding setbacks in some states) and it was obvious that the party has mass appeal, at least within the Hindu community. L. K. Advani's Rath Yatra (a Hindu religious procession) and the movement to construct the temple in Ayodhya demonstrated the growing strength of the party and in the Lok Sabha elections of May–June 1991 the BJP emerged as the second largest party in the house with 119 seats and a popular vote share of 20.2 per cent. It also won a majority of seats in the Uttar Pradesh legislative assembly elections, mainly at the expense of the Congress (I).

The BJP is a right-wing party and gives priority to the unity of the country; it is in favour of using force to deal with militant and secessionist movements in the Punjab, Kashmir and the northeast. The BJP has not had much success with Scheduled Castes and Muslim voters. Some of its policies have even led to communal tension and violence. However, Brass (1994: 88) contends that the BJP is not a 'fundamentalist' Hindu party. It uses Hindu religious beliefs and symbols as a focus for creating a national identity, 'but the party's goals are secular: to transform India into a modern, industrial, military power with a united nation and a disciplined work force'. The BJP's 2004 election manifesto stated: 'We believe that Indian nationhood stems from a deep cultural bonding of the people that overrides differences of caste, region, religion and language. We believe that Cultural Nationalism for which Indianness, Bharatiyata and Hindutva are synonyms – is the basis of our national identity'.[9] The BJP accepts the multifaith character of India and considers it to be a source of strength and not weakness. However, the BJP also 'unflinchingly holds that differences in faith cannot challenge the idea of India as One Nation or undermine our millennia-old identity as One People … Thus, Cultural Nationalism is the most potent antidote to communalism, divisiveness, and separatism of every kind, and a guarantor of our national unity and national integration.' The BJP's 'cultural nationalism' is described by the Congress as 'a device for dividing Indians emotionally'. The Congress claims that it 'unites the Indian nation through consensus'. It asserts that its policies 'have always been anchored in a vision of an economically prosperous, socially just, politically united and culturally harmonious India'.[10]

The BJP supported the economic reforms introduced by the Congress (I) in the early 1990s that aimed to bring about the transformation of the economy into one based on the market and private enterprise. The BJP is of the view that a big shift is taking place in the global economy, and India should be prepared to take advantage of it.[11] Its members and supporters are not uneducated and parochial Hindus but intellectuals, retired army generals, ex-civil servants and prominent businessmen, as well as teachers, professional people and engineers. Brass (1994: 88–9) describes the BJP in almost glowing terms: 'the BJP must be seen as the latest and currently the most vital political force striving to build a united Indian nation, a dynamic economy, and a strong state. It seeks to overcome the heterogeneity and caste divisiveness of Indian society by consolidating a sense of Hindu nationalism around symbols common to all who claim to be Hindus.' According to a 'mood of the nation' opinion poll conducted by *India Today*-ORG-MARG in January 2003, Vajpayee (BJP) was the most popular candidate for the prime-ministerial post, followed by Sonia Gandhi (Congress (I)) and his performance as prime minister was rated as good or outstanding by 40 per cent of the respondents (*India Today*, 10 February 2003).

On the other hand, Echeverri-Gent argues that a decentring of India's party system is taking place. Decentering involves the growing pluralism of political parties wielding power in India's federal system, especially the rise of single-state parties or regional parties that win parliamentary seats in only one state. Moreover, the mobilization of the lower castes has increased the decentring of India's party system. The poor have higher rates of participation than the upper classes. In 1999, the voter turnout of the SC communities was 2.2 per cent higher than the national average. The biggest increase has been among the STs, whose participation has traditionally been below average. In 1999, their rate of participation was 0.4 per cent above the national norm. The mobilization of these groups has coincided with the decline of the Congress (I) and the rise of parties with narrower social bases. The process began in the 1960s when OBCs in south India were mobilized by regional parties such as the DMK. This trend then spread to north India and led to defections from the Congress and the creation of new opposition parties such as the Bahujan Samaj Party, the Samata Party, and the SP, representing the OBCs, SCs and STs (Echeverri-Gent, 2002)

However, the empowerment of the disadvantaged sections of the society also includes the empowerment of women, especially in rural areas. The late Gita Mukherjee, a member of the CPI, a member of parliament from West Bengal and chairperson of the special parliamentary committee on the Women's Reservation Bill had always asserted that the first step was to allow women to break into politics. The *Panchayati Raj* institutions were the real nurseries of political leadership for women. The battle against poverty and violence can be won if women form a critical mass in all decision-making bodies, from village *panchayats* to the parliament. The reservation of seats for women in local government by the 73rd and 74th amendments of the Indian constitution (1993) has led to women wielding power effectively at the village level and challenging feudal traditions. However, the passage of the Women's Reservations Bill, which seeks to reserve 33 per cent of all seats in the national parliament and state assemblies for women, has been repeatedly blocked. Opponents of the bill include centre-left parties such as the Rashtriya Janata Dal and the SP that want subquotas for OBCs and Muslim women (*India Today*, 19 May 2003). Many organizations are encouraging women to participate in politics and are providing education and training. However, barriers to participation are not easy to surmount. Rural areas are plagued by illiteracy and poverty, and patriarchy remains deeply entrenched. The adult literacy rate for women in India was still only 46.4 per cent in 2002, as against 69 per cent for men (UNDP, 2003). Practices such as wife-beating and dowry deaths are still prevalent. Moreover, rural women do not represent a unified group. Caste, clan and family considerations often take precedence over the empowerment of women in rural areas (Pande, 2000). The new UPA government has promised to introduce legislation for the reservation of seats for women in the state legislative assemblies and the Lok Sabha and also on domestic violence and gender discrimination (Common Minimum Programme, May 2004). But the emancipation of women is not just a women's issue; it is an integral part of social progress. Economic growth can lead to more opportunities for women to acquire skills, including literacy skills, start their own business and find employment. However, it does not automatically lead to a decline in gender inequality. Public action has to be taken to bring about radical and rapid social change (Dreze and Sen, 1999).

Parliamentary democracy

Judith Brown (1994) comments that India's ability to sustain democratic forms of government and politics through the second half of the twentieth century is in sharp contrast to the experience of her Asian neighbours and of most former colonies in Africa. India has never been under military rule and elections to the parliament and state legislatures are regularly held. Brown reckons that these have been no rubber stamp: the people's verdict has produced major and sometimes dramatic results. However, as Thakur (1995) points out, the Congress Party exercised a commanding influence on Indian politics from 1947 until 1967. It was the party which had fought for independence and under Nehru became the embodiment of a remarkable consensus for such a diverse country, on social, economic and foreign policies. It was able to accommodate diverse interests and factions within its fold (Baxter, 1998: 95). Jalal (1995: 40), too, argues that 'in the absence of any national alternative ... Congress had little difficulty romping home to victory in the first three general elections, further confirming its dominance at the national as well as the state levels'. Critics point out though that the Congress attained its dominant position in rural India by making alliances that enforced the traditional patterns of domination (Sorensen, 1993: 22). Focusing on the identity of the electorate, both Jalal and Brown agree that caste loyalties still help to determine political loyalties. Political parties, therefore, have to select candidates carefully to match each local constituency, taking into account its caste, communal and economic characteristics. Nonetheless, political parties seeking national status cannot afford to rely on a single caste appeal, hence the Congress strategy.

The adoption of a parliamentary system of government has not automatically led to 'democratization'. Corbridge and Harriss (2000) write that the founding fathers' understanding of democracy and government had been shaped by the Raj and Westminster and the reforms introduced by the Indian Councils Government of India Acts of 1909, 1919 and 1935. The preamble to the Indian constitution defines the founding mythologies of modern India. In reality the power of the Indian state was enhanced because the state was the initiator and instigator of development and nation-building. This weakened democracy. However, India has not remained static and entirely dependent on a nexus between the wealthier classes and the government; the marginalized communities also are gradually beginning to play a role in the democratization of Indian politics. The problem is that globalization may not facilitate this process. Accountability of the government to the governed may be overshadowed by accountability to market forces. Mittelman (1997: 9) comments that 'there is a marked contradiction between the emerging global preference for electoral democracy and the increasing economic polarization generated by world capitalism, which is not held accountable to elected officials'. This argument is valid and can potentially pose a dilemma for the Indian government.

Notes

1 See also http://en.wikipedia.org/wiki/Government_of_India_Act_1935#Genesis_of_the_Act.
2 'Scheduled' means a schedule to the Indian constitution. Scheduled Castes and Scheduled Tribes are castes, races and tribes deemed as such under Articles 341 and 342 of the Indian constitution. Members of the SCs and STs are entitled to positive discrimination in certain areas such as the reservation of seats in educational institutions, jobs in government services, seats in legislative bodies and the allocation of funds for preferential welfare programmes.
3 Available at www.pmindia.nic.in/cmp.htm.
4 Available at www.hindu.com/2005/02/18/stories/2005021802021000.htm.
5 Available at www.lawmin.nic.in/ncrwc/ncrwcreport.htm.

6 Dalits are the depressed classes and the lowest castes in Indian/Hindu society. They have traditionally done menial work and been denied educational opportunities. They are also considered to be ritually 'polluting' and are segregated from the upper castes.
7 In December 2004 the state chief electoral officer of Bihar, K.C. Saha, lodged an FIR against the RJD president and union railway minister, Mr Lalu Prasad, for distributing hard cash among the rural masses in Bihata before an election rally in Patna on 23 December 2004 in violation of the model code of conduct for politicians. ('FIR against Lalu for "cashing" popularity', *The Statesman*, 21 December 2004).
8 Available at www.aicc.org.in/manifesto-2004.htm.
9 Available at www.bjp.org/Press/mar_3104a.htm.
10 Available at www.aicc.org.in/manifesto-2004.htm.
11 Available at www.bjp.org/Press/mar_3104a.htm.

References

Agarwal, R. C., 1981, *Constitutional History of India and National Movement*, S. Chand, New Delhi.

Baxter, C. et al., 1998, *Government and Politics in South Asia*, Westview, Boulder, CO and Oxford.

BBC4, 2004, *Indira Gandhi: The Killing of Mother India*, 7 November.

Brass, P., 1994, *The Politics of India since Independence*, Cambridge University Press, Cambridge.

Brown, J., 1994, *Modern India: The Origins of an Asian Democracy*, Oxford University Press, Oxford.

Corbridge, S. and Harriss, J., 2000, *Reinventing India: Liberalization, Hindu Nationalism and Popular Democracy*, Polity Press, Cambridge.

Dhume, S., 2002, 'From Bangalore to Silicon Valley and back: how the Indian diaspora in the US is changing India' in Ayres, A. and Oldenburg, P. (eds), *India Briefing: Quickening the Pace of Change*, M. E. Sharpe, New York and London.

Dreze, J. and Sen, A., 1999, *Economic Development and Social Opportunity*, Oxford University Press, New Delhi.

Dutt, S., 1993, 'India in strife: the Ayodhya crisis', *New Zealand International Review*, March/April.

Echeverri-Gent, J., 2002, 'Politics in India's decentered polity' in Alyssa, A. and Oldenburg, P. (eds), *India Briefing: Quickening the Pace of Change*, M. E. Sharpe, New York and London.

Fukuyama, F., 2001, 'The West has won', *Guardian*, 11 October, p. 21.

Hewitt, V. 1997, *The New International Politics of South Asia*, Manchester University Press, Manchester.

Indian National Congress, *Lok Sabha Elections 2004, Manifesto of the Indian National Congress*, available at: www.aicc.org.in/manifesto-2004.html.

Jaffrelot, C., 1996, *The Hindu Nationalist Movement and Indian Politics, 1925 to the 1990s*, Hurst and Co., London.

Government of India, Ministry of Law, Justice and Company Affairs, *The Constitution of India*, as on 1 January 2000, Government of India, New Dehli.

Jalal, A., 1995, *Democracy and Authoritarianism in South Asia*, Cambridge University Press, Cambridge.

Jayal, N. J., 2001, *Democracy and the State*, Oxford University Press, New Delhi.

Jayal, N. J., 2001, *Democracy in India*, Oxford University Press, Oxford.

Khosla, A., 2004, 'Civil service reforms', *The Statesman*, 13 December.
Mehta, K. (dir.), 1993, *Sardar: The Iron Man of India*, film.
Ministry of Law, Justice and Company Affairs (Government of India), Department of Legal Affairs, *Report of the National Commission for Reviewing the Working of the Constitution*, March 2002.
Mittleman, J. H., 1997, *Globalization – Critical Reflections*, Lynne Rienner Publishers, Boulder, CO and London.
Mukherjee, J., 2002, 'The Indian economy: pushing ahead and pulling apart' in Alyssa, A. and Oldenburg, P. (eds), *India Briefing: Quickening the Pace of Change*, M. E. Sharpe, New York and London.
Nehru, J., 1969, *The Discovery of India*, Asia Publishing House, London.
Palkhivala, N. A., 1984, *We the People: India the Largest Democracy*, Strand Book Stall, Bombay.
Pande, M., 2000, 'India's nurseries of politics', *UNESCO Courier*, June.
Pylee, M.V., 1994, *India's Constitution*, S. Chand and Co., New Delhi.
Sharma, R. S., 1996, *Aspects of Political Ideas and Institutions in Ancient India*, Motilal Banarsidas Publishers, New Delhi.
Saez, L., 1999, 'The Sarkaria Commission and India's struggle for federalism', *Contemporary South Asia*, 8: 1.
Shourie, A., 1998, *Worshipping False Gods*, HarperCollins, New Delhi.
Singh, J., 'Dialogue among civilizations', New York, 5 September 2000, Ministry of External Affairs, Government of India, *Foreign Relations of India, Select Statements*, January 2000–March 2001.
Sorensen, G., 1993, *Democracy and Democratization*, Westview, Boulder, CO, San Francisco, Oxford.
Thakur, R., 1995, *The Government and Politics of India*, Macmillan, Basingstoke.
UNDP, *Human Development Report 2003*, available at http://hdr.undp.org/statistics/data/cty/cty_f_IND.html.

3 Identities and the Indian state[1]

The study of Indian politics has traditionally centred on the political system: government, political parties, elections and so on. However, a strong central government, a *dirigiste* state and the dominance of the Congress Party promoted a strong national focus. Globalization and economic liberalization has changed all that. A decentralization of power is taking place. And, as regions and constituent states of the Indian union are beginning to compete with one another for investment in their economic development,[2] regionalism in Indian politics is becoming more important. Globalization has not eliminated diversity between local sites. On the contrary, 'the process has on numerous occasions encouraged a reinvigoration of substate territorial identities' (Scholte, 1996: 50). Similarly, the study of IR which had traditionally focused on the state, has begun to give more importance to culture and identity in the post-Cold-War era. The reason is, as Lapid (1997: 10) explains, 'IR's fascination with sovereign statehood has greatly decreased its ability to confront complex issues of ethnic nationhood and political otherhood'. IR theorists have turned to culture and identity better to understand, describe and explain novel issues of global heterogeneity and diversity. Commenting on IR's preoccupation with sovereign statehood, Ferguson and Mansbach (1997: 21) write that 'the demise of the Soviet empire surprised state-centric theorists in part because their theories could not accommodate a revival of old identities. Such theories are equally useless when it comes to addressing mini-nationalisms, tribal violence in Africa, the globalization of business and finance, or criminal cartels.' It is, therefore, time to look at other multi-ethnic states as well.

The concept of nation-state in international relations is based on certain assumptions, for example that humanity is divided into nations and each nation is entitled to the right to self-determination, i.e. a state of its own. Although a state can exist without a nation it does not have the same legitimacy as a nation-state. Thus post-colonial states which are often considered to have artificial boundaries and clearly encompass many ethnic groups feel obliged to embark on nation-building and prove that they are a nation-state even though, as Lapid and Kratochwil (1997: 123) point out, homogeneous nation-states are a dwindling minority and the two principles of socio-political organization – territory and ethnicity – have become contradictory in our multicultural world. However, if we believe that a state should be a nation-state, a multiethnic nation-state is a contradiction in terms. Unless, of course, we accept that ethnicity does not have to form the core of the nation, which is an 'imagined community' and is constructed, a process in which intellectuals play an important role and so do political elites. In theory, there can be a civic, liberal nationalism which does not place much importance on ethnicity. However, is it suitable for India?

According to Smith (1991: 14), the fundamental features of national identity are an historical territory or homeland, common myths and historical memories, a common mass public culture, common legal rights and duties for all members and a common economy with territorial mobility for members. However, as Bhikhu Parekh (1994: 498–9) points out, modern Indian leaders who wanted to regenerate India did not want to base the new national identity on history and culture, and resisted the temptation to evoke historical memories and draw historical parallels. In 1947, when India became independent, Prime Minister Nehru insisted that it must be based on a new liberal, democratic and secular national philosophy. Even if we accept that a nation is not a primordial entity but a construct, this still does not provide an answer to the question posed by the noted Indian jurist Nani Palkhivala (1996: 7): 'Is India a collection of communities or is it a nation?' In his opinion, the paramount need of India is to preserve the unity and integrity of the country. The policies of the Indian government do tend to give priority to this objective. However, it is difficult to say how far India has progressed since 1947 beyond mere political integration and towards the creation of a nation-state through the spread of national sentiment among the masses and the transfer of loyalties from regional or ethnic groups to the nation whose legal expression is the Indian Union. In the long run, only the loyalty of all Indian citizens to the nation will preserve the Indian state as it exists today. However, centrifugal forces are strong in India and prompts Palkhivala (1996: 7) to write that 'it is doubtful whether this mosaic of humanity will survive unfractured for any length of time'.

This chapter argues that there has always been a tension between national and subnational identities in India. Not everyone who lives within the territorial borders of India considers him/herself to be an Indian nationalist, for example – Kashmiris seeking independence. The country is subject to unrelenting tension because of the abundance of centrifugal and particularistic forces. While these may be suppressed in times of national crisis, such as war, particularism is the normal condition and universalism the exception. Policy-makers in New Delhi must act on the assumption that political unity is fragile can never be taken for granted, but instead must always be assiduously cultivated (Thakur, 1995: 4).

However, the main reason why the issue of political unity and loyalty to the Indian nation became salient in the 1990s is because the Congress – which has played such a major role in Indian politics and was considered for many years to be the embodiment of Indian nationalism and undertook the construction of an Indian national identity – was going to rack and ruin. C. R. Irani, editor of *The Statesman* in Calcutta, commented in August 1997, that 'the party is going about celebrating the golden jubilee of 1947 on the fallacy that freedom was secured by the shapeless mass which now masquerades as the Congress. The Mahatma's Indian National Congress was a national platform on which all citizens in good conscience could stand ... it has been broken into pieces and it is purely an accident that the name Congress sticks to the rump' (Irani, 1997). At the eightieth All-India Congress Committee (AICC) plenary session in Calcutta in August 1997, the Congress admitted its 'mistakes and weaknesses' in a political resolution which was passed, and stated that these had led to an 'erosion of the party's credibility'. The party also emphasized the need to consolidate its support base among the minorities, SCs and STs (*The Statesman*, 8 August 1997) who together constitute about 42 per cent of India's population.

The BJP, the Congress Party's main political and ideological rival, has made electoral gains in recent years, mainly at the expense of the Congress. Its fundamental objective is the same, i.e., to maintain the unity and integrity of the Indian state. However, it aims to create a new national identity. The objectives of the party are very clearly stated in Article II of its constitution:

> The party is pledged to build up India as a strong and prosperous nation, which is modern, progressive and enlightened in outlook and which proudly draws inspiration from India's ancient culture and values and thus is able to emerge as a great world power playing an effective role in the comity of Nations for the establishment of world peace and a just international order.
>
> The Party aims at establishing a democratic state which guarantees to all citizens irrespective of caste, creed or sex, political, social and economic justice, equality of opportunity and liberty of faith and expression.
>
> The Party shall bear true faith and allegiance to the Constitution of India as by law established and to the principles of socialism, secularism and democracy and would uphold the sovereignty, unity and integrity of India.[3]

The BJP's election manifesto of 1996 (the year in which it emerged as the single largest party in the Lok Sabha and formed a coalition government) stated unequivocally that the 'BJP is committed to the concept of one nation, one people, one culture', and asserted that its nationalistic vision is defined by the nation's ancient cultural heritage; 'from this belief flows our faith in cultural nationalism which is the core of Hindutva. That, we believe, is the identity of our ancient nation – Bharatvarsha' (BJP, 1996). However, the main problem the BJP faces is that Hinduism is not a monolithic and unitary religion. Brass comments that there is in contemporary India considerable ambiguity concerning the use of the word 'Hindus' to define any clearly demarcated group of people in the subcontinent and considerable doubt about the existence of a Hindu political community (Brass, 1994: 16; Chiriyankandath, 1996: 44–66). Kaviraj argues that one of the fundamental difficulties for the BJP is how it can mobilize Hindu sentiments without inflaming the question of caste. He writes: 'caste is so fundamental to traditional Hindu doctrine and social practice, and it has been so strongly emphasized by electoral politics, that to ask Hindus to forget their caste while asserting their Hindu identity is to offer a deeply untraditional and paradoxical programme' (Kaviraj, 1997: 325–44).

The BJP's notion of cultural nationalism is still very vague, as Irani points out. The party's main objective seems to be to make electoral gains rather than reconstructing national identity or promoting a coherent national ideology. And to do this it has either to set aside some of its core beliefs and principles, or reinterpret them radically so as to make them acceptable to groups, communities and classes that have until now remained hostile to it (*The Statesman*, 21 August 1997).

This chapter argues that the constitution of India, to which all political parties swear allegiance, promotes liberal values but gives priority to the unity and integrity of the Indian state. Even the Indian government's programmes of socio-economic development are geared to this goal. Moreover, identities based on caste, tribe, language and religion are given selective recognition. This means that some ethnic groups may not get any official recognition at all or are merged with other ethnic groups. Moreover, groups which are potentially anti-national are suppressed and denied political expression. Therefore there is always a tension between national and subnational identities which political parties aspiring to form a government at the centre get around by forming social coalitions, something the Congress did very successfully for forty years. As Bhagwan Dua (1987: 358) explains, while most of the national leaders, especially Nehru, emphasized goals such as national integration, secularization and economic strength, a 'new breed of Congressmen "parochialized" party structures and formed winning coalitions to control the levers of power' and 'the Congress was transformed into a political machine, adjusting its programs and practices to the caste and parochial orientations of the electorate'. It used and misused its political resources and its advantages as a ruling party to undercut the strength of the opposition parties.

Kedourie's (1993: 1) argument that nationalism is a doctrine invented in Europe at the beginning of the nineteenth century is accepted by a lot of scholars. To this, Partha Chatterjee (1993: 18) adds that the assertion of national identity, in India, was a form of struggle against colonial exploitation. However, as the national movement recedes further back into history, the Congress Party loses its dominance in Indian politics and ethnic groups become politicized, it is necessary to take a fresh look at the importance of ethnicity in India.

The invention of India

Fieldhouse (1981: 12) points out that India in the eighteenth century bore little resemblance to the modern state of the same name. It did not even see itself as a nation-state, that is, as a 'distinct, integrated political unit, held together and delimited by its common and coextensive culture, institutions and history'. The 'thing' that 'became independent' wrote Salman Rushdie (1997: 58) on the occasion of India's fiftieth anniversary, 'had never previously existed, except that there had been an area, a zone called India. So it struck me that what was coming into being, this idea of a nation-state, was an invention. It was an invention of the nationalist movement. And a very successful invention.'

Indian historians, litterateurs and poets, educationists and politicians committed to the promotion of national integration see India as a natural geographical entity. Bounded by mountains and seas on all four sides, through the centuries it has remained politically distinct from the rest of Asia. Deudney (1997: 132) remarks that 'evidence for topophilia in modern national identity can be found in the symbolic content of various mottoes, anthems, monuments, and literary works. "National" anthems often evoke the particular places.' The Indian national anthem, *Jana gana mana*, composed by Rabindranath Tagore, is a good example of this. Before the coming of the European colonizers, especially the British, no significant part of the subcontinent had ever been annexed to any kingdom outside of it (except in the sixth and fourth centuries BC when parts of the north-west were annexed to the Persian empire and later to the Macedonian empire). Few Indian rulers succeeded in extending the boundaries of their kingdom beyond the natural boundaries of the area. To establish an empire covering the whole of the subcontinent was the ambition and life-time mission of many a great king, as discussed in Chapter 1. However, this factor by itself has never been sufficient to promote the growth of a single nation, and has had very little effect on national integration.

In ancient times, the Indian subcontinent was divided into a large number of states and principalities, some of which were republics while others were constitutional monarchies or kingdoms ruled by Hindu kings. Political boundaries usually corresponded to ethnic boundaries, though not always, and certainly not in the case of the larger kingdoms or empires. It must be pointed out, however, that it is rather difficult to define 'ethnic' in the Indian context.[4] As Brass (1974: 13) has rightly observed, India is characterized by an extraordinary abundance of ethnic dimensions, of which some are cumulative, i.e. they reinforce each other, and some are not. For example, the caste system has prevented (in most parts of India) the formation of ethnic groups on the basis of religion or language, or rather it has led to the existence of ethnic groups within ethnic groups. In ancient times too, the two upper castes or *varnas*, i.e. the Brahmins and Kshatriyas, dominated the two lower *varnas*, i.e. the Vaishyas and Shudras, who were excluded from all political offices and consequently had neither wealth nor political power. B. C. Smith (1996: 274) points out that some post-colonial societies are collections of tribes and/or ethnic groups and lack at least two of the seven features of a nation – cultural differentiation and group sentiment of a nation – as defined by A. D. Smith (1991). This applies to India, which cannot therefore be considered a nation. However, as Smith also points out, a subjective belief that people constitute a nation is more important than objective definitions of historians and social scientists.

In spite of the insularity of the Indian subcontinent, foreign invasions were not infrequent in ancient times. The north-west, which borders Iran and Afghanistan, was the most susceptible to these invasions. The foreign invaders included the Persians, the Macedonians, and tribes from Central Asia – the Shakas, Parthians and Kushans, some of whom succeeded in establishing large empires in the Indian subcontinent as discussed in Chapter 1. In the main, however, foreign invaders were kept in check by powerful Hindu kings. The political unification of almost the whole of the subcontinent was accomplished twice, before the arrival of the Muslims: once in the third century BC by Emperor Ashoka and once in the fourth century AD by Emperor Samudragupta (Wolpert, 1993).

Salman Rushdie (1997: 58) writes that the history of India 'is a history of independent nation-states. It is a history of Oudh or Bengal or Maratha kingdoms. All those independent histories agreed to collectivize themselves into the idea of the nation of India.' However, the standard history of India which is taught in its schools and universities, is still to a large extent based on the research done by British and European indologists. It is a political history of dynasties and empires and highlights high cultures and the identities of political elites. Romila Thapar (1996: 19–21) explains that the concentration on dynastic histories in the early studies was based on the assumption that in 'Oriental' societies the power of the ruler was supreme even in the day-to-day functioning of the government. This also led to the division of the history of India into three periods, ancient (Hindu), medieval (Muslim) and modern (British). However, Thapar explains that the understanding of the functioning of power in India lies in analyses of the caste and sub-caste relationships and of institutions such as the guilds and village councils, and not merely in the survey of dynastic power. She also explains that the study of institutions did not receive much emphasis because it was believed that they did not undergo much change. This belief fostered the theory that Indian culture has been a static, unchanging culture for many centuries.

Muslim rule in India

From the point of view of Hindu-Muslim relations, however, the invasion in the twelfth century of Mohammad of Ghur, an Ilbari Turk, is significant. His successors established the Delhi Sultanate which lasted until the sixteenth century. The Turko-Afghan sultans succeeded in subduing the Hindu kings and at the peak of its glory the empire of the Delhi Sultanate extended to almost the whole of the subcontinent. The disintegration of the empire led to the establishment of independent sultanates and Hindu kingdoms in various parts of the country (Wolpert, 1993).

What is noteworthy about this period of Indian history is that political rivalries were not based on religious differences. There was a lot of in-fighting among the Muslims rulers and also among the Hindu rulers, and the Muslim and Hindu rulers often helped each other in fighting against their co-religionists. Moreover, the Muslim rulers employed a large number of Hindus, many of whom held high positions in the army or government. The only discriminatory measure adopted against the Hindus was the imposition of the *jizya,* or tax imposed on all non-Muslims (Wolpert, 1993).

Through the centuries, the Hindus and the Muslims maintained their separate identities, although religious conversion was not uncommon. However, the fusion of the two cultures gave rise to new styles of art, architecture and music and a new language, Urdu, which is a mixture of Persian, Arabic, Turkish and local vernaculars of Sanskritic origin. Many Hindu and Muslim scholars studied each other's religions, while the common people co-existed peacefully.

The rule of the Delhi sultans and of the last Lodhi ruler, Ibrahim Lodhi, was ended by Babur, a Chaghtai Turk from Turkestan and a descendant of Timur and Ghengiz Khan, in 1526 AD. Thus began the rule of the Mughals. Babur was succeeded by his son Humayun, who in turn was succeeded by his son Akbar, the greatest of the Mughal rulers. A great imperialist who achieved the political unification of nearly the whole of northern and central India, Akbar was also a statesman *par excellence.* He recognized the importance of the Hindu Rajput princes, some of whom were quite powerful and were well-known for their bravery and valour, and adopted a policy of conciliating them and thus securing their help in expanding his empire.

Akbar was succeeded by his son Salim (Jahangir), who in turn was succeeded by his son, Shah Jahan. The Mughal rulers practised religious toleration and Akbar even abolished the discriminatory *jizya*. They were also great patrons of art, architecture, literature and music. However, Shah Jahan's son and successor, Aurangzeb, reversed the policies of his predecessors. An orthodox Muslim and a puritan, he re-imposed the *jizya*. He also waged several wars against the Rajputs and thus alienated them. The persecution of the Sikhs and martyrdom of their gurus finally led to the formation of the *Khalsa*. Aurangzeb's successors were weak and incompetent rulers and the Mughal empire began to disintegrate after his death. The last Mughal emperor, Bahadur Shah, was imprisoned and deported to Rangoon by the British in 1857.

There are values implicit in this account of Indian history which applauds the policies of rulers who aimed to promote good governance, public welfare, religious tolerance and cultural activity. However, Naipaul does not agree that the Mughal period was a time of glory. In his opinion, 'the Mughals were tyrants, every one of them. India is a country that, in the north, outside Rajasthan, was ravaged, and intellectually destroyed to a large extent, by the invasions that began in about 1000 AD by forces and religions that India had no means of understanding' (Naipaul, 1997: 37).

Feudal societies are not conducive to the growth of nationalist feelings, and Hindu religion, with its caste system, is not a unifying force. However, something akin to nationalism did fire the spirit of some Hindu rulers, such as the Rajput princes, the Marathas – especially under their illustrious chief, Shivaji, in the seventeenth century – and the Sikhs under Maharaja Ranjit Singh, in the late eighteenth and early nineteenth centuries. The power of both the Marathas and the Sikhs was finally crushed by the British.

British rule in India

British rule paved the way for the establishment of a modern state. First, it led to the growth of nationalism and nationalist feelings, and second it introduced the Indian people to modern (European) democratic ideas, principles and institutions. While the former served to unify the Indian people, the second led to 'force' being supplanted by the 'will of the people' as the basis of the state. However, none of this was achieved in a day and neither were these achievements the objective of British rule in India.

The British rulers, like the Muslim rulers before them, were foreigners in India. But they differed from the Muslims in one important respect. They did not consider India to be their home. For them it was only a colony to exploit. Economic gain was their primary objective, to which everything else, including the welfare of the people was subordinated.

The growth of Indian nationalism and Muslim communalism

From the point of view of national integration/disintegration, British rule gave rise to three significant developments: Indian nationalism, Muslim communalism, and Hindu-Muslim conflict. These developments need to be discussed in detail in order to understand how they affected the future of the subcontinent.

Indian nationalism was the product, on the one hand, of anti-British and anti-colonial feelings and, on the other hand, of Hindu revivalism. One of the primary causes of anti-British feeling was the policy of racial discrimination practised by the British rulers. The nineteenth century also saw the revivalism of Hinduism and the birth of several socio-religious movements which tried to revive pride in India's ancient culture and heritage, and tried to reform Hindu society and rejuvenate it. Meanwhile, western education introduced the Indians to the political philosophies of western thinkers such as Milton, Burke, Mill and Spencer, which led to aspirations for self-government and representative institutions (Mukherjee, 1975; Wolpert, 1993).

The growth of nationalism received a further boost with the creation of the Indian National Congress in 1885, which led to the emergence of an indigenous national political elite. The Congress spearheaded the national movement for independence. It imparted political education to the masses, united them and mobilized them in the struggle for freedom.

The leaders of the national movement, such as Bal Gangadhar Tilak, Lala Lajpat Rai and, of course, Mahatma Gandhi, became the focus of loyalty. Their personal contribution towards unifying the Indians and furthering the national cause is tremendous. These national leaders are the architects of modern India, and their ideals are its *raison-d'être*, and still a strong binding force which holds the country together.

However, Hindu revivalism and western education, which were the two main bases of Indian nationalism, did not have any influence on the Muslims. The Muslim orthodoxy rejected western education as un-Islamic. This hindered their progress under the British. The man who was responsible for bringing about a *rapprochement* between the Muslims and the British and changing the Muslims' attitude to western education was Sir Syed Ahmad Khan. In 1875 he founded the Mohammadan Anglo-Oriental College at Aligarh, which promoted Muslim solidarity. Sir Syed was considerably influenced by Theodore Beck, the English principal of the college, and on his advice kept aloof from the Congress and persuaded other Muslims to do the same. He felt that the Congress' demand for representative government would injure the interests of the Muslims who were in a minority in India. The fear of majority rule first expressed by Sir Syed was echoed half a century later by Jinnah, and finally led to the partition of India and the creation of the separate state of Pakistan (Mukherjee, 1975).

In 1906 a Muslim deputation to the Viceroy made a strong claim for communal representation with which the Viceroy expressed complete sympathy. Encouraged by the success of the Muslim deputation, Nawab Salimulla Khan of Dacca founded the Muslim League in 1906 with the object of promoting the loyalty of the Muslims to the British government and of safeguarding their political and other interests. However, the League did not have the support of all educated Muslims, many of whom were nationalists and whole-heartedly supported the Congress and the national movement. The Muslims were granted separate electorates for the first time by the Indian Councils Act of 1909. The Government of India Act 1919 granted separate electorates to Sikhs and Europeans also (Mukherjee, 1975).

Although the Muslim League made half-hearted attempts at *rapprochement* with the Congress for a while, a spate of communal riots across the country once again strengthened the communal stance of the Muslim League. From 1940 the Muslim League began to demand a separate state comprising the Muslim majority provinces of Kashmir, the whole of the Punjab, Sind, North West Frontier Province, the whole of Bengal, Assam and Hyderabad. The basis of the League's demand was its 'Two Nation Theory', which was first enunciated by Sir

Wazir Hussain in his presidential address at the Bombay session of the League in 1936. He said, 'The Hindus and Mussalmans inhabiting this vast continent are not two communities but should be considered two nations in many respects' (Mukherjee, 1975).

To consider the Hindus and the Muslims inhabiting the Indian subcontinent to be two distinct nations would, however, be erroneous for many reasons, one of which is that it overlooks ethnicity. Ethnically, neither the Hindus nor the Muslims are a homogeneous group. Pakistan, which came into existence in 1947, consisted of five distinct linguistic and cultural ethnic areas: East Bengal, Sind, the North-West Frontier, Baluchistan and the Punjab, inhabited by the Bengalis, Sindhis, Pathans, Baluchis and Punjabis respectively. Pakistan was therefore the product, not of genuine Muslim nationalism, but of the communal politics of the Muslim League (Levak, 1974: 205).

In fact, the Hindu community itself was not considered to be homogenous, and narrowly escaped being split up. In 1932, British prime minister Ramsay Macdonald made his 'communal award' on account of the inability of the leaders of the various Indian communities to come to an agreement regarding the representation of minorities in the provincial legislature. The award granted separate electorates to the Harijans or 'depressed classes' (Untouchables). However, Gandhi, who was strongly opposed to the idea of splitting up the Hindu community, made a pact with Ambedkar, which was ratified by the Hindu Mahasabha and accepted by the British government. Under the pact, joint electorates were to be retained but the number of seats reserved for the Harijans was to be considerably increased (Mukherjee, 1975).

It is also important to note that when India got its independence in 1947, there were 500-odd princely states within India's borders which had the choice of either acceding to India or Pakistan or remaining independent. That they did not readily identify with India is quite clear. Sardar Vallabhbhai Patel, a senior congressman, had to persuade them to accede to the new Indian state.

The Indian constitution and national integration

Although the Indian national movement was strong enough to free the subcontinent from foreign rule, it was mainly a political movement, spearheaded by leaders who had common political ideals, the principal one being the political integration of the subcontinent and the creation of a single independent state, India. This ideal is reflected in the Indian constitution, which is federal in form but has a strong unitary bias. The constitution provides for a division of powers between the central government and the state governments, and for a Supreme Court to act as the guardian of the constitution and decide all constitutional disputes between the central and state governments. However, the distribution of power favours the centre. Moreover, in certain circumstances the union parliament can make laws on any subject in the state list. Although the states, like the union, have a parliamentary form of government, each state has a governor who is not elected by the people but appointed by the president of India. The governor is expected to work as the agent of the central government. The constitution also empowers the union parliament to alter the boundaries and name of any state, and does not give the states the right to secede from the union. Moving the draft constitution for the consideration of the constituent assembly on 4 November 1948, Ambedkar, the chairman of the Drafting Committee, stated that 'the Drafting Committee wanted to make it clear that though India was to be a federation, the federation was not the result of an agreement by the States to join in a federation' and therefore 'no state has the right to secede from it'. He also explained that it was for this reason that the constitution described India as a Union of States instead of a federation: 'The federation is a Union, because it is indestructible.'[5] This has implications for the development of political identities which grow in opposition to the Indian state. In response to the DMK's secessionist propaganda, the central government amended the constitution in 1963 and made it compulsory for all candidates contesting elections to the state legislatures or the parliament to take an oath to uphold the sovereignty and integrity of India and not produce any secessionist propaganda.

Fully recognizing that national integration in India could be impeded by social inequities and injustices, the framers of the Indian constitution incorporated in it a list of fundamental rights: the right to equality, the right to freedom, the right to freedom of religion, cultural and educational rights, the right against exploitation, and the right to constitutional remedies.

Article 14 of the constitution guarantees equality of all persons before the law. Article 15 prohibits any discrimination on grounds of religion, race, caste, sex or place of birth, as between citizens, while Article 17 abolishes untouchability. In 1955 the Indian parliament passed the Untouchability (Offences) Act, which prescribed the punishment for this offence. In order to uplift the socially and educationally 'backward classes' and the SCs and STs, the constitution has introduced the principle of positive discrimination and allowed the government to grant these classes certain privileges, such as the reservation of a certain percentage of government jobs, and seats in educational institutions.

Article 20 allows all the minorities in India to preserve and promote their language, script and culture, while Article 25 says that all persons shall be entitled to freedom of conscience and the right to practise and propagate their religion freely. In 1976, the constitution was amended and the word 'secular' was included in the preamble to the constitution which now reads, 'We, the people of India, having solemnly resolved to constitute India into a sovereign, socialist, secular, democratic republic and to secure to all its citizens: justice, social, economic and political; liberty of thought, expression, belief, faith and worship; equality of status and opportunity; and promote among them all fraternity assuring the dignity of the individual and the unity and integrity of the nation.' Most of this has so far only been realized on paper, however. With the achievement of independence, nationalism in India entered a new phase. Nation-building was now the principal task and challenge for the new state.

The policies of governments of multi-ethnic states with regard to national integration can be either pluralist or assimilationist or a mixture of both. The policy laid down by the Indian constitution is essentially a pluralist one, although there are a few deviations from this norm. The constitution has adopted Hindi as the national language, although it is spoken by only 42 per cent of the population as their mother tongue. This adoption was in fact a highly controversial issue and was achieved by a margin of only one vote in the constituent assembly. Second, the state and the constitution has given recognition to and thus privileged eighteen Indian languages, although more than 1000 languages and dialects are spoken in India.

Society and culture in modern India

Constitutional and legal provisions notwithstanding, untouchability continues to be practised in India. Religion, caste and language have created social as well as communication barriers which have existed for centuries and which laws cannot eliminate. People from different religions, castes and regions do not intermarry and social interaction among them is limited. It is interesting to note in this regard that the Indian government has adopted a policy of encouraging inter-caste/communal marriages. However, although nationalist leaders have always hoped to achieve unity through cultural assimilation, any attempt to impose an assimilationist policy on the people would lead to serious consequences. For example, the people of south India have always been opposed to Hindi, a north Indian language, and secessionist tendencies were strong in the southern state of Tamil Nadu in the 1950s (Barnett, 1976). The process of cultural assimilation cannot be unduly hastened or forced. Karl Deutsch's (1969: 73) observation that it took centuries to make Englishmen and Frenchmen, and that it is difficult for variegated tribal groups to become Tanzanians, Zambians or Malavians in one generation, applies equally to the different ethnic groups which make up India.

In 1961, Jawaharlal Nehru set up the National Integration Council (NIC) with the objective of promoting communal harmony and national integration. It was, however, not very effective. In 1968 J. P. Narayan, a veteran politician, wrote to Nehru that the composition of the NIC, which was made up of ministers and parliamentarians, was likely to give the impression that the task of national integration was one that was largely, if not wholly, to be accomplished by the state. He wrote, 'This, as you know, is far from being the case. Indeed, more has to be done at the people's level than by the state' (Sarhadi, 1974: 164–5). In fact, the NIC has not even been very effective in ironing out differences between political parties and their leaders on communal issues. In recent years, the NIC has attempted but failed to arrive at a consensus on the Ayodhya issue, which has created communal disharmony in the country.

Anderson et al. (cited in Smith, 1996: 276) have argued that 'Afro-Asia, in particular, is dominated by new states that face agonising problems in winning the full commitment of their citizenry which is taken for granted in most Western societies'. The leaders of these states face intense competition from diverse forms of subnational loyalties, which may be based on race, ethnic identity, language, caste, religion, or region.

In spite of the fact that India is officially a secular nation, caste and religion play an important role in the electoral politics of many of its states. This is because politicians have always recognized the potency of ethnic identities and do not hesitate to 'use' caste or religion to win votes or increase their personal power. They try to mobilize the masses by appealing to their religious or caste sentiments. Some even ignite communal conflicts (Desai, 1992: 9).

Religious identities

The two main religions in India are Hinduism and Islam. The Hindus constitute about 80 per cent of the population, while the Muslims form about 13 per cent. Sikhs, Christians, Buddhists and Jains together make up less than 7 per cent of the total population. However, the Hindus are not homogeneous. They belong to different castes, speak different languages, have different customs and live in and/or identify with different regions. The Muslims in India are not ethnically homogenous either. They are dispersed in all the twenty-eight states and six union territories, although a little over half of them live in the three large states of Uttar Pradesh, West Bengal and Bihar. They are in a majority only in the state of Jammu and Kashmir and in Lakshadweep. Urdu is the mother tongue of about half of the Muslim population. The rest of the population speak Kashmiri, Bengali, Gujarati and so on. They are also divided along sectarian lines: Shia, Sunni, Aga Khani Khoja and at least two sects of the Bohras (Khalidi, 1995: 2).

However, from the primordialist point of view, which was also the view of the leaders of Muslim separatism, Hindus and Muslims constituted in premodern times distinct civilizations destined to develop into separate nations once political mobilization took place. The differences between the two cultures, it was argued, were so great that assimilation could not take place and a single national culture could not be created. Others held the view that the cultural and religious differences between Hindus and Muslims were not so great as to rule out the creation of either a composite national culture or at least a secular political union in which those aspects of group culture that could not be shared would be relegated to the private sphere. Some historians have also pointed out that 'Muslim social identities in late-nineteenth century India remained fractured by class, region and the rural-urban divide' (Bose and Jalal, 1998: 167). Thus Muslim separatism was the result of the conscious manipulation of selected symbols of Muslim identity by Muslim elite groups in economic and political competition with each other and with elite groups among Hindus (Brass, 1991: 71–6). Khalidi (1995: 3) however, argues that 'a whole generation of young Muslims has grown up looking upon India as the land of their birth. This new generation neither shares the sense of participation in the struggle for Pakistan nor feels the separation of the close kinsmen and relatives across the border as deeply as its preceding generation did. Moreover, it is not saddled with "guilt" over the partition of the country.'

Imtiaz Ahmed writes that, for nearly four decades, the belief has persisted that Muslims vote *en bloc* in elections and mainly for the Congress. This was true up to the third general elections in 1962, but is no longer. The Muslim vote is split among a number of different political parties. In recent years, after the demolition of the Babri Masjid, Muslim public opinion was greatly alienated from the Congress. However, for obvious reasons, they see the BJP as their primary enemy. Ahmed (1996: 47) remarks that in future elections, 'wherever a viable third force does not exist, the Muslim vote will go in favour of the Congress'.

Caste identities

The caste system, as mentioned in Chapter 1, is a hierarchical structure consisting of four *varnas*: the Brahmins (priests and custodians of sacred knowledge), Kshatriyas (warriors and rulers), Vaishyas (traders), and Shudras (persons performing manual labour and menial jobs). In this hierarchical social order, the Brahmins are the highest caste and the Shudras the lowest. The caste system was not originally so rigid, but has become ascriptive so that people who belong to a higher caste also have a higher status, irrespective of their talents and achievements. The caste system has led to social and residential segregation, and in the rural areas the Shudras live on the outskirts of the villages and towns, away from the high-caste neighbourhood, as they are considered to be unclean and therefore 'untouchable' (Baxter et al., 1993: 42–4).

However, in reality the caste system is not a simple fourfold division. It is estimated that there are about 3,000 subcastes into which the present Hindu society is divided. These castes are known as *jatis*, the size of which can range from a few hundred people to millions. However, unlike the universal fourfold *varna*, the *jati* is geographically and linguistically bounded. It provides the social identity and an unofficial but effective social security system for village individuals and defines a person's *dharma*, which is a Hindu concept encompassing every aspect of an individual's conduct and social relations including his duty towards his fellow human beings (Baxter et al., 1993).

Jayaram writes that social scientists influenced by Marxist, as well as Weberian, theories of socio-economic change, which had evolved in the context of industrialization and the development of capitalism in western Europe, had assumed that the process of modernization would gradually dissolve the caste system and the collectivist ethos, and replace it with a class system and an individualist ethos. However, anthropological and sociological studies on the caste system in India undertaken since the 1960s have revealed this assumption to be untenable. Modernization does not, *ipso facto*, tear apart the basic fabric of the caste system (Jayaram, 1996: 70).

But, at the same time, Jayaram and other social scientists do not argue that the caste system has not changed at all. Indeed, Jayaram (1996: 70) notes that the caste system 'has been the most flexible of the primordial institutional arrangements anywhere in the world, and it has shown an extraordinary capacity to adapt itself to a variety of changing, and often apparently contradictory, socio-economic conditions'.

That the caste system is not egalitarian is immediately obvious. It has led to inequality, exploitation and educational and economic 'backwardness'. To redress the situation and guided by the liberal values of justice and equality enshrined in the constitution of India, the government of India classified certain castes as 'Scheduled Castes' (see Chapter 2, footnote 2). According to the census of 2001, about 16.2 per cent of India's total population was classified as SCs. The total number of SCs was 1,666 *lakhs*. In some Indian states, SCs constitute almost or more than 25 per cent of the total population, for example Punjab (28.90 per cent); Himachal Pradesh (24.70 per cent) and West Bengal (23 per cent) (Census of India 2001).

However, although the Directive Principles of State Policy enjoins the government of India to promote the welfare of the weakest sections of Indian society, this often leads to the selection of some and not others for preferential treatment. Castes which are unable to present their case convincingly are excluded from preferential policies. However, as long as this does not lead to social unrest and anti-national feelings it does not threaten the security of the state, and the government can afford to ignore it. According to an opinion poll conducted by *India Today* and OGR-MARG in May 1997, apart from the SCs and STs, all other social groups have misgivings over caste-based reservations. About 52 per cent of the people feel that the best criterion for reservations is economic status and not caste, while 28 per cent feel that there should be no reservations at all (*India Today*, 18 August 1997: 32).

A lot of research has been done on caste and electoral politics in India. In some states, such as Bihar, 'caste plays a vital role in forging electoral and political alliances'. In the general elections of 1996, the caste factor gave Laloo Prasad Yadav, leader of the RJD, a clear edge (Narayan, 1996: 7) and the situation had not changed in 2004. Thakur (1995: 12–13) writes that caste is now being used in Bihar as a system for the distribution of political spoils. It is 'organised for capturing political power and the social and material benefits that flow from it, whether it be a government job, preferential entry into an educational institution or a government licence'. He asserts that if secularism is understood as the gradual displacement of ascriptive ties of religion, caste and ethnicity by achievement-based calculations, then the opposite has happened in India. The Akbarpur

(Uttar Pradesh) by-election of 20 December 2004 highlighted the importance of the Dalit vote even in the twenty-first century. The political parties contesting the election, the BSP and the SP were acutely aware of the importance of the Dalit community. Moreover, the scrapping of Ambedkarnagar district (in which Akbarpur is located) had become a controversial issue as it is associated with the name of B. R. Ambedkar, a leader of the Dalit movement. The High Court eventually reinstated the district.[6]

However, in other states, such as West Bengal, caste does not play an important role in electoral politics. According to the above-mentioned opinion poll covering a sample of 12,651 respondents and a wide cross-section of the population of India, 52 per cent of the voters said that they would vote on the basis of a candidate's merit and only 3 per cent said that they would vote on the basis of caste (*India Today*, 18 August 1997: 28; *India Today*, 31 August 1997: 40). This confirmed the trend detected by a poll conducted the previous year by ICSSR-CSDS and *India Today*. However, the poll analysts emphasize that it may be hasty to conclude that voting according to caste-community has ceased to take place. The trend might be the result of the recent rise in the politics of coalition-building among castes and communities.

Caste identities *per se* do not pose a threat to India's territorial integrity, unless they appear under the guise of regionalism, and are able to build coalitions with other castes in their region, provide political leadership and identify a common ethnic characteristic, for example language.

Tribal identities

Tribals comprise 8 per cent of India's population (Census of India 2001). They are heterogeneous and scattered over different parts of the country. Chatterjee's (1996: 101–18) research reveals that the communities are ethnically and culturally diverse and varied from the point of view of ethnic identity, language, culture, customs and rituals, religious practice, economic activities, geographical location and much more. However, they are often united in their efforts to keep non-tribal outsiders out of their territory. The Indian states that have the largest tribal populations include Madhya Pradesh, Maharashtra and Orissa. However, in the north-eastern states of Meghalaya, Mizoram and Nagaland, the percentage of ST population to total population is 86 per cent, 95 per cent and 89 per cent respectively (Census of India 2001).

Modernization and development have had adverse consequences for the tribals. They have led to their marginalization, encroachment on their land and forests and sometimes their displacement. The Indian government's policy of giving preferential treatment to the STs has not proved satisfactory for several reasons. Firstly the educational backwardness and poverty of the tribals often renders them incapable of availing themselves of many of the benefits offered by the state, and second, as in the case of the SCs and OBCs, the government has given only selective recognition to the tribals. For example, Chatterjee's (1996) research reveals that only about one-third of Uttar Pradesh's total tribal population is listed and that only since as recently as 1967.

However, Chatterjee also points out that there is no absolute cultural or social distinction between all tribal folk and all caste members. The reality is 'a wide spectrum with varying degrees of caste and tribal traits. Some tribals are closer to the jati side than others, while some jatis show greater resemblance than other jatis to one or other tribe' (1996: 108) She emphasizes that there is an ongoing process of tribalization of certain *jati*s and also the *jati*fication of certain tribes, although the latter is taking place on a much wider scale than the former.

The alienation of tribals does pose a threat to India's security. As alienation 'afflicts wider sections of the tribal community, protest tends to move from the individual to the aggregative form. There is a reassertion of tribal values and institutions and the desperate search for roots' (Chatterjee, 1996: 113). The entire case is presented in nationality terms and the tribals demand greater socio-political and economic autonomy and greater participating rights in the context of the national economy and politics. A good example of this is the movements for the creation of the states of Jharkhand and Uttaranchal. The government of India initially gave Jharkhand more autonomy and eventually a separate state was created in 2000. As Chatterjee (1996: 113) argues, if demands remain unfulfilled and the psyche unappeased, there is always a lurking risk of the tribals taking up more militant and intolerant positions and playing into the hands of secessionist forces, as has happened in the north-eastern states of the country.

Linguistic identities

Although, in a country with cross-cutting cleavages, language is not and cannot be the only basis of ethnicity, major linguistic groups in India have never been willing to submerge their identity. Thus the demand for linguistic provinces, which was made in pre-independence days, finally led to the creation of the States Re-organization Commission in 1953 and the passage of the States Re-Organization Act in 1956, although not until considerable pressure was put on the government.[7] The Act created fourteen states and five union territories. However, it did not satisfy everyone. Because of agitation for the creation of two separate states for the Marathi- and Gujarati-speaking populations of Bombay, the Bombay Re-organization Act was passed in 1960, dividing the province into Maharashtra and Gujarat. Agitations in the Punjab finally led in 1966 to the creation of the state of Haryana out of the Hindi-speaking areas of the Punjab. The demand of the Naga hill tribes of the north-east for a separate state was finally conceded by the central government in 1962, although only after years of insurgent activity, and the state of Nagaland was created out of three districts of Assam. It must, however, be noted that the Nagas are not ethnically homogenous. According to a memorandum presented by the Naga National Council to

Gandhi and the constituent assembly in 1947, the Nagas are 'not a single tribe but a whole group of them, each differing from the others in customs and dialect'. However, they have a distinct culture of their own which is different from those of the plains people of Assam (*The Statesman*, 2 August 1947: 1).

Meghalaya too was carved out of Assam and given statehood in 1972, together with Manipur and Tripura, which were previously union territories. However agitations continued in various parts of the country for the creation of more states, or for effective autonomy. For example, Jharkhand in Bihar, Gorkhaland in northern West Bengal, Bodoland in Assam, Vidarbha in Maharashtra and Uttarakhand in Uttar Pradesh. The BJP government decided to create three more states and accordingly Jharkhand, Chhattisgarh and Uttaranchal were created in 2000 (*The Times of India*, 8 April 1998: 8). At present there are twenty-eight states and six union territories in India, but more may be created such as Telengana.

The British rulers never accepted language as the sole basis for any territorial or provincial re-organization of the country. They feared that linguistic provinces would strengthen nationalist feelings. The Indian National Congress accepted the idea of linguistic provinces, although only after much hesitation. The Congress leaders were acutely aware of the dangers of creating linguistic states from the point of view of national integration. They feared that it would lead to the 'Balkanization' of the country. This fear increased after the country was partitioned in 1947.

However, the 1956 re-organization of states took place on the basis of the languages listed in the eighth schedule to the constitution. The 1961 census of India recorded 1,652 mother tongues in India, of which at least 200 had over 10,000 speakers. However, official recognition has been given to only eighteen Indian languages, which are included in the eighth schedule. None of the tribal languages, such as Santhali, Bhili and Lammi, spoken by thousands of people, are given official recognition. Saxena (1997) notes that there do not appear to be any demographic, cultural or linguistic criteria for inclusion or non-inclusion. She argues that 'a number of languages with developed literary traditions and large numbers of speakers do not find any place in the Eighth Schedule. Language policy having been inherently ambiguous, inclusion in the Eighth Schedule has evidently depended largely on the ability of a language group to influence the political process' (Saxena, 1997: 270).

The adoption of Hindi as the national language seems unfair considering that it is an Indo-Aryan language which is spoken only in parts of northern India, and Khari Boli is, of course, the language of the northern Hindi-speaking elites. The languages spoken in south India are all Dravidian languages. However, in its anxiety to hasten cultural assimilation, the central government has even encouraged the cultural imperialism of northern India over the rest of the country. This is often resented by the people of South India. An important means of promoting national integration, especially cultural integration, in India is

Doordarshan (Indian television). However, *The Hindu*, a newspaper published in south India, observed on the occasion of Doordarshan's thirty-third birthday, that it purveys a 'distinctive Hindi belt kitsch' and that 'on Doordarshan today ethnic diversity is not the norm, it is show-cased as being Naga dancers with feathers or a self-consciously announced Tamil *bhakti geet*' (religious song). The norm is 'a mish-mash, semi-prosperous northern urban culture' (Ninan, 1992: 3).

Insurgency and state repression

Insurgent groups abound in the north-eastern states of Assam, Nagaland, Tripura, Mizoram, Manipur and Meghalaya, and in the northern states of Jammu and Kashmir and the Punjab. However, the central government does not consider insurgent activity in any of these states to be a national liberation struggle, but rather looks on them as attempts (both from within and without the country) to destabilize India's frontier states. The centre has, therefore, treated the situation prevailing in these states as a law-and-order problem, and dealt with it by the deployment of military and paramilitary forces, the suspension of the democratic process, and imposition of president's rule, incidentally a power which the central government has exercized quite frequently and freely over the years (Brass, 1994). In 1996 even the chief minister of Assam, Prafulla Mahanta, had to renege on his pre-poll promise that the army would not be used to handle internal problems, when he decided to extend army operations to Kokrajhar in August 1996, following the eruption of violence in the state.

However, state repression is not the answer to the problem of militancy, insurgency and terrorism. A political solution is necessary. A senior government official in the ministry of home affairs, Mr Padmanabhaia, admitted this to the Star Plus TV channel in August 1997. He further explained that violence must not be allowed to 'escalate' and this was the main reason for deploying the army in these areas. If violence were to escalate negotiations would not take place.[8] One of the insurgent groups operating in north-eastern India, the United Liberation Front of Asom (ULFA) was willing to negotiate with the Indian government. It did not make withdrawal of the army a precondition for talks. It said that it was open to talks as long as they revolved around the 'sovereignty' and the right to self-determination of the Assamese people; were held in a 'third country'; and in the presence of a United Nations representative. The ULFA also succeeded in taking its case to the United Nations Working Group on Indigenous Populations in Geneva. That ensured that an extended presence of the army in the state would mean increased pressure on the government from civil rights groups (*India Today*, 31 August 1996: 16). However, the ULFA did not succeed in bringing about a political solution and at the time of writing (January 2005), it continued to operate, often from bases across India's north-eastern borders, in neighbouring countries. In late 2003 the Indian government had thanked the government of Bhutan for not allowing the ULFA to set up bases in Bhutan. It was estimated that there were between 400 and 500 members of the various rebel groups from the north-east in various camps along the Indo-Myanmar border (Hazarika, 2004: 4). In Manipur, however, the people of the state have had enough of the Armed Forces Special Powers Act and have called for its removal (NDTV, 28 December 2004). Anti-insurgency military operations also continue in Jammu and Kashmir. Meanwhile the All-Assam Students' Union has announced its decision to constitute a new regional outfit, Asom Sena, to fight for the protection of the rights of indigenous people. The youth of the province are disillusioned with the best-known regional party, the Asom Gana Parishad (AGP) and have become 'directionless'.

However, explaining the Naga problem, as he perceives it, Mr Imchalemba (Nagaland's lone member in the Lok Sabha in 1992) is reported to have complained that there is a large communication gap between the Naga psyche and the policy-makers in New Delhi, who, he feels, are incapable of appreciating the Naga urge for reform if not resurgence in the social, political and economic arenas. He also suspects a politico-bureaucratic design to perpetuate strong-arm methods in Nagaland and believes that army operations carried out in Nagaland for more than four decades have not done the state any good, yet this is not conceded (*The Statesman*, 29 August 1992: 9). A retired army officer, J. R. Mukherjee (2005), also argues that inward migration, lack of development and neglect have caused unrest in Meghalaya, Mizoram and Tripura. New Delhi must deal with these issues. He admits, however, that the Mizo Accord of the late 1980s that led to insurgents coming overground and forming the government has brought peace to the Mizo Hills.

The eleventh Lok Sabha: a microcosm of the nation?

The results of the 1996 general elections reflected the trend towards pluralism and away from single-party dominance. After four decades of steadily gaining political power in local and state governments, the OBCs occupied an unprecedented number of seats in the Lok Sabha. The growth of the regional parties led to the eleventh Lok Sabha comprising twenty-eight different parties, which is unparalleled in Indian parliamentary history. The strength of farmers increased from 33 per cent to almost 52 per cent. There were fewer Congress MPs in Nehru jackets and *dhoti-kurta*, but more saffron clad BJP members and also some navy-blue turbaned Akali Dal MPs.[9] Subhash Kashyap, former Lok Sabha general secretary, described it as 'a microcosm of the nation' (Baweja, 1996: 37).

Although the BJP emerged as the single largest party, it did not have enough members in the house to form a government. This was formed by the United Front, a coalition of thirteen political parties, including the Janata Dal, the Samajwadi Party, the CPI, the AGP, the TMC, the DMK, the Maharashtra Gomantak Party (MGP) and the Telegu Desam (Dutt, 1997). Many of them are regional political parties which, a few years ago, were not even considered to be eligible to contest elections to the national parliament. However, Prime Minister Gowda claimed that he tried to give representation to as many states as possible (*The Statesman*, 29 June 1996: 1).

So what implications does this have for India's political future? Former MP A.K. Roy commented that what we are witnessing is not a reflection of plurality in our society or a new model of federalism, but a 'show of fractured polity threatening the country and unleashing forces of disintegration'. He does not accept that it is a projection of unity in diversity. The 'division of parties and rise of regional forces show the growth of centrifugal forces' (Roy, 1996: 8). A senior congressman is reported to have offered the explanation that it is first, the lack of a charismatic leader like Indira Gandhi and second, the 'Mandalization', (the policy of positive discrimination for OBCs) and 'Mandirization' (Hindu communal politics) of the polity which has broken the society into groups and subgroups. Also, the former prime minister, Narasimha Rao, was 'unable to translate economic liberalization and national security as attractive alternatives' (Baweja, 1996: 38).

The twelfth Lok Sabha: a victory for the BJP

The results of the twelfth general elections confirmed the trend towards the assertion of regional political identities. More than thirty political parties were represented in the twelfth Lok Sabha, although some of them had only one or two seats. It would be inaccurate to say that the BJP had come to power. It won 179 of the 539 seats contested but had to seek the support of twenty small parties and independents. Its allies included the Shiv Sena, Samata, Haryana Vikas Party (HVP), Akali Dal, AIADMK, BJD, Trinamool, Lok Shakti, Pattali Makkal Katchi (PMK), Marumalarchi Dravida Munnetra Kazhagam (MDMK), Revolutionary Communist Party of India (RCP) and the Janata Party. A hung parliament for the fourth successive election confirmed that it is 'the age of coalitions' in India and that the path to power lies in the creation of political, regional and social alliances (*The Economist*, 21 March 1998: 83–4).

However, the BJP had won sixty-three more seats this time than it did in 1996. An analysis of the *India Today*-CSDS post-poll survey of the 1998 election showed that the BJP is no longer an exclusivist party, but one that now reaches out to a much wider range of the electorate in terms of class, caste and religion. As a right-wing party, the BJP had initially obtained more votes from the privileged sections of society: the higher castes, upper classes, men (rather than women) and educated people. According to the results of the *India Today*-CSDS poll, the BJP has taken a significant step towards becoming a more broad-based party. Its political coalition has also helped it to build a social coalition. The party still gets more than half the votes of the upper castes, but the key to the gains made in 1998 is its inroads into OBC votes. More OBCs have swung towards the BJP in these elections than any other community. Also, more OBCs supported the BJP front in 1998 than any other grouping, including the United Front (UF), which was the main OBC party in 1996 (*India Today*, 16 March 1998: 29–35).

The BJP has increased its base among the SCs and STs at the cost of both the Congress and the United Front. It is still the least popular political party with the Muslims, but in 1998 increased its support among them by about three per cent compared with the 1996 elections. This happened mainly because it formed alliances with parties considered to be more secular.

However, the BJP cannot ignore its allies. As Aroon Purie, the editor of *India Today*, wrote, 'once again a government, in a sense, was being held to ransom, dictated to not by ideology but by individual agendas' (*India Today*, 23 March 1998: 1). In 1998 the prime minister, Vajpayee, was seriously tempted to give in to the demands of his infamous AIADMK ally, Ms. Jayalalitha of Tamil Nadu, who had been trying to bring about the dismissal of the democratically elected DMK government of M. Karunanidhi. However, as the editor of *The Statesman* remarked, 'if he gives the impression ... that he places the survival of his government higher than principles of governance, more than his government will be lost' (*The Statesman*, 20 April 1998: 8).

The BJP has also been obliged to dilute its agenda to ensure its government's survival. It did not immediately implement its three central commitments that distinguish it from other parties: legislating to build a temple at Ayodhya; scrapping Kashmir's special status; and enacting a common civil code. Instead, it emphasized the importance of its National Agenda for Governance which is a variant of the United Front's Common Minimum Programme. The BJP claims that it wants to usher in an era of national reconciliation and consensus and avoid the politics of confrontation.

However, within weeks of being appointed prime minister, Vajpayee inaugurated a grand temple of International Society for Krishna Consciousness (ISKCON) and a Vedic cultural centre at New Delhi. He asserted that the application of the work-related ideology of the Bhagavadgita could create a new work culture in India. Mr Vajpayee is in favour of what he calls the 'globalization of the message of the Gita' and the messages of all the sacred books of the world, with which the message of the Gita bears close conformity. The temple and the cultural centre have been jointly set up by ISKCON and the Hinduja Foundation at a cost of more than Rs 20 *crores* (*The Times of India*, 6 April 1998: 1). The Communist Party of India objected to the prime minister inaugurating the ISKCON temple. The secretary to the CPI national council, D. Raja, asserted that heads of government should keep away from religious functions (*The Times of India*, 7 April 1998: 9).

However, Vajpayee assured parliament that India would not become a theocratic state. He said that the BJP-led government had no hidden agenda and denied any attempt to change the basic structure of the constitution (*The Asian Age*, 1 April 1998: 2). The Congress party vowed to do 'anything' required to ensure that 'the Bharatiya Janata Party (BJP) government does not tamper with the basic secular, democratic and egalitarian fabric of the nation'. A political resolution was passed at the AICC meeting on 6 April 1998 in New Delhi, which said that the Congress was prepared to face the challenge of all communal, divisive and authoritarian forces and pledged to safeguard the identity of a pluralistic India which is the only guarantee of its unity and integrity (*The Times of India*, 7 April 1998: 11).

Like all his predecessors, Vajpayee vowed to protect India's territorial integrity. The National Agenda for Governance committed the BJP-led government to re-assess India's nuclear policy. It emphatically declared that 'to ensure the security, territorial integrity and unity of India we [i.e. the BJP government] will take all necessary steps and exercize all available options. Towards that end, we will re-evaluate the nuclear policy and exercize the option to induct nuclear weapons'. According to an official in Islamabad, the main purpose of testing the Ghauri missile, which was apparently capable of targeting Delhi, Mumbai and even Chennai, was to send a signal to New Delhi. Pakistan could match India's nuclear plans and was not about to bow out of the nuclear race (Baweja, 1998: 34–5). In May 1998 first India and then Pakistan carried out nuclear tests. However, the escalation of the arms race in South Asia was condemned by the international community and the BJP was also faced with the task of creating a national consensus on the subject at home.

According to the *India Today*-CSDS post-poll survey, the most dynamic and economically vibrant sections of Indian society feel that they can entrust the BJP with their future. Indian industry strongly supports the BJP government and the BJP will not abandon its emphasis on *swadeshi* (indigenous). It will go out of its way to be partial to the interests of Indian-owned businesses and make a sharp distinction between *swadeshi* and *videshi* (foreign). It is not just Hindu nationalism but also economic nationalism which the BJP is promoting and going by the results of the twelfth general elections, 'modern India' sees no apparent contradiction in supporting a party that emphasizes Indian identity and *swadeshi* (Dasgupta, 1998: 21; Dasgupta and Bhaumik, 1998: 14). This brand of economic nationalism may help the BJP to win votes, but may not be the best economic policy in an increasingly globalizing world.

But even more than the BJP ideology, India's victory in the Kargil war of 1999 united 'a normally apathetic' nation and the surge of patriotism swept Prime Minister Vajpayee back to power at the thirteenth general elections. For the Indian army the Kargil war had been one of the harshest its soldiers had ever fought. There were no tanks or air strikes to back infantry. The battle in the world's highest mountains led to the death of many brave soldiers, 'heros' who had died defending their motherland. The nation mourned them, shared the grief of their families but also expressed pride in their achievement; in the process it united behind the political leadership (*India Today*, 28 June 1999; 3 January 2000). However, Kumar argues that the National Democratic Alliance

(NDA) and especially the BJP made militarism and chauvinism the central themes of their 1999 election campaign. The campaign also confirmed that the United Front, a coalition of regional, caste-based and left-wing parties, that had attempted to offer an alternative to the BJP, had eased to exist; some of these parties had defected to the NDA (Kumar, 1999).

The fourteenth Lok Sabha: the return of the Congress?

In May 2004 the Congress won 143 seats in the elections to the fourteenth Lok Sabha. The total number of seats won by the party and its allies was 219. The BJP won 136 seats and its allies won an additional forty seats (*The Statesman*, 14 May 2004). The allies of the Congress include the RJD, DMK, PMK and the Nationalist Congress Party (NCP), all members of the UPA which became the ruling coalition of political parties at the centre. This alliance is externally supported by the four left parties; CPI/M, CPI, RSP and the All-India Forward Bloc. In order to co-ordinate the co-operation, a UPA-Left Co-ordination Committee has been formed.

In Chapter 2 it was argued that the thirteenth general elections confirmed that a decentring of the Indian polity was taking place. Economic reforms are having the effect of decentralizing authority by curtailing central government dirigisme (Echeverri-Gent, 2002). At the same time state governments are becoming more active than ever in promoting economic development. Globalization has intensified the competition between states and promoted the reassertion of regional identities in India. Single-state parties or regional parties are representing the interests of particular states and regions as well as those of OBCs, SCs and STs. This trend has continued notwithstanding the return of the Congress in May 2004. Irani comments that 'this election has shown that India is too fractured to be won by a pan-Indian theme' (*The Statesman*, 14 May 2004: 8). Indian voters voted on local and regional issues and not on the economic achievements of the BJP government. Mehta writes:

> Although I am tempted to declare that pseudo-secularism has triumphed, it is Indian democracy (pseudo-secularism included) which has triumphed. Not only has the country been stunned by the awesome verdict, the entire free world must learn from the courage of the poor, the illiterate, the voiceless and the underprivileged of the earth's largest democracy as they punish rulers who thought their realm consisted of 15 million for whom India was definitely 'shining'. (Mehta, 2004)

Conclusion

The spread of national political consciousness began in India only in the late nineteenth century. However, this consciousness had an anti-colonial and not an ethnic basis. Nevertheless, it helped in the creation of the Indian union. At independence, the Indian nationalist elite wanted 'sovereignty, unity, order, a strong state, secularism, democracy and parliamentarism, economic self-sufficiency, and social and economic reform'. They also declared 'for all the world to hear and for any internal dissidents who had a different view that India was to be a sovereign independent republic' (Brass, 1994: 10). However, it cannot be denied that the maintenance of the unity and territorial integrity of the Indian state is heavily dependent on constitutional provisions rather than on the national consciousness of the people. The unity of the country is also dependent on the existence of a strong and competent government at the centre, which is responsive to the needs of the people. In order to assimilate people into one community, the government must be responsive to human needs. The record of the Indian government on this count has been fairly good so far, although there are several discontented ethnic groups in the country. The spread of literacy, social and political mobilization and rising economic aspirations will make the government's task even more difficult in the years to come.

The factors responsible for insurgency in the states of the north-east, Jammu and Kashmir and the Punjab are numerous and include rising economic aspirations, perception of a threat to their political, economic and cultural interests, a communication gap between the central government and the people of these states, and loss of faith in the central government's ability and willingness to solve regional problems. The pursuit of power by political leaders and parties, political mobilization along communal and ethnic lines for political and electoral gain, conflict between different ethnic groups and power struggles between political parties and leaders, often aggravate the situation.

Brass argues that the policies pursued by the Indian government after Nehru's death have played a major role in the intensification of conflicts in these regions, and have in the process highlighted a major structural problem in the Indian political system. That problem arises 'from the tensions created by the centralizing drives of the Indian state in a society where the predominant long-term social, economic, and political tendencies are toward pluralism, regionalism, and decentralization'. During Nehru's time, central government policies had favoured pluralist solutions, non-intervention in state politics except in a conciliatory role or as a last resort, and preservation of a separation between central and state politics, allowing considerable autonomy for the latter. However, from the early 1970s Indira Gandhi's government reversed these policies for short-term political gain (Brass, 1994: 227).

Western political scientists had previously believed that ethnic groups in both western and Third World countries would become irrelevant because the particularism and 'backwardness' associated with them would be replaced by a progressive and inclusive 'national' political community organized on the basis of 'functional' criteria and informed by universal and democratic aspirations (Safran, 1995: 1). However, experience has shown that neither socialism nor urbanization, industrialization and the spread of education have eradicated ethnic consciousness and replaced particularism with universalism (Sen Gupta, 1995: 37). Moreover globalization has enhanced pluralism by 'loosening the hold of the state', although it also has the potential to decrease diversity (Scholte, 1996).

Sen Gupta (1995: 37) comments that 'ethnic consciousness has taken a firm root in India' and 'some of us are fearful of India's unity'. According to the opinion poll conducted by *India Today* in August 1997, 41 per cent of the Indian people think that India will stay united in the next fifty years, 36 per cent think that India will disintegrate into independent nations and 23 per cent are not sure (*India Today*, 18 August 1997: 35). While it is difficult to predict what will happen in the next fifty years, it cannot be denied that ethno-nationalism does pose a threat to India's unity. Moreover, if globalization widens the gap between the richer and poorer regions it may lead to separatist movements, although in the past, states that were performing relatively well, in economic terms, but felt that their economic growth was being hampered by the central government's policies also felt alienated from New Delhi. On the other hand, Indian society is characterized by cross-cutting ethnic cleavages which hinder the development of intense solidarity at the state level. Loose integration does not lead to calls for secession. As such, India may not meet with the same fate as the former USSR.

Notes

1 An earlier version of this paper was published in the *Third World Quarterly*, 19:3 (1998).
2 The state of Gujarat, for example, organized the Vibrant Gujarat – Global Investors Summit in 2005.
3 Available at www.bjp.org.
4 Bell and Freeman (1974: 13) write that at minimum, ethnicity may be defined as 'characteristic, distinctive, cultural or subcultural traits that set one group off from another. Different beliefs, values and patterns of behaviour are involved as well as self and other identifications. Language differences may be so intertwined that they may in circumstances be considered part of the definition, and this may be inherently so, given the important connections between language and culture.'.
5 Constituent Assembly Debates, Vol. VIII, p. 43, cited in Agarwal (1981: 19). Also see Verney, 1995, pp. 19–50.
6 'Battle for Akbarpur: Caste's the key', *The Statesman*, 18 December 2004.
7 For a history of the demand for linguistic states see Phadke, 1974, pp. 1–30; Brass, 1994, chapter 5, 'Language Problems'.
8 Interview with Star Plus (India), 17 August 1997.
9 *Dhoti-kurta* is a traditional Indian dress for men consisting of a piece of white cotton cloth tied around the waist and reaching down to the ankles and a long, full-sleeved, white cotton shirt. Members of the Congress have traditionally worn this dress, especially at official functions. The colour saffron represents Hindu religion and is the colour of the traditional garments worn by members of various Hindu religious orders, members of the BJP with close connections to right-wing Hindu organizations, or Hindu religious leaders. The navy-blue turban is worn by members of the Akali Dal, the premier political party for the Sikhs.

References

Agarwal, R. C., 1981, *Constitutional History of India and National Movement*, S. Chand and Co., New Delhi.
Ahmed, I., 1996, 'The Muslim-vote myth', *India Today*, Elections 1996, 30 April.
Anderson, C.W., Von der Mehden, F. R. and Young, C., 1974, *Issues of Political Development*, Prentice Hall, Englewood Cliffs.
Arora, B. and Verney, D. (eds), 1995, *Multiple Identities in a Single State*, Konark Publishers, New Delhi.
Barnett, M. R., 1976, *The Politics of Cultural Nationalism in South India*, Princeton University Press, Princeton.
Baweja, H., 1996, 'Changing face of parliament', *India Today*, 15 July.
Baweja, H., 1998, 'Fire in the sky', *India Today*, 20 April.
Baxter, C., Malik, Y., Kennedy, C. and Oberst, R., 1993, *Government and Politics in South Asia*, Westview, Boulder, CO and Oxford.
Bell, W. and Freeman, W. (eds), 1974, *Ethnicity and Nation-building*, Sage, Beverly Hills and London.
Bharatiya Janata Party (BJP), 1996, Election Manifesto.
Bose, S. and Jalal, A., 1998, *Modern South Asia*, Routledge, London.
Brass, P., 1974, *Language, Religion and Politics in North India*, Cambridge University Press, Cambridge.
Brass, P., 1991, *Ethnicity and Nationalism*, Sage, Beverly Hills and London.
Brass, P., 1994, *The Politics of India since Independence*, Cambridge University Press, Cambridge.
Brass, P. and Robinson, F. (eds), 1987, *Indian National Congress and Indian Society, 1885–1985*, Chanakya Publications, Delhi.
Chatterjee, P., 1993, *Nationalist Thought and the Colonial World*, Zed Books, London.
Chatterjee, D., 1996, 'Tribals in India: deepening identity crisis and India's security', *Jadavpur Journal of International Relations*, 2.
Chiriyankandath, J., 1996, 'Hindu nationalism and regional political culture in India: a study of Kerala', *Nationalism and Ethnic Politics*, 2:1 (spring).
Desai, N., 1996, 'How VHP planned the Gujarat riots', *The Telegraph* (Calcutta), 12 July.
Dasgupta, S., 1998, 'Swadeshi as modernity', *India Today*, 23 March.
Dasgupta, S. and Bhaumik, S. N., 1998, 'Crown of thorns', *India Today*, 16 March.
Deudney, D., 1997, 'Ground identity: nature, place, and space in nationalism' in Lapid, Y. and Kratochwil, F. (eds), *The Return of Culture and Identity in IR Theory*, Lynne Rienner, Boulder, CO and London.
Deutsch, K., 1969, *Nationalism and its Alternatives*, Alfred Knopf, New York.
Dua, B., 1987, 'Indian Congress dominance revisited' in Brass, P. and Robinson, F. (eds), *Indian National Congress and Indian Society, 1885–1985*, Chanakya Publications, Delhi.
Dutt, S., 1997, 'India after the 1996 elections', *CAPS News*, The Nottingham Trent University.
Ferguson, Y. H. and Mansbach, R. W., 1997, 'The past as prelude to the future? Identities and loyalties in global politics' in Lapid, Y. and Kratochwil, F. (eds), *The Return of Culture and Identity in IR Theory*, Lynne Rienner, Boulder, CO and London.
Fieldhouse, D. K., 1981, *Colonialism 1870–1945: An Introduction*, Weidenfeld and Nicolson, London.
Hazarika, S., 2004, 'Myanmar military ups border vigil', *The Statesman*, 20 December.
Irani, C. R., 1997, 'Cry, the beloved country!', *The Statesman*, 9 August.
Jayaram, N., 1996, 'Caste and Hinduism: changing protean relationship' in Srinivas, M. N. (ed.), *Caste, Its Twentieth Century Avatar*, Penguin Books, India.

Kaviraj, S., 1997, 'Religion and identity in India', *Ethnic and Racial Studies*, 20:2 (April).
Kedourie, E., 1993, *Nationalism*, Blackwell, Oxford.
Khalidi, O., 1995, *Indian Muslims since Independence*, Vikas Publishing House, New Delhi.
Kumar, A., 1999 'Indian elections: a further shift to the right by the main parties', 7 September, available at www.wsws.org/articles/1999/sep1999/indi-s07_prn.html.
Lapid, Y., 1997, 'Culture's ship: returns and departures in International Relations Theory' in Lapid, Y. and Kratochwil, F. (eds), *The Return of Culture and Identity in IR Theory*, Lynne Rienner, Boulder, CO and London.
Lapid, Y. and Kratochwil, F. (eds), 1997, *The Return of Culture and Identity in IR Theory*, Lynne Rienner, Boulder, CO and London.
Lapid, Y. and Kratochwil, F., 1997, 'Revisiting the "national": Toward an identity agenda in neo-realism?' in Lapid, Y. and Kratochwil, F. (eds), *The Return of Culture and Identity in IR Theory*, Lynne Rienner, Boulder, CO and London.
Levak, A. E., 1974, 'Provincial conflict and nation-building in Pakistan' in Bell, W. and Freeman, W. E. (eds), *Ethnicity and Nation-building*, Sage, Beverley Hills and London.
Mehta, V., 2004, Editorial, 'You can't buy the people of India', *Outlook*, 24 May.
Mukherjee, J. R., 2005 'Tale of three states', *The Sunday Statesman*, 6 March.
Mukherjee, L., 1975, *A History of India (British period)*, Mondal Brothers, Calcutta.
Naipaul, V. S., 1997, 'A million mutinies', *India Today*, 18 August.
Naliwal, R. P., 1998, 'Government calls meeting to discuss Uttarakhand', *The Times of India*, 8 April.
Narayan, H., 1996, 'Caste factor gives Laloo a clear edge', Elections '96, *The Sunday Statesman*, 7 April.
Ninan, S., 1992, Media pulse, *The Hindu*, 20 September.
Palkhivala, N., 1996, 'A state without a nation?', *The Statesman*, 30 May.
B. Parekh, B., 1994, 'Discourses on national identity', *Political Studies*, 43:2.
Phadke, Y. D., 1974, *Politics and Language*, Himalaya Publishing House, Bombay.
Roy, A. K., 1996 'Parliament today', *The Statesman*, 5 July.
Rushdie, S., 1997, ' A fantasy called India', *India Today*, special issue, 1947–1997, 18 August.
Safran, W., 1995, 'Nations, ethnic groups, states and politics: a preface and an agenda', *Nationalism and Ethnic Politics*, 1:1 (Spring).
Saxena, S., 1997, 'Language and the nationality question', *Economic and Political Weekly*, 8 February.
Sarhadi, A. S., 1974, *Nationalisms in India – The Problem*, Heritage Publishers, Delhi.
Scholte, J. A., 1996, 'Globalisation and collective identities' in Krause, J. and Renwick, N. (eds), *Identities in International Relations*, Macmillan, Basingstoke.
Sen Gupta, P., 1995, 'Ethnic discontent and India's unity' in Banerjee, A. (ed.), *Integration, Disintegration and World Order*, Allied Publishers, Calcutta.
Smith, A. D., 1991, *National Identity*, Penguin Books, London.
Smith, B. C., 1996, *Understanding Third World Politics*, Macmillan, Basingstoke.
Srinivas, M. N. (ed.), 1996, *Caste, Its twentieth Century Avtar*, Penguin Books, India.
Thakur, R., 1995, *The Government and Politics of India*, Macmillan, Basingstoke.
Thapar, R., 1996, *A History of India*, Penguin Books, London.
Verney, D., 'Are all federations federal? The United States, Canada and India' in Arora, B. and Verney, D. (eds), *Multiple Identities in a Single State*, Konark Publishers, New Delhi.
Wolpert, S., 1993, *A New History of India*, Oxford University Press, Oxford.
Yadav, Y. and Mcmillan, A., 1998, 'Results: how India voted', *India Today*, 16 March.

4 Economic development: from import-substitution industrialization to economic liberalization

When India became independent in 1947 Indian leaders were aware that India was a developing country even though the concept of development was not given sufficient international recognition before the launch of the UN Development Decades in 1961. This chapter will comment on the diversity of approaches to development, although its main focus will be the Indian government's policies. However, one cannot understand these policies without some knowledge of their antecedents. India's first prime minister, Nehru, wanted to modernize and industrialize India. He wrote: 'I believe in industrialization and the big machine and I should like to see factories springing up all over India' (cited in Seth, 1993: 461). He believed that industrialization would increase the wealth of India and raise the standard of living of the Indian people. He also felt that the real difference that we observe today between the east and the modern west was introduced by the industrial age. Nehru believed in reason. He argued that 'our chief enemy [in India] today is absence of reason…we must cultivate the spirit of enquiry and welcome all knowledge whether the source of it is the East or the West' (cited in Seth, 1993: 459). Progress for him was the development and spread of science and industry – the progressive universalization of reason. But at the same time he cautioned that science is almost unconcerned with our application of the knowledge it puts at our disposal and that 'the competitive and acquisitive characteristics of modern capitalist society, the enthronement of wealth above everything else, the continuous strain and the lack of security for many, add to the ill health of the mind and produce neurotic states' (Nehru, 1969: 556–7).

A 'low-income' developing country:[1] problems holding India back

India is a developing nation and, according to the World Bank's criteria, can be classified as a low-income country. Its gross national income (GNI) per capita was US$480 in 2002 and $530 in 2003. However, with a population of over a billion, its share of the world's population is about 17 per cent while it accounts for only 1.5 per cent of world GNI. If purchasing power is taken into account, according to some estimates, India's GNI per capita was around $2,880 in 2003. Low per capita income is, however, one of the characteristics of India as a developing economy. India's per capita GNI is even lower than that of China ($940 in 2002 and $1,100 in 2003) and much lower than those of the US ($35,060 in 2002 and $37,610 in 2003), Japan ($33,550 in 2002 and $34,510 in 2003) and the UK ($25,250 in 2002 and $28,350 in 2003) (*World Development Report 2004*, Select Indicators; *World Development Report 2005*, Select Indicators). But as mentioned above, if the domestic purchasing power of currencies is taken into account, the gap between India and the developed economies narrows slightly. In general, the gap between the rich and poor countries is continuing to grow. The only positive development, as far as India is concerned, relates to growth rates. In the 1960s and 1970s the developed economies grew at a faster rate than the Indian economy but since the 1990s the Indian economy has grown at a faster rate.

Agriculture

Another characteristic of the Indian economy is the high percentage of the working population engaged in agriculture (including subsistence farming). Farming and agriculture continues to be the main occupation even after more than fifty years of independence and the drive for industrialization. Agriculture accounts for 22 per cent of the gross domestic product (GDP) and provides livelihoods for 58 per cent of India's population (Government of India, *Economic Survey 2003–2004*: 169). Unfortunately, however, agricultural productivity is low and there are historical reasons for this. The agricultural sector has not received as much attention and investment as other sectors of the economy, i.e., services and manufacturing. The Indian government recognizes that the dependence of agriculture on the monsoons should be reduced by extending irrigation facilities. The development of rural infrastructure is also essential. Moreover, there is growth potential in emerging areas like horticulture, floriculture, organic farming, genetic engineering, food processing, branding and packaging.

Agricultural exports constitute around 13 per cent of total merchandise exports. The value of agricultural exports increased from US$5.9 billion in 2001–02 to $6.7 billion in 2002–03. Marine products contributed around 20 per cent of the total agri-products. India also exports foodgrains (rice and wheat), tea, coffee, sugar and molasses, tobacco, spices, cashew nuts, sesame and niger seeds, fruits and vegetables, meat and meat preparations and oil meals. The Indian government has announced certain policy measures to boost agri-exports such as the free exportability of all agricultural products except onion and niger seed; the setting up of agri-export zones to enhance international market access, improve infrastructure facilities and ensure better flow of credit; and financial assistance for improved packaging, strengthening of quality-control mechanisms and the modernization of processing units. The share of agricultural imports in total merchandise imports grew slightly from 4.5 per cent in 2001–02 to 4.6 per cent in 2002–03. Their value increased to US$2.8 billion in 2002–03 from $2.3 billion in 2001–02. Edible oil accounts for almost two-thirds of the total agri-imports (*Economic Survey 2003–2004*: 168–9).

On 7 March 2005, while inaugurating the New Delhi office of the International Food Policy Research Institute, the prime minister, Manmohan Singh, said that his government was committed to launching the 'second green revolution' (the first had been launched in the 1960s). He promised rural India a 'New Deal' to reverse the decline in investment in agriculture. More funds would be made available for agricultural research, irrigation and wasteland development. The New Deal aimed to ensure the food and nutritional security of the people, augment farm incomes and increase employment (*The Statesman*, 8 March 2005). However, left parties are not impressed. The increase in expenditure on agriculture in the union budget for 2005–06 is small (*The Statesman*, 1 March 2005). Even Federation of Indian Chambers of Commerce and Industry (FICCI) president, Kanwar, is in favour of increasing investment in agriculture and a higher allocation for the sector in the union budget (*The Statesman*, 26 February 2005). Professor Bagchi, an Indian economist, has asked a more fundamental question, 'why is there no mention of incentives to states for introducing pro-peasant land reforms [in the union budget]?' (Bagchi, 2005).

Population 'explosion'

One of the main characteristics of India as a developing economy is the rate of growth of the population. The total population of India crossed the 1 billion mark in March 2000.[2] India has high birth rates and declining death rates, thanks to modern science and improved health facilities. Although birth rates have fallen from 36.9 per thousand in 1971 to 29.5 per thousand in 1991 and 25.8 per thousand in 2002, death rates have fallen even more steeply, from 14.9 per thousand in 1971 to 9.8 per thousand in 1991 to 8.5 per thousand in 2002 (Central Statistical Organization, 2002: 1). Population growth has to be matched by economic growth if a decent standard of living is to be maintained.

A growing population leads to an increase in the labour force. According to the tenth five-year plan (2002–07) 'there is … every likelihood that the labour force will increase faster than the economy's current ability to provide gainful and decent work opportunities' (Chapter 1, tenth plan). If the supply of labour outstrips the demand for it, it naturally leads to unemployment. However, Indian economists argue that unemployment in India is structural and is the result of a deficiency of capital. Industries cannot expand to absorb the entire labour force. Even in agriculture there is (disguised) unemployment. In other words, a much larger number of labourers are engaged in production than are really needed. According to Chapter 10 of the third five-year plan (1961–66), 'in the villages unemployment ordinarily takes the form of underemployment'.[3] Overall, the rate of growth of employment declined in the 1990s, indicating a decline in the labour intensity of production. The absolute number of unemployed increased from 20 million in 1994–94 to 27 million in 1999–2000. Also, the incidence of unemployment (expressed in terms of unemployed as a percentage of the labour force) increased from 5.99 per cent in 1993–94 to 7.32 per cent in 1999–2000. However, employment growth in the services sector exceeded 5 per cent per annum (*Economic Survey 2003–2004*: 207–09). According to the tenth plan 'the composite incidence of unemployment and underemployment, as captured by the current daily status (CDS) basis, presently stands at nearly 9 per cent of the labour force and at almost 13 per cent for the youth' (tenth plan, Chapter 1). The incidence of underemployment among rural males increased during the mid to late 1990s. The principal cause of this is the steadily worsening land–man ratio and the continued dependence of a high proportion of the population on agriculture. A rapidly growing population needs a relatively high rate of capital formation to improve living standards, and the present rate is not adequate.

Quality of human capital

A large population can be an asset. However, a more significant factor is the quality of human capital as it contributes to economic development. Poor quality of human capital is a problem that most developing countries face. According to the *Human Development Report 1997* India was ranked at number 138 on the basis of the United Nations Development Programme's Human Development Index (UNDP/HDI) that takes into account life expectancy, adult literacy and so on, and did not compare favourably with countries like China, which was ranked number 108 (UNDP, 1997: 44–5). Critical factors include, for example, expenditure on education and health. The Indian expenditure on education in 1993–94 was about 3.8 per cent of the GNP. This grew to 3.99 per cent in 2001–02 (*Economic Survey, 2002–2003*: 222; UNDP, 1997: 181). The corresponding figure for the US in 1993–94 was 5.5 per cent of GNP (UNDP, 1997: 208). However, the Indian government claims that plan expenditure on education has increased since the first five-year plan, although it admits that the goal set by the national policy on education (1986) of 6 per cent of GDP has not been achieved. Critics point out that expenditure on education (in percentage terms) had actually declined in the post-reform period (Datt and Sundharam, 2001: 257). A high priority has been accorded to this sector in the tenth five-year plan, with an allocation of Rs 43,825 *crores*[4] as against Rs 24,908 *crores* made available in the ninth plan (1997–2001), representing an increase of 76 per cent (*Economic Survey 2003–2004*: 213). The national health policy 2002 envisages increasing public health investment from the current level of 0.9 per cent of GDP to 2 per cent of GDP by 2010 (*Economic Survey 2003–2004*: 216). India's UNDP/HDI rank in 2001 was 127 among 175 countries while China's was 94 (*Economic Survey 2003–2004*: 201; *Human Development Report 2003*).

Table 4.1 *Selected health indicators (person years)*

Serial no.	Parameter	1951	1981	1991	Current level
1	Crude birth rate (per 1,000 population)	40.8	33.9	29.5	25.0 (2002★)
2	Crude death rate (per 1,000 population)	25.1	12.5	9.8	8.1 (2002★)
3	Total fertility rate (per woman)	6.0	4.5	3.6	3.2 (1999)
4	Maternal mortality rate (per 100,000 live births) NFHS	NA	NA	437 (1992–93)	407 (1998)
5	Infant mortality rate (per 100,000 live births)	146 (1951–61)	110	80	64 (2002★)
6	Child (0–4) mortality rate (per 1000 children)	57.3 (1972)	41.2	26.5	19.5 (2000)
7	Couple protection rate (%) NFHS	10.4 (1971)	22.8	44.1	48.2 (1998–99)
8	Life expectancy at birth Male	37.2	54.1	59.7 (1991–95)	63.9 (2001–06)
	Female	36.2	54.7	60.9 (1991–95)	66.9 (2001–06)

Note: The dates in the brackets indicate years for which latest information is available.
Key: NFHS – National Family Health Survey; NA – not available; ★ – provisional.
Source: Government of India, Ministry of Health and Family Welfare, *Economic Survey, 2003–2004*.

About 25 to 40 per cent of the population also suffers from malnutrition, a result of the low calorie intake and low level of consumption of protein that prevails in India (Datt and Sundharam, 2001: 8). Prime Minister Manmohan Singh has indicated that the Planning Commission is considering setting up a food and nutrition security watch to function as a 'think tank' on food and nutrition security issues as well as a programme reviewing agency (*The Statesman*, 8 March 2005). The tenth plan asserts that notions of national security today are broader than merely that of defence or military preparedness. The two most critical aspects of this wider view are energy and food security. However, Table 4.1 shows that some progress has been made.

Inequitable distribution of assets/wealth

Yet another problem that leads to low living standards is the inequitable distribution of assets and wealth. Assets constitute the resource base of households and it is argued have an impact on their income. According to a survey carried out by the Reserve Bank of India and covering the period July 1991 to June 1992, 9.6 per cent of the rich households in rural areas owning assets worth Rs 2.5 *lakhs* or more accounted for nearly 49 per cent of total assets. The concentration of wealth in urban areas is, however, worse. Nearly 66 per cent of the total assets of all urban households were held by 14.2 per cent of the wealthiest households owning Rs 2.5 *lakhs* or more (cited in Datt and Sundharam, 2001: 8). About 65 per cent of Indian households do not have a bank account. A higher percentage of urban households (50 per cent) have bank accounts while only 30 per cent of rural households have one. However, the demand for consumer products is growing. Homes without a kitchen or toilet have TVs and two-wheel vehicles such as scooters, mopeds or motorbikes. According to some estimates 61 million Indian families, constituting about 32 per cent of the total population, own a TV set (*India Today*, 28 July 2003: 17).

Technological 'backwardness'

Another undesirable characteristic of the Indian economy is 'technological backwardness'. Primitive technology is still used even though it does not enhance productivity. The absorption of modern technology is hindered by the lack of capital and the lack of skill. The low productivity per hectare in Indian agriculture and the low level of productivity per worker in agriculture and industry are largely a consequence of this 'backwardness'. Farmers are often too poor to buy improved seeds, fertilizers and insecticides, and equipment such as harvestors, tractors and sowing machines.

Demographic characteristics

India also possesses certain demographic characteristics that impede rapid economic growth and development. The density of population is high: 358 per square kilometre in 2003. This is much higher than the density of population in developed countries and even China (a country with a large population) has a lower density of population – 138 per square kilometre in 2003 (*World Development Report 2005*). Life expectancy at birth was 63.7 in 2002, lower than in most developed countries, but it has improved over the years. China's life expectancy at birth in 2002 was 70.9 (*Human Development Report 2003*). Death rates have declined, although infant mortality rates are still relatively high. According to the census of India 2001, 37.3 per cent of the total population is in the age group 0–14, 55.4 per cent is in the working age group, i.e. 15–59, and only 7.3 per cent is in the age group 60 and above (Central Statistical Organization, 2002: 7). The density of population becomes a problem when there is a shortage of affordable housing as there is in India. According to the 2001 census, the total slum population in the country is 40.3 million, comprising 22.6 per cent of the total urban population of cities and towns that have slums.

Greater Mumbai has the largest slum population, with 48.9 per cent of the total population.

According to a New Delhi Television (NDTV) survey broadcast on 20 December 2004, 88 per cent of respondents felt that India needs compulsory birth control while 12 per cent disagreed. Saroj Pachauri, regional director of the Population Council of India, also disagreed, arguing that the rate of population growth was coming down. It was 1.9 per cent in the 1990s and is declining further.

The Indian government introduced family planning in the early 1950s. According to the ninth five-year plan three principal factors are responsible for population growth in India: the large size of the population in the reproductive age group, high fertility rates and relatively high infant mortality rates. In 2000 the National Democratic Alliance (NDA) government adopted a national population policy. Its aim was to promote the two-child norm and stabilize the population by 2046. The Indian government also decided to freeze Lok Sabha seats on the basis of the 1971 census; thus more populous states such as Uttar Pradesh, Bihar and Madhya Pradesh will not be 'rewarded' for having larger populations and states such as Tamil Nadu and Kerala that have adopted the small family norm will not be unfairly penalized. The measures proposed by this policy include the reduction of infant mortality rates, the reduction of maternal mortality rates, universal immunization, incentives to adopt the two-child small family norm, a strict enforcement of the Child Marriage Restraint Act and Pre-Natal Diagnostic Techniques Act, access to information on Aids and the prevention and control of communicable diseases. It also recommended the appointment of a National Commission on Population to be headed by the prime minister to monitor the implementation of the population policy (Datt and Sundharam, 2001: 67–9).

Poor infrastructure

Finally, another characteristic of the Indian economy, and one that is impeding development, is poor infrastructure. Apart from roads, electricity and airports, financial institutions are needed to mobilize savings in the rural sector, to grant loans to farmers on easy terms and to provide medium and long-term loans to industries. In other words, better infrastructure and infrastructural improvements will not only promote indigenous development but will also attract foreign investment. This is discussed further in Chapter 5.

The issues relating to development in India therefore include low per capita income (one of the lowest in the world), a high proportion of people (34.7 per cent in 1999–2000 according to the *World Development Report 2005*) below the poverty line (despite the progress made in the last three or four decades), a low rate of economic growth (although this is now changing), a low level of productivity, the rate of growth of population that puts pressure on finite resources, unemployment, uncertainty of agricultural production due to dependence on monsoons, poor infrastructure, an imbalance between heavy industry and wage goods and finally a wide gap between the rich and poor.

However, it is not enough to raise the level of investment in order to initiate economic growth, it is also necessary to gradually transform the social, religious and political institutions which act as obstacles to economic progress. Moreover, it is wise to heed the warning of the *Human Development Report 1996* that economic growth must be matched by advances in human development if it is to be sustained. Human development requires that greater attention be paid to the problems of unemployment, poverty reduction, empowerment of the weaker and underprivileged sections of the society, and greater participation of the people in the process of growth and long-term sustainability. In other words, human development encompasses three broad objectives: growth, equity and democracy. Development in India should generate employment, be equitable, involve wider participation and growth from the grassroots and be sustainable.

A centrally planned economy

A mixed economy

The Industrial Policy Resolution (1948) envisaged a mixed economy for India, i.e. an economy in which public and private enterprises co-exist. In India the state demarcated the areas for the promotion of industries in the public and the private sectors. This division was initially specified in the Industrial Policy Resolution of 1948 and then in the Industrial Policy Resolution of 1956 which replaced it.

Industries which would be the exclusive responsibility of the state were listed in schedule A of the Industrial Policy Resolution of 1948 and 1956 and included arms and ammunition; atomic energy; iron and steel; heavy machinery required for iron and steel production; mining and machine tool manufactures; heavy electrical industries; coal; air transport; rail transport; shipbuilding; telephone, telegraph and wireless equipment; generation and distribution of electricity.

Industries listed in schedule B included chemical industries, drugs and pharmaceuticals, fertilizers, synthetic rubber, road transport and sea transport and were to be progressively state owned. Private enterprise was expected only to supplement the efforts of the state. All remaining industries (in Schedule C) were to be left to the initiative and enterprise of the private sector but had to respect the social and economic policy of the state and were subject to control in terms of relevant legislation.

The industrial licensing policy was laid down by the Industries (Development and Regulation) Act of 1951. According to this, no new industrial units could be established or substantial extension to existing plants made without a licence from the central government and, while granting licences for new undertakings, the government could specify conditions regarding location, minimum size and so on. Critics pointed out that large industrial houses such as the Birlas often did not utilize the licences issued to them and as there was no system for revoking licences, this practice prevented the entry of new entrepreneurs. The 1951 Act was replaced by a new industrial licensing policy in 1970. However, the 'license-permit raj' continued for another twenty years.

The Indian government also vigorously pursued a policy of Indianization. The industrial policy of 1956 made it clear that 'as a rule, the major interest in ownership and effective control, should always be in Indian hands. In all cases, however, the training of suitable Indian personnel for the purpose of eventually replacing foreign experts will be insisted upon.' The nationalization of banks was another policy pursued by the government. In 1969 fourteen major banks were nationalized, followed by six more in 1980 (Manorama yearbook 1996; *India Today*, 18 August 2003). In 1994 however this policy was abandoned in keeping with the policy of economic liberalization. Economic reforms also led to the growth of capital markets and reduced the reliance of companies and firms on government-controlled banks and other financial institutions as well as on a heavily regulated stock market. Private-sector banks held 20 per cent of total deposits at the beginning of the twenty-first century, compared with around 11 per cent in 1992 (Mukherjee, 2002: 59–60). Foreign institutional investors were also allowed to register and invest in India's stock markets, subject to a ceiling determined by the Indian government (*Human Development in South Asia 2001*: 67). The government had moved from direct to indirect control through regulatory bodies such as the Securities and Exchange Board of India (SEBI) (Mukherjee, 2002: 63).

Critics of the Congress Industrial Policy Resolution of 1956 argued that it had led to unemployment, rural–urban disparities, industrial 'sickness', slow growth of industrial output and no real growth in investment (Datt and Sundharam, 2001: 168). All these issues have continued to plague the Indian economy. The criticisms about 'sick' industries have now given way to criticisms about the lack of progress made in disinvestment in public-sector enterprises (PSEs). The most serious problems identified in the public sector are a low rate of return on investment, a large number of loss-making units and an accumulation of losses which have ultimately to be paid out of the general revenues by the state exchequer. The public sector grew from five PSEs at the beginning of the first five-year plan (1951–56) and an investment of Rs 29 *crores* to 242 PSEs at the end of the eighth five-year plan (1992–97) and an investment of Rs 206,655 *crores* (Bose, 2000). Congress MP Pranab Mukherjee told Star television news on 16 August 2001 that 'sick' PSEs should not be bailed out by the government – if they could not perform they should disinvest. However, maximum autonomy should be given to PSEs that are performing well. Mukherjee (2002: 72) comments that the failure to privatize has been one of the biggest shortcomings of the first decade of reform while Bose asserts that disinvestment is geared to meeting the government's short-term financial needs; the emphasis is on asset disposal to cover revenue expenses (Bose, 2000). The Indian government proposed granting autonomy to many PSEs including the Indian Oil Corporation (IOC), Oil and National Gas Corporation (ONGC), Steel Authority of India Limited (SAIL) and Bharat Heavy Electricals Limited (BHEL), in order to make them more efficient and competitive. This measure would enable them to incur capital expenditure, decide upon joint ventures, set up subsidiaries abroad, enter into technological strategic alliances, raise funds from capital markets (domestic and international) and enjoy substantial operation and managerial autonomy. A list of PSEs was also referred to the Disinvestment Commission for its advice and recommendations (*Economic Survey 1997–1998*: 102).

The Congress's industrial policy of 1980 endorsed the policy of 1956. However, after 1980 the industrial licensing policy was liberalized in favour of large business houses. A particularly significant move was making them free from the provisions of the Monopolies and Restrictive Trade Practices (MRTP) Act and the Foreign Exchange Regulation Act (FERA). In July 1991 Narasimha Rao's Congress government announced a new industrial policy whose main aim was to remove bureaucratic control, integrate the Indian economy with the world economy, remove restrictions on direct foreign investment and liberate the domestic entrepreneur from the restrictions of MRTP. The number of industries in respect of which licensing was compulsory was reduced to eighteen. In April 1993 the government removed three more items from this list: motor cars, white goods (refrigerators, washing machines, air conditioners, etc.), and raw hides and skins and patent leather. As demand for these goods was growing they were no longer regarded as luxury goods, moreover, the government hoped that the removal of compulsory licensing would encourage potential investors and increase the flow of investment in these industries. Some of these goods, for example leather and leather products, could also boost exports. In order to attract foreign capital the Indian government also decided to provide approval for direct foreign investment of up to 51 per cent equity in high priority industries. Nine industries were identified for 74 per cent automatic approval and included construction and maintenance of roads, ropeways, ports, harbours, and power plants. The main aim was to attract foreign direct investment in certain sectors such as infrastructure and export-oriented industries. The government would also permit 100 per cent equity in cases where the entire output was exported (Datt and Sundharam, 2001: 171–5).

The five-year plans

India has a centrally planned economy. The Planning Commission was set up in 1950 to assess the country's need of material, capital and human resources in order to formulate plans for their balanced and effective utilization (first five-year plan, Introduction). The first five-year plan commenced in 1951 and was followed by ten more five-year plans and three annual plans between 1966 and 1969. Certain long-term objectives were set out by the planners in India:

1. to increase production to the maximum possible extent so as to achieve a higher level of national and per capita income;
2. to achieve full employment;
3. to reduce inequalities of income and wealth;
4. to set up a socialist society based on equality and justice and absence of exploitation.

The first plan's (1951–56) immediate objectives were the rehabilitation of refugees, rapid agricultural development and achievement of food sufficiency, and control of inflation. It stated that 'in an underdeveloped economy with low yields in agriculture, there is of course no real conflict between agricultural and industrial development. One cannot go far without the other; the two are complementary. It is necessary, however, on economic as well as on other grounds, first of all to strengthen the economy at the base and to create conditions of sufficiency and even plenitude in respect of food and raw materials. These are the wherewithals for further development' (first five-year plan, Chapter 2). Sectors given importance included power and transport. The annual average growth rate during this plan period was 3.61 per cent as against a target of 2.1 per cent. Having achieved the agricultural targets set by the first plan, the government decided to give priority to industrial development in the second plan (1956–61), and in 1956 announced its industrial policy. It aimed to promote a socialist economy: 'our second five-year plan seeks to rebuild rural India, to lay the foundations of industrial progress, and to secure to the greatest extent feasible opportunities for weaker and under-privileged sections of our people and the balanced development of all parts of the country. For a country whose economic development was long retarded these are difficult tasks but, given the effort and the sacrifice, they are well within our capacity to achieve' (second five-year plan). The plan achieved a growth rate of 4.32 per cent (Government of India, Factsheet 2000).

The third five-year plan (1961–66) set as its goal the establishment of a self-sustaining economy. The emphasis on industrial development continued, however agriculture was also given priority as it was realized that India's economic development was also dependent on the rate of growth of agricultural production. But India faced several problems during this plan period: a growing trade deficit, mounting debt obligations, conflict with neighbouring countries and droughts. The country had to resort to borrowing from the IMF and the rupee was devalued for the first time in 1966. According to the Indian government's assessment this plan was a relative failure (Government of India, Factsheet 2000).

Following the wars with China in 1962 and Pakistan in 1965, the focus of the third plan shifted from development to defence and development. India's external relations had to be factored in; India could not just concentrate on its economy and economic development. By 1985 India spent 2.5 per cent of its GNP or US$7,207 million on defence. This rose to US$10,600 million in 1998 although it is estimated that as a percentage of the GNP it remained the same. Nevertheless, the *Human Development in South Asia 1997* report asserts that 'widespread human deprivation in south Asia contrasts sharply with large armies, modern weapons, and expanding military budgets in the region. Two of the largest armies in the world are in South Asia.' The countries in the region are much poorer than Saudi Arabia, an oil-rich country, yet the region spends 'twice as much [as Saudi Arabia] each year on the purchase of high-tech arms'. South Asia is 'the only region where military spending (as a proportion of GNP) has gone up since 1987; it has declined substantially in all other parts of the world after the end of the cold war' (ul Haq, 1997: 2–3). The Indian union budget for 2005–06 has increased the allocation for defence to Rs 83,000 *crores* from Rs 77,000 *crores* in the previous year (Flory, 2005). It is not an increase in real terms but a Pakistani foreign affairs spokesperson has said that it is not a 'helpful trend' (*The Statesman*, 1 March 2005: 5).

The Indian planners did realize that for a poor country such as India with a majority of people steeped in poverty, national income was not a suitable indicator of economic development. Thus from the fourth plan (1969–74) onwards the objective of planning was not simply growth but raising the standard of living of the people and the removal of poverty. There was, therefore, an ideological shift. However, achieving a higher national income is easier than achieving a more equitable distribution of national income. The removal of poverty is therefore not an easy task.

The fourth plan should have been launched in 1966 but was abandoned because the economy was going through a particularly difficult phase due to two years of drought, devaluation of the rupee and an inflationary recession. It was replaced initially by three annual plans between 1966 and 1969 and then by a new fourth five-year plan covering the period between 1969 to 1974. It had set two principal objectives: growth with stability and progressive achievement of self-reliance. The fourth plan aimed at a target growth of 5.7 per cent and laid emphasis on improving the condition of the underprivileged and weaker sections of the community through the provision of education and employment – the latter came to be known as the objectives of 'growth with social justice' and '*garibi hatao*' (remove poverty), a slogan associated with Indira Gandhi. The growth rate achieved by this plan was 3.21 per cent (Government of India, Factsheet 2000). The fifth five-year plan was supposed to cover the period between 1974 and 1979 but was terminated in 1978 by the Janata Party after it won the elections. When it was introduced the country was facing an economic crisis. The hike in oil prices after the Yom Kippur war of 1973 had contributed to rising inflation. *Garibi hatao* remained one of the main concerns but approaches to tackling poverty varied. One approach (that was not eventually adopted) claimed that the main causes of abject poverty were open unemployment, underemployment and the low resource base of a very large number of producers in the agriculture and service sectors. Poverty could not be removed simply on the basis of higher rates of growth of the economy. The approach that was eventually adopted outlined two objectives: the removal of poverty and the attainment of self-reliance, through promotion of higher rates of growth, better distribution of income and a very significant increase in the domestic rate of saving. The main objective of the plan changed from growth with social justice to growth for social justice. The fifth plan achieved a growth rate of 4.8 per cent, which was slightly higher than the target rate of 4.4 per cent (Government of India, Factsheet 2000).

The first sixth plan (1978–83) adopted by the Janata Party openly praised the achievements of planning in India but held the Nehru model of growth responsible for growing unemployment, for the concentration of economic power in the hands of a few powerful business and industrial families, for the widening of inequalities of income and wealth and for mounting poverty. The Janata plan focused on the enlargement of the employment potential in agriculture and allied activities, encouragement to household and small industries producing consumer goods for mass consumption and on raising the incomes of the lowest income classes through a minimum needs programme. The Janata plan was terminated by the Congress after they won the elections of 1980 and replaced by a new sixth plan, covering the period 1980–85, that went back to the goal of achieving higher rates of growth. However, the main objective of the plan was the removal of poverty. Infrastructure was also given importance. The growth rate achieved was 5.7 per cent and exceeded the target (Datt and Sundharam, 2001: 271; Government of India, Factsheet 2000).

A new economic policy – 1985

The seventh plan (1985–90) gave importance to foodgrains production, increasing employment and raising productivity. These were short-term goals but were geared to achieving the long-term goals of planning in India determined in the early 1950s. In 1985, Rajiv Gandhi's government announced a new economic policy – a policy of economic liberalization – which was directed towards creating the right sort of climate for the private sector. Gandhi's key aims were to improve productivity, absorb modern technology and promote fuller utilization of capacity. To provide larger scope to the private sector, a number of changes in policy were introduced with regard to industrial licensing, export-import policy, technology upgradation, fiscal policy, foreign equity capital, removal of controls and restrictions, and rationalizing and simplifying the system of fiscal and administrative regulation. All these changes were aimed at increasing private-sector investment to modernize the economy and usher in rapid growth. The new policy offered greater scope for expansion to the private sector, particularly in the corporate segment of the manufacturing industry, and opened up opportunities for multinational enterprises. The seventh plan was heralded as a great success since the economy recorded 6 per cent rate of economic growth during this plan as against the targeted 5 per cent. The average annual rate of growth in the 1980s was 5.8 per cent as against the average of 3.5 per cent in the previous five plans. The Indian economy, finally, crossed the barrier of what Professor Raj Krishna called 'the Hindu rate of growth' (Datt and Sundharam, 2001: 230, 276).

A balance-of-payments crisis leads to economic reforms

However, the balance-of-trade deficit, instead of narrowing down, increased. The country was faced with a serious balance-of-payments crisis. Whereas the average deficit in trade balance during the sixth plan (1980–85) was around Rs 5,930 *crores*, it increased to Rs 10,840 *crores* during the seventh plan (1985–90). There was also a decline in the receipts on invisible account, from Rs 19,070 *crores* during the sixth plan to Rs 15,890 *crores* during the seventh. India was affected by the Gulf War in 1990, and remittances from Indian workers in the Gulf, an important source of revenue, also declined (Datt and Sundharam, 2001: 231).

The government of India was forced to approach the World Bank and the IMF and secured a loan of about US$7 billion, given on condition that a number of policy measures would be initiated to bring about the structural readjustment of the economy. The government responded by adopting a programme to reduce fiscal deficits supported by reforms intended to promote the growth of the economy. In July 1991, the Congress government, led by Narasimha Rao, announced a new industrial policy as discussed above. In a memo to the IMF dated 27 August 1991, Manmohan Singh, finance minister, stated: 'The thrust will be to increase the efficiency and international competitiveness of industrial production and to utilize foreign investment and technology to a much greater degree than in the past, to improve the performance and rationalize the scope of the public sector, and to reform and modernize the financial sector so that it can more efficiently serve the needs of the economy' (cited in Datt and Sundharam, 2001: 231).

Industrial licensing was to be abolished for all projects except for a short list of industries related to security and strategic concerns, hazardous chemicals, elitist consumption, social objectives and over-riding environmental concerns. In order to encourage foreign investment in high-priority areas requiring large investments and advanced technology, it was decided that approval would be given for direct foreign investment of up to 51 per cent foreign equity ownership in such industries. The major areas of the second wave of economic reform were: fiscal policy; monetary policy; pricing policy; external policy; industrial policy; foreign investment policy; trade policy; and public-sector policy (Datt and Sundharam, 2001: 232).

The eighth five-year plan was originally supposed to cover the period 1990–95. However, as indicated above, the country was undergoing severe economic problems in the early 1990s caused by a balance-of-payments crisis, a rising debt burden, ever-widening budget deficits, mounting inflation and recession in industry. The Planning Commission was reconstituted several times and finally the plan was adopted to cover the period 1992–97. It may be recalled that the Congress had lost the elections of 1989; after a brief interlude during which non-Congress political parties were in power, P. V. Narasimha Rao of the Congress became the prime minister in 1991 and his government initiated the process of fiscal reforms and also economic reforms with a view to providing a new dynamism to the economy. The main aims of this plan were to stabilize the adverse balance-of-payment situation, focus on human development and bring about an improvement in trade and current account deficits. The plan was also to manage the transition from a centrally planned economy to a market-led economy. During the eighth plan India achieved an average annual growth of 6.5 per cent, exceeding the growth rate of the previous plan period as well as the targeted rate of growth for the eighth plan of 5.6 per cent (Government of India, Factsheet 2000). This was achieved even though the share of the public sector in total investment had declined considerably to about 34 per cent (Datt and Sundharam, 2001: 276). Private-sector investment and the movement towards a market-based economic system were some of the factors responsible for the higher rate of economic growth during the eighth plan. It should also be noted that the agricultural sector performed relatively well, despite a setback in 1995–96. Although the Congress lost the elections of 1996, successive governments (including those dominated by the BJP) remained committed to the process of economic liberalization.

However, some Indian economists argue that 'the new Industrial Policy may be able to attract foreign investment and give a boost to domestic investment, but whether it will lead to more employment along with higher output growth is doubtful. Besides, excessive freedom to foreign capital may ultimately affect our economic sovereignty and also push the country into a debt trap further' (Datt and Sundharam, 2001: 176). In 2000 the Indian government raised the ceiling on investment by foreign multinationals in their Indian subsidiaries and new joint ventures from 51 per cent to 74 per cent. The Indian government also issued a notification on 5 March 2004 enhancing the foreign direct investment (FDI) limit in private sector banks from 49 per cent to 74 per cent. Mr P. Chidambaram, the finance minister, told the Lok Sabha on 15 December 2004 that 'the revision in FDI limit will create an enabling environment for higher FDI inflows, along with the infusion of new technology and management practices, resulting in enhanced competitiveness' (*The Statesman*, 16 December 2004). Table 4.2 shows which sectors are attracting the highest numbers of FDI approvals as well as FDI inflows.

Nonetheless, India's desire to remain self-reliant has not waned; it is worth noting that of the three sources of plan finance, domestic, external and deficit, the most important are still the domestic budgetary resources. They accounted

Table 4.2 Sectors attracting the highest FDI approvals with inflows (January 1991–March 2004)

Amount: Rs in crores (US$ in billion)

Rank	Sector	No. of FDI approval	FDI approved	Percentage of total FDI approved	FDI inflows	% of total FDI inflows* (Rs)	% of inflows over approval (Rs)
1	Energy	701	77,828 (20.99)	26.62	9,802 (2.32)	10.21	12.59
	of which power	362	43,703 (11.90)	14.95	–	–	–
	of which oil refining	339	34,125 (9.09)	11.67	–	–	–
2	Telecommunications	803	57,328 (15.43)	19.61	10,725 (2.56)	11.17	18.71
3	Electrical equipment (incl. computer software & electronics)	4,495	28,072 (7.29)	9.94	13,930 (3.32)	14.50	47.92
4	Transportation	1,069	21,966 (5.73)	7.51	11,517 (2.78)	11.99	52.43
5	Services sector	1,102	19,261 (4.27)	6.59	8,134 (0.31)	8.47	42.23
6	Metallurgical industries	407	15,534 (4.27)	5.31	1,254 (0.31)	1.31	8.07
7	Chemicals (other than fertilizers)	1,053	13,090 (3.73)	4.48	5,692 (1.49)	5.93	43.48
8	Food & food processing	771	9,620 (2.77)	3.29	4,346 (1.09)	4.53	45.18
9	Hotels & tourism	504	5,215 (1.45)	1.78	899 (2.14)	0.87	17.24
10	Textiles	641	3,517 (1.02)	1.20	1,163 (0.31)	1.21	33.07

Note: *Percentage figures do not take into account the amount of FDI Inflows for ADRs/GDRs/FCCBs, RBISs NRI schemes, acquisition of existing shares (up to 1999), stock swapped & advance pending for allotment of shares, as these are not categorized sector-wise.

Source: Government of India, Economic Survey 2003–2004.

for 73 per cent of the total funds raised during the first plan and 86 per cent of the total funds raised for the eighth plan (Datt and Sundharam, 2001: 276).

The Approach Paper to the ninth five-year plan (1997–2002) announced that its principal task was to 'usher in a new era of people-oriented planning, in which not only the Governments at the Centre and the States, but the people at large, particularly the poor, can fully participate. A participatory planning process is an essential precondition for ensuring equity as well as accelerating the rate of growth of the economy.' It noted that 'although the macro-economy performed reasonably well in the Eighth Five Year Plan, some major weaknesses have also emerged. In particular, the growth pattern has not benefited the poor and the underprivileged'. It was further noted that 'economic growth and employment opportunities in themselves may not be sufficient to improve the living conditions of the poor'. Emphasis was put on a basic minimum services programme. The ninth plan aimed to build on the successes of the eighth, while tackling the problems that had emerged, particularly in areas such as capital formation in agriculture, living standards of the poor, infrastructure, social sector, regional disparity and fiscal deficits. It was also noted that resources continued to be limited and that the Indian economy was still vulnerable and the operation of a more open economic system had to be tempered by judicious public and state interventions to ensure that these vulnerabilities are gradually overcome.[5]

The ninth plan aimed to achieve an annual average growth rate of 6.5 per cent for the economy as a whole. It sought to achieve 'growth with equity', which needs to be seen in the context of four important dimensions of state policy: the quality of life of the citizens and the generation of productive employment, regional balance and self-reliance. The plan's specific objectives were as follows:

1. priority to be given to agriculture and rural development with a view to generating adequate productive employment and eradication of poverty;
2. accelerating the growth rate of the economy with stable prices;
3. providing the basic minimum services of drinking water, primary health care facilities, universal primary education, shelter and connectivity to all in a time-bound manner;
4. containing the growth rate of population;
5. ensuring environmental sustainability of the development process through social mobilization and participation of people at all levels;
6. empowerment of women and socially disadvantaged groups such as SCs, STs, OBCs and minorities as agents of socio-economic change and development;
7. promoting and developing people's participatory institutions like *panchayati raj* institutions, co-operatives and self-help groups;
8. strengthening efforts to build self-reliance.

The Approach Paper to the tenth five-year plan (2002–07) stated that it was being prepared against the backdrop of high expectations and pointed out that 'GDP growth in the post-reforms period has improved from an average of about 5.7 per cent in the 1980s to an average of about 6.5 per cent in the eighth and ninth plan periods, making India one of the ten fastest growing developing countries'. Encouraging progress has also been made in other dimensions. At the time of writing the percentage of the population in poverty has continued to decline, even if not as much as was targeted. Population growth has decelerated below 2 per cent for the first time in four decades. Literacy increased from 52 per cent in 1991 to 65 per cent in 2001 and the improvement has been evident in all states. Sectors such as software services, entertainment and IT-enabled services have emerged as new sources of strength, creating confidence about India's potential to be competitive in the world economy. The prime minister has directed the Planning Commission to examine the feasibility of doubling per capita income in the next ten years. With population expected to grow at about 1.6 per cent, this target requires the rate of growth of GDP to be around 8.7 per cent over the tenth and eleventh plan periods. The planners were also directed to set monitorable social targets such as increase in the literacy rate to 75 per cent within the plan period, the reduction of gender gaps in literacy and wage rates by at least 50 per cent by 2007, and provision of employment for the addition to the labour force over the tenth plan period (Planning Commission, 2001). The mid-term appraisal of the tenth plan noted that the economy is doing well in many areas but that there are also important weaknesses. GDP growth has averaged 6.5 per cent in the first three years, which is below the target of 8.1 per cent. Growth in 2005–06 is projected to accelerate to 7.6 per cent. The factors responsible for the lower growth rate include insufficient investment, inadequate infrastructure and high oil prices (Planning Commission website). According to the *Economic Survey 2004–2005*, the Indian economy is poised to achieve 6.9 per cent growth. The agriculture and allied sector is looking up despite deficient rainfall, and industrial production will increase by 8.4 per cent. The survey states that the initiatives taken under the National Common Minimum Programme, enhanced FDI flow, buoyancy in investments and exports, policy for public private participation in infrastructure and priority to agriculture, manufacture and resource mobilization etc. will go a long way in furthering economic growth.

Achievements of planning in India

India's national income has increased over the decades. It was Rs 40,450 *crores* at the beginning of the first plan and Rs 2,58, 470 *crores* at the end of the eighth plan (Datt and Sundharam, 2001: 281). However, the rate of growth of per capita income was much lower and slower, indicating that population growth was having an effect.

Another achievement was that agricultural production increased considerably, though not to the extent planned by the government. Initially this was achieved by bringing more land under cultivation, but from 1960–61, the emphasis was on increasing production per hectare. The 'green revolution' was also initiated in the 1960s. To increase agricultural productivity, efforts were made to enlarge the supply of water, fertilizers, pesticides, improved seeds etc. in selected areas. Between 1950–51 and 1996–97 the consumption of chemical fertilizers had gone up from less than a million tonnes to over 14 million tonnes, and the area under irrigation had gone up from around 23 million hectares to nearly 81 million hectares. Furthermore, the High Yielding Varieties Programme, started during the third plan, covered over 76 million hectares of land by the end of the eighth plan. Although targets were not always met, the production of foodgrains, rice, wheat and potatoes has increased steadily. For example, foodgrains production went up from 51 million tonnes at the beginning of the first plan to 199 million tonnes by the end of the eighth plan. The Planning Commission's target is to increase foodgrains production to 300 million tonnes in 2007–08 from 204 million tonnes in 1998–99 (Datt and Sundharam, 2001: 282–3). However, as regards the green revolution, critics have pointed out that it 'greened only certain areas in the north and benefited only the better-off sections of the peasantry' (Swamy, 1994: 121).

Since the first plan was adopted in the early 1950s, the Indian government has invested heavily in the development of industries, on the expansion of transport and communications and the generation and distribution of electricity. Between 53 to 55 per cent of all planned outlay of the government in each five-year plan was on these sectors. Industrial production has not only gone up, the diversification of Indian industries has also taken place. The industries that have done well include steel, aluminium, engineering goods, chemicals, fertilizers and petroleum products. During the second plan period three major steel plants were set up at Durgapur, Bhilai and Rourkela. The demand for electric power has been increasing continuously and the government has struggled to meet it. The problem is that the generation and distribution of power has not matched demand even though power generation in India increased from 5 billion kilowatts in 1950–51 to 481 billion in 1999–2000 (Datt and Sundharam, 2001: 103). India uses mainly thermal power which accounts for around three-quarters of total installed capacity, followed by hydro-electric power which accounts for about a quarter of total installed capacity, and finally nuclear power which accounts for only 3 per cent. The *Economic Survey 2003–2004* asserts that a rapid enforcement of the Electricity Act (2003) is necessary for a durable solution to the power problem, including the problems of generation, transmission and distribution. This Act introduces competition and removes barriers to the entry of the private sector. It also lays down the framework for the reorganization of the state electricity boards. Another problem associated with the generation of electricity relates to the construction of river valley projects. In the 1950s, the government invested in the massive Bhakra-Nangal dam in the Punjab, the Tungabhadra project on the Andhra Pradesh-Karnataka border and the Rihand dam in Uttar Pradesh. However, they displaced thousands of people and 'over time the Indian villager was to develop a marked unwillingness to make way for "nation-building" projects' (Gadgil and Guha, 1995). The government had simply not done enough to resettle the displaced people. Social movements have begun to oppose government policy and are discussed in Chapter 6. Nevertheless, the Janata Party's sixth plan noted in the late 1970s that 'the country is self-sufficient in consumer goods and in basic commodities like steel and cement, while the capacity of other industries like fertilizers is rapidly expanding' (Datt and Sundharam, 2001: 283). India had, in other words, adopted a policy of import-substitution industrialization. India's dependence on foreign countries for the import of capital goods and consumer goods has declined and India is now exporting manufactured goods herself. The emphasis on self-sufficiency has led to the development of science and technology and technical and managerial cadres as well as a comprehensive educational system.

However, it is also necessary to note some of the problems that planning was unable to deal with. They include the inefficiency of many public-sector enterprises. Second, despite the growth of the industrial sector, the occupational structure has remained more or less unchanged with about 58 per cent of the population still working in the agricultural sector. Third, non-implementation of land reforms and the persistence of traditional agriculture is a problem that retards progress. Indian economists berate the plans for failing to eliminate poverty (although it has been reduced), to provide employment to all able-bodied persons and reduce inequalities of income and wealth. According to the Indian government's estimates 260 million people still live below the poverty line. Slogans such as *garibi hatao* are meaningless unless there are tangible results. It should be noted, however, that in 1973–74 half the population lived below the poverty line, according to these estimates. Poverty removal programmes were made an integral part of the fifth and subsequent plans, but the Indian government has been criticized for adopting an approach that provided temporary relief rather than emphasizing sustainable employment creation. Datt and Sundharam (2001: 285) write that a 'basic failure of planning in India was the emphasis on growth rather than on employment' and the adoption of capital-intensive production rather than labour-intensive production. Critics have also pointed out that fiscal measures to unearth unaccounted money have failed and the planners have also failed to reduce the concentration of economic power in the hands of a few. The irony is that the policies adopted to make India self-sufficient benefited businessmen and industrialists while the licensing and quota system led to corruption often benefiting senior civil servants and politicians.

But the reforms introduced since the early 1990s have not benefited the poor either. An *India Today*-ORG-MARG 'mood of the nation' poll conducted between 24 July 2003 and 6 August 2003 revealed that over 52 per cent of the respondents feel that reforms have only benefited the rich and not the middle class or the poor (*India Today*, 25 August 2003). Corbridge and Harriss comment that 'the reforms are not simply about the renegotiation of India's relationships with the global market-place, nor even are they about the relationships of private capital with the Indian state in the formal economy; the reforms are also about the reworking of the idea of the state itself and of the state's capacity to work on behalf of those who stand outside India's (expanding) social and economic elites' (Corbridge and Harriss, 2000: 169). They believe that the interests of the Indian elites are determining the changes that are taking place and not the needs of the poor. The impact of the economic reforms on Dalits in India has been analyzed by Teltumbde. He concludes that the free-market reforms should take into consideration the fact that even today India is predominantly an agrarian economy, with over 70 per cent of its population living in villages. Moreover, socio-cultural inequality is an abiding feature of Indian society. Therefore, '[u]nless there is a wide spread purchasing power in the economy the market can never be free and sustainable. The reform strategy thus should embody sustainable economic empowerment of rural masses; investments to enhance their capability and effective measures for accelerated development of the disadvantaged sections like dalits' (Teltumbde, 1996).

Another point that needs to be made is that economic liberalization appears to have aggravated regional disparities. Certain states of the Indian union have always performed better than others. These states include the Punjab, Gujarat, Maharashtra and Tamil Nadu. The states that are at the bottom of the Indian league tables include Bihar, Orissa, Madhya Pradesh and Uttar Pradesh (Central Statistical Organization, 2002: 7; *India Today*, 19 May 2003). The tenth plan confirms that the per capita incomes in the various states have 'started diverging rapidly during the past decade' and there are also disparities in social attainments. It expresses the concern that a growing polarization of the country can have an extremely damaging effect on national unity and harmony (Planning Commission, 2001). Kurian notes that 'the ongoing economic reforms since 1991 with stabilisation and deregulation policies as their prime instruments and a very significant role for the private sector seem to have aggravated the inter-state disparities' and that 'the better-off states are able to attract considerable amounts of private investment, both domestic and foreign, to improve their development potential because of the existing favourable investment climate including better socio-economic infrastructure' (Kurian, 2000). The backward states are unable to attract private investment because they do not have resources to invest in infrastructure and cannot offer a favourable investment climate in general. Table 4.3 gives the shares of the top five states attracting FDI approvals.

A study conducted by *India Today* (19 May 2003) has also discovered that some of the smallest states such as Delhi, Goa and Himachal Pradesh are attracting new investment, especially in the services sector. Their success is mainly due to a more accessible investment environment and infrastructure facilities.

Table 4.3 *Shares of top five states attracting FDI approvals (January 1991–March 2004)*

Name of state	No. of FDI approvals			Amount of FDI		% of total FDI approved
	Total	Tech.	Financial	Rs in crores	US$ in billion	
1 Maharashtra	4,816	1,308	3,508	51,114.68	13.18	17.48
2 Delhi	2,638	304	2,334	35,250.74	9.78	12.06
3 Tamil Nadu	2,607	613	1,994	25,071.77	6.52	8.58
4 Karnataka	2,467	494	1,973	24,138.44	6.15	8.26
5 Gujarat	1,204	556	648	18,837.30	4.81	6.44

Source: Government of India, *Economic Survey 2003–2004*.

However, India is not the only country in the world where there is a wide gap between the rich and the poor; and it is not the only problem that the Indian government has to deal with. India is currently facing a HIV/Aids explosion. According to the World Bank, 'the number of Indians contracting Aids could rise to 5.5 million a year by 2033 – more than the total number of current cases – unless urgent steps are taken.' It could become the single largest cause of death in the world's second most populous nation. India has the largest number of people with HIV/Aids outside South Africa; the number of people living with Aids in India rose to 5.1 million in 2003 according to the government.[6]

However, since the issue of 'development' is being addressed at the global level and since it is people-centred development, the Indian government can pacify its citizens by endorsing international targets. The Millennium Development Goals to be achieved by 2015 were adopted by the UN General Assembly in 2000. They are:

1 Eradicate extreme poverty and hunger:
  • halve the proportion of people living on less than US$1 a day
  • halve the proportion of people suffering from hunger.
2 Achieve universal primary education
  • ensure that children everywhere – boys and girls alike – complete a full course of primary education.
3 Promote gender equality and empower women
  • eliminate gender disparities in primary and secondary education, preferably by 2005, and in all levels of education by 2015.
4 Reduce child mortality
  • reduce infant and under-five mortality rates by two-thirds.
5 Improve maternal health
  • reduce maternal mortality ratios by three-quarters.

6 Combat HIV/Aids, malaria and other diseases
 • halt and begin to reverse the spread of HIV/Aids
 • halt and begin to reverse the incidence of malaria and other major diseases.
7 Ensure environmental sustainability
 • integrate the principles of sustainable development into country policies and programmes and reverse the loss of environmental resources
 • halve the proportion of people without sustainable safe drinking water
 • achieve, by 2002, a significant improvement in the lives of at least 100 million slum dwellers.
8 Develop a global partnership for development.
 (UNDP, *Human Development Report 2002*, cited in Government of India, *Economic Survey 2002–2003*: 210).

The government's *Economic Survey 2002–2003* states that the Millennium Development Goals comprise quantifiable, monitorable targets to assess progress achieved against standards set by the international community. The UNDP/HDI helps the government to compare the progress made by India with the achievements of other countries. The HDI measures the overall achievements of a country in three basic dimensions of human development – longevity and health; education and knowledge and a decent standard of living. Countries such as China, Indonesia and even Sri Lanka are performing better than India. Within India, Kerala has the best performance and Orissa and Bihar the worst in the area of human development, according to the National Human Development Report (NHDR) brought out by the Planning Commission. The survey asserts that 'the ongoing economic reforms have a human face and in pursuance of the commitment towards development of human resources and enhancement of human well being, additional resources for the social services sector are being allocated by the Government. Suitable targets for the reduction of poverty, hunger, mortality and illiteracy have also been incorporated in the Tenth Five Year Plan (2002–07)' (*Economic Survey 2002–2003*: 211).

The British government's Department for International Development (DFID) also accepts the tenth five-year plan as the basis for development co-operation between itself and the Indian government: 'It represents a broader approach than earlier plans. Economic growth is still a central priority, but it is complemented by themes of equity and social justice, human development and governance reform.' The DFID acknowledges that 'India has substantially reduced poverty in the last twenty years, nearly halving the proportion of people below the poverty line. There has been good economic growth, and considerable progress in a number of areas, including education.' However, the benefits of India's development and growth have been uneven; there are still around 350 million below the US$1 per day international poverty line, and many people do not have access to essential services. Therefore renewed efforts have to be made to achieve India's development targets as well as the Millennium Development

Goals. India is the DFID's largest country programme. In the New Delhi Declaration of January 2002, the UK government stated its intention to increase its assistance to India to £300 million a year (DFID, 2004: 1). The World Bank also announced in June 2004 that it would double its loans to India to nearly $3 billion a year in order to develop infrastructure projects and help the poor. Its additional funding will go towards schemes including irrigation, power, water supply and road development. It also aims to increase access to education and healthcare. The most impoverished states such as Bihar, Uttar Pradesh and Orissa will get extra assistance but the World Bank will not fund free electricity for farmers as that may encourage some farmers to waste water resources. The World Bank will lend India $2.15 billion annually, in addition to $750 million a year from the International Development Association, a World Bank arm created in 1960 to help support the world's poorest nations (BBC News, 25 June 2004). There is, therefore, no doubt that India's agenda for development links up with the global agenda and that developed states as well as international institutions are in favour of helping countries like India to reduce poverty and meet international development targets.

During a visit to New Delhi in November 2004, the former president of the World Bank, James D. Wolfensohn, commended the National Common Minimum Programme of the government of India which deals with employment, agriculture, education, health, women and children, food and nutrition security, scheduled castes and scheduled tribes, social harmony and welfare of minorities, infrastructure, industry, economic reforms and so on (Wolfensohn, November 2004). However, there is a fundamental difference between the approach of the World Bank and that of the left parties in India. Wolfensohn is in favour of investing in the social sector and infrastructure. He asserts that as 'five billion people live in developing countries and … have about 20 per cent of global income' as opposed to the one billion who live in 'the wealthy world' and have a little more than 80 per cent of global income, leaders of the world want to promote the Millennium Development Goals and if problems such as poverty, disease and environmental degradation are not dealt with, 'you will have a world that was lopsided and unstable'. His critics, however, do not believe that he is interested in promoting global equity. Wolfensohn is concerned that the lack of economic opportunities and the resulting competition for scarce resources will lead to conflict. He states that 'the position of the Bank is very simply this: that if you really want to have stability, if you really want to fight against instability, or even terror, the best way to do it is to project hope and growth and business'. Wolfensohn is interested in stability whereas the Indian Left parties want to increase investment in the social sector in order to empower the poor and overthrow the 'iniquitous system' (Wolfensohn, March 2004: 1–3; Jhunjhunwala, 2004).

Notes

1. The term 'developing' is preferred to 'underdeveloped' as it implies that though still underdeveloped, the process of development has been initiated in these countries. The *World Development Report 2005* classifies countries whose GNI was US$765 per capita or less in 2003 as low-income countries; countries whose GNI was between $766 and $9,385 in 2003 as middle-income countries and countries whose GNI was $9,386 or more in 2003 as high-income countries.
2. Available at www.rationalistinternational.net/archive/en/rationalist_2000/40.htm.
3. The plans are available at www.planningcommission.nic.
4. 1 *crore* is equal to 10 million units (e.g. of money/people).
5. Available at http://shikshanic.nic.in.cd50years/15/8P/HM/8PHM0101.htm.
6. GuardianUnlimited, 2004, available at www.guardian.co.uk/india/story/0,12559, 1282852,00.html.

References

Bagchi, A. K., 2005, 'Towards rural India', *The Statesman*, 1 March.
Central Statistical Organization, 2002, *Statistical Pocketbook, India 2002*, Government of India, New Delhi.
Corbridge, S. and Harriss, J., 2000, *Reinventing India: Liberalization, Hindu Nationalism and Popular Democracy*, Polity Press, Cambridge.
Datt, R. and Sundharam, K. P. M., 1995 and 2001, *Indian Economy*, S. Chand and Co., New Delhi.
DFID, 2004, *Country Plan, India*, DFID, London.
Dutt, S., 2000, 'Megacities of joy: The environmental problems of Calcutta in the age of globalization', *Australian Journal of International Affairs*, 54: 3.
Flory, K., 2005, 'Defence expenditure', *The Statesman*, 5 March.
Gadgil, M. and Guha, R., 1995, *Ecology and Equity*, Routledge, London and New York.
Government of India, *Census of India, 2001*, Government of India, New Delhi.
Government of India, *Economic Survey*, various years, Government of India, New Delhi.
Government of India, Factsheet 2000, available at: http://pib.nic.in/archieve/factsheet/fs2000/planning.html.
ul Haq, M., 1997, *Human Development in South Asia*, Oxford University Press, Oxford.
Jhunjhunwala, B., 2004, 'World Bank and the left', *The Statesman*, 19 December.
Kurian, N. J., 2000, 'Widening regional disparities in India', *Economic and Political Weekly*, 12–18 February.
Mahbub ul Haq Human Development Centre, 2002, *Human Development in South Asia 2001*, Oxford University Press, Oxford.
Mukherjee, J., 2002, 'The Indian economy: pushing ahead and pulling apart' in Alyssa, A. and Oldenburg, P. (eds), *India Briefing: Quickening the Pace of Change*, M. E. Sharpe, New York and London.
Nehru, J., 1969, *The Discovery of India*, Asia Publishing House, New Delhi.
Perdikis, N., 2000, *The Indian Economy: Contemporary Issues*, Ashgate, Aldershot.
Planning Commission, Government of India, 1996, *Approach Paper to the Ninth Five-Year Plan*, Government of India, New Delhi, available at www.planningcommission.nic.in.
Planning Commission, Government of India, 2001, *Approach Paper to the Tenth Five-Year Plan*, Government of India, New Delhi, available at www.planningcommission.nic.in.

Rothermund, D. (ed.), 1996, *Liberalising India: Progress and Problems*, Manohar, New Delhi.
Seth, S., 1993,' "Nehruvian socialism", 1927–1937: nationalism, Marxism and the pursuit of modernity', *Alternatives* 18.
Swamy, D. S., 1994, *The Political Economy of Industrialisation from Self-Reliance to Globalization*, Sage, London.
Teltumbde, A., 'Impact of new economic reforms on Dalits in India', available at www.foil.org/inspiration/ambedkar/ecoreforms.html.
UNDP, 1997, *Human Development Report 1997*, Oxford University Press, Oxford.
Wolfensohn, J. D., 2004, '2004 Krasnoff lecture', Stern School of Business, New York University, 8 March.
Wolfensohn, J. D., 2004, 'India: opportunity and challenge in a globalizing world', Teen Murti, New Delhi, India, 17 November.
World Bank, *World Development Report 2004*, available at www.worldbank.org.
World Bank, *World Development Report 2005*, available at www.worldbank.org.

5 India in the global (political) economy

Following the analysis of economic development in India in Chapter 4, a discussion of India in the global political economy is important for several reasons. As international and global political economists assert, there is no clear division between the national economy and the international/global economy. Michalet (cited in Tooze, 1997: 213) argues, for example, that 'ideas of national and international, of domestic and foreign, of exterior and interior, and of frontier limits that used to define the existence of an international economy, are losing their validity. The outline of nation-states is becoming blurred and the power of the state over economic activity is lessened.' So, for example, states may not be able to control the activities of multinational corporations, and this is seen as undermining their sovereignty. The inability to exercise control over multinationals could also lead to the exploitation of labour, consumers and the environment or increase the gap between the rich and the poor. This explains the ambivalence towards globalization shown by many national governments and political or interest groups. During a debate on 'Globalization and interdependence' in the Second Committee (Economic and Financial) of the United Nations on 26 October 1999, Jayant Malhoutra, a member of the Indian parliament declared:

> We believe that we should carry out a far more incisive analysis, both of the opportunities and drawbacks of globalization. This is particularly necessary at the national level by individual countries where we need to define what the objectives of globalization are. Clearly, if globalization is to be meaningful at the national level, it cannot lead only to enhanced international trade or financial flows per se, but to raising of standards and quality of life all around. Specifically, at the national level, globalization needs to address poverty, unemployment, education, health etc. and lead to higher living standards and for this we need to assess how globalization is impacting each individual developing country. (Malhoutra, 1999)

The point is that globalization benefits some more than others and this will be explored further in this chapter.

Another reason why a discussion of India in the global political economy is important is that politics and economics affect each other. Hirst and Thompson (1996: 14) argue that the term 'international economy' 'has always been shorthand for what is actually the product of the complex interaction of economic relations and politics, shaped and reshaped by the struggles of the Great Powers'. This argument will be borne out, albeit indirectly, by an examination of the impact that colonial rule had on the economy as well as the external constraints facing the Indian economy in the post-independence period. The issue of internal constraints has been discussed in Chapter 4, however, the external constraints on the Indian economy need to be explored further here. On a more general note, Tooze (1997: 222) remarks that 'the way that any national economy fits into the international economy produces distinct political problems – for the state and international relations – depending on the nature of that state's economic activity and the power it has to structure the system'. This implies that a discussion of the economy of any state is bound to be inadequate if it is carried out without any reference to the international/global economy. However, before proceeding any further, we should make it explicit that the international economy is an economic system based on world markets and production and that the market economy has its origins in the industrial revolution. Moreover, the system is a capitalist system, notwithstanding the existence of the communist bloc from the late 1940s to the late 1980s.

In a similar vein to Hirst and Thompson, Rothermund (1993) argues that there is a relationship between power and wealth or between the political and economic domains. Of course, markets have always existed for the exchange/buying and selling of goods. However, prior to the eighteenth century there was no market system based on industrial production. The emergence of the market economy had an impact on the economy of the Indian subcontinent. However, given that the Indian economy was not completely transformed by capitalism, our discussion of India in the global economy has to start long before capitalism was introduced in the subcontinent. Most scholars would agree, for example, that we cannot treat the mercantilist period as irrelevant to any discussion of the evolution of the Indian economy, as mercantilism promoted colonial rule in India which, in turn, determined how India was to be integrated into the capitalist world economy. An examination of contemporary India in the global political economy, therefore, could benefit from some knowledge of the past, especially of the colonial period which has left its mark on the Indian subcontinent and its relations with the rest of the world. The first chapter on the history of the subcontinent dealt with the political aspects of colonial rule; this section will deal with the economic aspects. Another point that needs to be made at this juncture is that, regardless of the views of the Indian government and political parties on contemporary globalization, India has for many centuries already been affected by it. In recent years, the debate in India has been about self-reliance and protectionism versus liberalization, and it is in the context of this debate that the potential impact of globalization is considered. However, the present author takes a much wider view of the phenomenon and this needs to be clarified at the outset.

Phases of globalization

While Giddens (1990) associates globalization with the development of modern societies, industrialization and the accumulation of material resources, other scholars such as Robertson (1992) see it as pre-dating modernity and the rise of capitalism. Robertson identifies five phases of globalization in Europe. The first lasted from 1400 until 1750, and saw the beginning of global exploration, the spread of the Roman Catholic Church, the widespread adoption of the Gregorian calendar, the advent of mapping and of modern geography, and the growth of national communities and of the state system. This period coincides with the mercantilist period. The second phase, between 1750 and 1875, saw non-European countries admitted to the Europe-dominated 'international' society. If the history of India is divided into three periods – ancient, medieval and modern – many scholars would agree that the modern period starts during this phase. Giddens, too, agrees that the colonization of different parts of the world by Europeans in the nineteenth century was one of the factors that resulted in contemporary globalization.

The third phase (1875–1925) was characterized by communicational advances (e.g. telegraphy, telephones, radio, railways, shipping, canals, etc.) and increasing economic and political connections. The First World War took place in this period. India participated in this war and many Indian leaders thought that India's great contribution of men and materials to the war effort would result in self-rule. After the war, the first universal international organization for the purpose of maintaining international peace and security, the League of Nations, was established in 1920, under the Treaty of Versailles. In the fourth phase (1925–69) the Second World War occurred and, after it ended, the UN was established. This was also the beginning of the nuclear age which affected conceptions of international security. The final phase is the contemporary period of globalization and will be discussed in greater detail in subsequent sections of this chapter. Held et al. (1999) also see contemporary globalization as the latest manifestation of a set of historical processes. These include the pre-historic and historic migration of people; the global spread of the major world religions; the impact of the great empires; the influence of powerful western nation-states and modern nationalism, including the outward expansion of Europe from the sixteenth century; the transnational flows of capital and of 'big' ideas (pertaining to science, liberalism, socialism, feminism, etc.); and of course, the hegemony of English as a truly 'global language'. Technological developments include the laying of the trans-Atlantic telegraph in the 1860s and cable communication across the British Empire by the 1880s. All these processes affected the Indian subcontinent, and it is for this reason that this chapter argues that India has been a participant in the process of globalization for a long time and that this has affected the politics, economy and culture of the subcontinent.

Foreign trade in pre-colonial India

Since ancient times, the Indian subcontinent had active maritime trade relations with many countries around the Indian Ocean. During medieval times, this benefited the kings of many south Indian states by augmenting their income and enhancing their power. European historians note that 'in the eleventh century Asia was definitely ahead of Europe in most respects, and its corporate empires, whose power was based on an ample supply of rice and a buoyant trade, were much more splendid even in cultural terms than the realms of the west' (Rothermund, 1993: 10). The powerful corporate empires that emerged simultaneously included the Chola empire of south India. The Cholas had trade relations with China, Burma, Srivijaya and other Southeast Asian countries. Access to the Chinese market, which developed very fast under the Sung dynasty, was an important goal. However, as these corporate empires declined, their navies also disappeared and the Indian Ocean emerged as a free trade zone not controlled by any sea power.

At about this time, the European traders arrived on the scene. The Portuguese were the first to arrive, followed by the Dutch who captured the spice trade and became major players in the textile trade. Nevertheless, the Europeans played a marginal role in Asia. There were Indian ship owners who had more ships in the Indian Ocean than the European companies. The European demand for Indian goods did not necessitate any restructuring of Indian production. However, silver brought in by traders had a major impact on the Indian economy, although not all of this silver came from Europe. Indian trade with Arabia, the Persian Gulf and Southeast Asia also resulted in remittances in silver. Most of it had originally come from America.

The mercantilist period and the 'sins' of the East India Company

However, the arrival of the English East India Company is probably one of the most important landmarks in the history of modern India. In 1600, a Royal Charter granted the company a monopoly on trade with the Indies. In 1608 it arrived in India and in 1619 built a factory in Surat. The company became masters of Bengal after winning the Battle of Plassey (1757). It soon eliminated all European competition and established its rule in India. This did not happen 'in a fit of absent mindedness'. During the mercantilist period between the fifteenth and eighteenth centuries, the powerful nation-states that had emerged in Europe competed with one another to enhance their power. This competition spilt into the economic realm. The mercantilists believed that wealth and power were closely associated with the possession of so-called precious metals. To attain this objective governments tried to maintain a favourable balance of trade. One way of achieving this was by acquiring colonies. Spero (1985: 6) comments that 'colonies existed to accommodate the mercantile interests of the metropole, and strict state regulation of the colonial economy existed to serve these ends. It was the reaction to such mercantilist policies – the regulation of production and exports and imports and the control of shipping – that led the American colonies to rebel against Europe'. In the nineteenth century, however, Britain's military and political dominance enabled it to adopt and internationalize a liberal economic system centred on Britain and London emerged as the financial centre of the world. The liberal economic system began to decline alongside the decline of British power towards the end of the nineteenth century. It was replaced by a new imperialist system, but the position of the colonies remained the same; they were integrated into an international economic system designed to serve the economic interest of the metropole.

Some scholars such as Bandyopadhyaya have suggested that the history of South Asia since 1750 should be reconceived as part of the development of a capitalist world system. The world system approach to the understanding of world politics contends that all politics, international and domestic, takes place within the framework of a capitalist world economy. Moreover, states are not the only important actors in international relations; social classes are also very significant. Patterns of interaction and domination are determined by the location of states and classes within the structure of the capitalist world economy. Although Marx's conception of capitalism is useful in some respects, Lenin's ideas are more relevant to our discussion. Lenin argued that imperialism had created a two-tier structure within the world economy with a dominant core exploiting a less-developed periphery. This chapter will attempt to ascertain to what extent this theory explains India's role in the global economy both during the colonial period and after political independence was achieved. Bandyopadhyaya asserts:

> the structure of the contemporary international system is the legacy of four and a half centuries of European imperialism. International relations in the second half of the twentieth century cannot be understood, analysed, interpreted, or altered, without reference to the preceding four centuries of imperialism. (1982: 8)

Returning to our discussion of the East India Company, we find that it has been described as 'a modern capitalist corporation of an advanced bourgeois nation' that 'entrenched itself like a parasite in the agrarian state dominated by a decaying military feudal regime. The parasite adjusted to the system of its host and benefited from it without changing it very much' (Rothermund, 1993: 16). The company succeeded in collecting more revenue than its feudal predecessors. This was one of its principal objectives along with the development of trade. However, not much of it was invested in India for the benefit of the Indians.

Some scholars are of the view that India could have benefited from territorial rule by a trading company. It could have led to economic growth. However, it did not. The reason is that the company was not interested in stimulating the economy.

Internal economic conditions were not good under the company. As mentioned above, its main objective was to extract as much revenue as possible and not introduce any economic reforms. As regards foreign trade, the company was interested in promoting exports in order to facilitate the remittance of tribute from India to Great Britain, but there was not much scope for 'export-led growth'. Moreover, due to the industrial revolution in Britain India became a supplier of raw materials and a market for British manufactured goods: the company did not organize commodity production in India on a large scale and India became a dependent agrarian state. In 1813, the British parliament abolished the trade monopoly of the company and, in 1833, its trading activities were terminated altogether. However, the company had to continue to make remittances to London in order to pay a dividend to its shareholders. Therefore, it had to promote exports and was even willing to finance the export of products that did not fetch a good price in London. Meanwhile, the peasants were forced to produce whatever they were asked to, even if they had to do so at a loss.

Bose and Jalal argue that trade with India also helped Britain to deal with its trade deficits. Between 1870 and 1914 India's export surplus was critical for Britain's balance of payments. The value of British imports from continental Europe and America was greater than the value of its exports to these regions. Protectionist policies made it difficult for Britain to export manufactured goods. Therefore, 'Indian raw-material exports to America and continental Europe proved vital for financing Britain's deficits with the USA and Europe. This was possible because Britain had a surplus with India and a huge deficit with the rest of the world, while India had a deficit with Britain and a huge surplus with the rest of the world' (Bose and Jalal, 1998: 100).

In the nineteenth century, the main commodities exported from India were indigo, opium and cotton as well as precious metals. However, the peasants who produced the indigo and opium did not get much out of this. Washbrook (1990: 41) argues that 'several characteristic features of India's "timeless" peasant economy may have emerged, or become general, only in the middle decades of the nineteenth century, and as a result of changes in the world economy … the desperate poverty and "backwardness" of peasant India were constituted as much by the forces of the international market economy as by anything else'. Fortunately for India, the cotton trade was in Indian (rather than British) hands to a large extent and based mainly in Bombay rather than Calcutta, the capital of British India until 1911. Some pioneering Indian industrialists accumulated a great deal of their capital in the cotton and opium trade in Bombay. Industries which were in Indian hands from the start fared much better in the longer term than industries such as jute which were in the hands of British managing agents who were mainly after short-term gains. Between 1906 and 1913, the jute industry in eastern India enjoyed a boom but collapsed during the First World War. These agents also did little to alleviate the suffering of the jute growers during times of hardship. The different pattern of development in western India partly explains why the performance of the economies of states such as Maharashtra and Gujarat was much better than that of West Bengal in the post-independence period despite the availability of raw materials, cheap labour, managerial skills and a major commercial centre such as Calcutta.

The end of company rule but not the end of exploitation

It may be argued that with the establishment of the first cotton textile mill in Bombay in 1855, a new age began. At about the same time, in 1858, the East India Company rule too came to an end following the Indian Mutiny which took place in 1857. This did not usher in a new, less exploitative age. The Indian experience was no different from the experiences of other Asian and African peoples colonized by the Europeans. Spero (1985: 8) observes that 'as in the days of mercantilism, colonies were integrated into an international economic system designed to serve the economic interest of the metropole. The political victors controlled the investment and trade, regulated currency and production, and manipulated labour, thus establishing structures of economic dependency in their colonies that endured far longer than their actual political authority'.

There was a steady expansion of foreign trade in the second half of the nineteenth century and India continued to have an export surplus. However, this did not benefit the Indians as the objective of maintaining this surplus was to provide the means for the transfer of tribute and other remittances to Britain. In fact, the takeover by the Crown meant more charges had to be met. The disloyalty of many Indian troops led to more British troops being stationed in India after the mutiny of 1857, the expansion of the Indian railways led to debts that had to be serviced and there was also the expansion of the British Indian administration. Silver remittances and the use of the India–China–Great Britain trade triangle were no longer enough. In the late nineteenth century, India exported more and more agricultural produce to Europe and imported industrial goods from there. India was an important market for the British cotton textile industry from 1870 to 1895 which benefited from the absence of protective tariffs. British industry even lobbied the government to remove import duties which had been imposed for purely fiscal reasons.

India also imported large quantities of silver and this helped to maintain the world silver price. Textiles and silver were thus the two main imports. However, India had to maintain an export surplus. India's exports increased rapidly and there was a trend towards diversification. The main exports were raw cotton, raw jute, cotton, tea and indigo. In the early twentieth century, the main exports were raw cotton, cotton textiles, raw jute, jute products, opium, rice and tea. However, the export surplus was not a genuine surplus (i.e. what is left after the home market is saturated with indigenous products). In Marxian terms, the surplus was what was expropriated. Moreover the development of the home market was determined by the forces of the world market. The silver currency strengthened the links between the two. But, as Marxists would argue, India was not at the core of the world market and consequently suffered.

Stunted industrial growth?

Colonial rule impeded India's industrialization. The British Indian government would not grant protection to Indian industries. It also abolished tariffs that had been imposed for purely fiscal reasons. Moreover, India's infant industry was adversely affected by an endemic shortage of capital and high interest rates. Nevertheless, due to the efforts of certain Indian entrepreneurs, the cotton textile industry and the jute industry did flourish in parts of India. However, these were industrial enclaves and the integrated industrialization of India did not take place. Moreover, there was no formation of industrial capital. There are several reasons for this. The production of raw materials for export attracted most of the available capital/credit. Second, the appreciation of the value of land meant that rural capital was used to purchase land and could not be used for industrial investment. Third, unlike Japan, India in the early nineteenth century lacked the necessary financial infrastructure for the formation of industrial capital. Thus the savings of ordinary people could not be mobilized for large-scale investment. The custom in India was to invest one's savings in gold ornaments which could be sold in times of crisis. (It is worth noting that until recently Japan had a high savings ratio (*Japan Times*, 28 June 2004)). The shareholders who contributed to the initial capital of the Tata Iron and Steel Company (TISCO) that was established in 1907 were all capitalists and Maharajas, for example. The average small entrepreneur found it difficult to raise capital.

In Japan, industrialization had been given a fillip by land mortgage banks, deposit bureaux and an industrial credit bank which attracted some rural capital and converted it into industrial capital. Such instruments were not available in India under colonial rule. The British Indian administration was more interested in collecting land revenue than in promoting economic growth and the development of financial institutions was, therefore, not given much importance.

Due to the lack of capital and demand (since real wages were not going up there was not much demand for industrial consumer goods) industry in India was taken over by managing agents who indulged in restrictive practices and financial speculation in order to make the most of the situation. Thus there was no real progress. Despite all this, however, some people did benefit from colonial rule: urban salaried employees (*boxwallahs*), traders and moneylenders. They could afford to buy luxury products and imported goods. The poor masses did not have much buying power and could only buy coarse grey cotton cloth.

The First World War and the Great Depression

The Indian economy was affected by the First World War, a war that started in Europe and in which thousands of Indian army personnel died. But the effects were not entirely adverse. Disruption of trade meant that industrial production had to be stepped up and the cotton textile industry benefited from this as did the coal mining industry and the cement industry. The jute industry benefited from new orders for sand bags for use during the war. The high profits of the industrialists in India were mainly due to the full utilization of capacities installed before the war and the general rise in the price of all commodities. At the end of the war, the high exchange rate of the rupee made imported investment goods comparatively cheap and this enabled industrialists to utilize their enormous wartime savings. From the Indian economy's point of view this was of doubtful value. Industry contributed only 3 per cent of the net domestic product and agriculture and animal husbandry still accounted for about 68 per cent (Rothermund, 1993: 75). Unfortunately, the internal terms of trade for agriculture deteriorated during the war and this had an impact on the peasants. Appreciation of the currency and inflation also adversely affected the real wages of the workers. The living standard of the poor declined and there was a redistribution of income in favour of the rich. However, the welfare of the peasants and workers had never been given much importance by the British Indian government. It was mainly the Indian nationalists who brought their plight to the attention of the world.

In 1921–22 the exchange rate declined sharply, and the British Indian government adopted a long-term policy of deflation in order to support it. However, Indian industrialists argued that a higher exchange rate would hit the indebted Indian peasant, whose debts had been incurred at the old rate. They also argued that the peasants would be even worse off if prices should fall; this is exactly what happened during the Great Depression. In the 1920s, prices remained high in India, in spite of the deflationary policy of the government, because world market prices were also high. As world prices declined in 1929 so did the prices of cash crops grown for export, although prices of grain for internal consumption did not as they were no longer tied to world prices as they had been before the war. Consequently rural people who had to pay rent, revenue and interest suffered, but the government would not devalue the rupee as it would diminish the value of the Home Charges (payments trsmsferred from India to Britain for administrative costs) (Stein, 1998: 313–14). Moreover, unlike in Britain and other countries such as the US, Canada and Australia, India's military budget was not reduced and expenditure for social welfare was not increased. Stein (1998: 330) writes that 'Indians suffered greater hardship than the poor of other countries, including Britain, where job-creating public investments were undertaken as anti-depression measures, some of which protected its manufactures at the expense of firms and workers in India, who continued to struggle for external markets with a rupee pegged at a punishing deflationary and uncompetitive rate'. A higher exchange rate made imported non-agricultural goods cheaper and this led to a demand from Indian industrialists for protective tariffs. In the 1920s India had a negative balance of trade with Britain but a positive one with Germany, Japan and the USA. The Great Depression hit India's foreign trade, especially exports which consisted mainly of agricultural products (Singh, 1965: 454–5).

Free trade versus discriminating protection

The instrument of 'discriminating protection', which was applied exclusively to steel in the 1920s was extended to other commodities during the Great Depression. This doctrine specified that in fields of production where India had a natural advantage (e.g. coal and ore resources), it was in India's interest to protect the respective industries. There should be no general protection of Indian industry, as this would be repugnant to the principle of free trade. But protection should be granted after careful discrimination between industries that met the test of 'natural advantage' and those that did not satisfy this test. However, it was not commitment to the principle of free trade but competition from the German and Belgium steel industries that prompted the adoption of this doctrine. The British steel-makers therefore supported the company TATA's demands for protective tariffs. However, the Indians had to accept 'imperial preferences', that is special rights for British exporters. This kind of protectionism did not benefit the Indian consumers as it did not extend to all industrial sectors and thus did not create linkages which would have promoted general economic growth. It also created an arbitrary division of labour; while Indian industry produced 'cheap' steel, 'high-quality' and highly priced steel was imported from Britain and British steel-makers were assured of a market. The cotton textile industry was next granted protection to keep the Japanese out of the Indian market. This benefited the Indian and British textile industries.

The booming sugar industry, which by the late 1930s was in a position to progress from import substitution to export production, suffered due to a glut in the world market and the subsequent International Sugar Agreement which fixed national quotas and classified India as an importing rather than exporting nation. It was not classified as a sugar-exporting nation in order to protect the interests of other sugar exporting British colonies.

The effects of the Second World War and the end of *laissez-faire*

During the Second World War, India experienced a kind of wartime stagflation. While real wages declined, profits were high but there was little scope for investment. The reasons were first that investment goods could not be manufactured in India during the war, and second that all available credit was used by the British Indian government to finance the war effort. In the agrarian sector too, prices rose but production did not as the mode of production of innumerable small peasants could not be changed overnight. The cotton textile industry and the steel industry continued to flourish both during and after the war, but the jute industry gradually declined.

The commitment to free trade and *laissez-faire* policies had been weakening for some time and with the outbreak of the Second World War, the British Indian government abandoned its policy of non-intervention. For the procurement of goods and for handling the food crisis, the government had to create a formidable interventionist machinery. This machinery was geared to solving immediate problems rather than designed in the interest of long-term planning. What is significant is that it created a faith in *dirigisme* that continued even after India achieved independence. The adoption of the method of central planning has been discussed in Chapter 4 and need not be repeated here. The emphasis was on heavy industry and import substitution, on controls and the expansion of the public sector. However, these policies led to poor industrial performance. India's decision to base economic growth on import substitution rather than export competitiveness had backfired.

Pioneers of industrialization in the Third World

It is ironic that India's industrial performance was not better in the post-independence period. India had been one of the pioneers of industrialization in the Third World in the nineteenth century and the rate of growth of Indian industry had been quite high: 10.4 per cent per annum during the period 1868–1900 (Lal, 1999: 16). During the period 1880–1914, the overall rate of industrial growth was higher in India (4-5 per cent per annum) than in most other tropical countries, and even exceeded that of Germany. By 1914 the Indian economy had developed the world's fourth largest cotton textile industry and the second largest jute manufacturing industry. The country's export performance should not be underestimated either. By 1913 about 20 per cent of Indian exports were modern manufactured goods. Total exports amounted to 10.7 per cent of national income. However, the growth rate of agricultural exports was much lower (1.4 per cent per annum) than the overall export growth rate, which was 3 per cent per annum between 1883 and 1913. Even between 1913 and 1938 Indian industrial growth was above the world average (Lal, 1999: 16–20). Thus writers such as Lal do not accept the argument that the policies of *laissez-faire* and free trade led to stunted industrial growth. On the contrary he argues that even if we judge performance by crude and inadequate criteria, such as rate of growth of manufacturing output, employment and investment, the performance during the pre-1913 free-trade period was better than in the protectionist 1919–39 period.

The need for foreign aid and foreign capital after independence

Indian independence coincided with the beginning of a new post-war era in the western world. The Bretton Woods conference was held in July 1944 and it led to the establishment of the IMF and the World Bank and to the General Agreement on Tariffs and Trade (GATT). The rules of the liberal international economic order that these institutions were set up to manage were written by the powerful states such as the USA and Britain. However, we find that while the western countries emphasized the importance of free trade and the dangers of economic nationalism, a neo-mercantilist conception of the state as having responsibility for the administration and development of the national economy was prevalent in the post-war period. Hoogvelt (1997: 49) writes that 'the dominance of Keynesianism as macro-economic theory, with its acceptance of state intervention in the economies of the advanced countries, ideologically spilt over into and converged with the developmentalist state notions of the liberal modernization theories. Less-developed countries were spurred on to take their economic destinies into their own hands.' But of course this was not possible given the economic dependency and unequal position of these countries in the world economic order. Additionally, the inability of national governments to promote development led to a deepening chasm between state and civil society within the Third World. However, as Hoogvelt points out, the 'national bourgeoisie' conveniently blamed the continuation of imperialist forms of domination of their countries for the perpetuation of the poverty of their people, while masking their own complicity in this domination. She adds that dependency theory did much to legitimize this analysis. This is borne out by the writings of Bandhyopadhyaya (1982: 8) in which he puts forward the argument that '[i]mperialism created a political structure of dominance and dependency, an economic structure of exploitation and impoverishment, and a cultural structure of contempt and humiliation across the globe', and that despite the fact that the decolonization process is now more or less complete, 'with minor exceptions the structures created by imperialism are still more or less intact'. What Bandyopadhyaya fails to mention or make explicit is the nexus between foreign capitalists and indigenous elites.

India's share of world trade is insignificant (less than 1 per cent). This knowledge may deter many scholars from taking an interest in India at all. However, given that it has a population of over one billion and that there is a glaring difference/mismatch between its share of world trade and its share of the world's population, an examination of India in the global political economy will help us to understand some of the issues of equity/inequity that plague many Third World countries and contribute to the creation of more conflict and insecurity in the world. The achievement of political independence of course did not improve India's position in the global economy. India's share of world trade began to decline in the post-independence period. This was partly due to the fact that exports were not given much importance, as it was believed that exports could not become the 'engine of growth' for underdeveloped countries, and imports were restricted. The emphasis was on self-reliance and not on export-led growth. Nevertheless, India needed foreign exchange in order to import essential commodities – capital goods, food grain and initially even consumer goods. As discussed in Chapter 4, India had opted for a capital goods-led industrialization model of development, favoured by India's first prime minister, Jawaharlal Nehru. When India became independent in 1947 the capital goods sector was not large enough to meet the country's needs, and neither had India achieved self-sufficiency in food production. By 1956, sterling reserves had been exhausted and there could have been a serious balance-of-payments problem. It is therefore clear why foreign aid was needed. During the first five-year plan period, India received 12 million tons of grain from the US. In the second and third five-year plan periods too India imported 17 million tons and 25 million tons of grain respectively from the US (Rothermund, 1993: 136).

Foreign aid and capital also was of vital importance for the ambitious programme of industrial growth. As mentioned above, that was the path to development that India had chosen . Domestic savings could not meet the investment requirements of the country and in addition there was a need for imported technology. During the second and third five-year plan periods, the foreign aid component of public investment was as high as 30 per cent (Rothermund, 1993: 137). After the third plan period foreign aid dwindled and this contributed to the industrial recession India experienced after 1965. The devaluation of the rupee in the 1960s under World Bank pressure did not have the desired effects. Imports became more expensive but exports did not grow. This was due to two reasons: the demand for Indian exports such as tea, spices and jute products in the world market was not that elastic; and second, Indian-manufactured goods were not of sufficiently high quality to be able to compete in the world market. Lower prices obviously did not compensate for inferior quality.

The Indian government's policy regarding foreign capital in the early years

In 1948, India had foreign capital worth Rs 256 *crores* (Swamy, 1994: 37). Most of it was British, almost entirely privately owned and concentrated in extractive and processing industries for exports. It is understandable that the inflow of British capital would have been seen as a form of neo-colonialism yet the Indian economy needed foreign capital. This led to a rapid increase in US investment in India, from Rs 40 *crores* in 1955 to Rs 400 *crores* in 1965. British investment fell by 50 per cent, while Japanese and German investment grew. India also received considerable aid from the Soviet Union and the Eastern European countries (Swamy, 1994: 113–14). This aid was mainly directed towards the public sector, the provision of defence equipment and petroleum, although the private sector too benefited through collaborations. However, foreign collaborations had to keep their equity within the ceiling of 49 per cent and allow the Indian counterpart a majority stake. Moreover, the government identified certain priority areas for foreign collaborations. The Industrial Policy Resolution of April 1948 also made it quite clear that while the government recognized the need for foreign capital in the industrialization of the economy, it would not be allowed to have a dominant position in the economy. The Resolution stated that 'as a rule, the major interest in ownership, and effective control, should always be in Indian hands. In all cases, however, the training of suitable Indian personnel for the purpose of eventually replacing foreign experts will be insisted upon' (Datt and Sundharam, 1995: 135). However, Indian economists have commented that there were many problems with private foreign capital. Often obsolete machines or technology was imported, or technologies that were not appropriate for the Indian situation. Some collaboration agreements made Indian industries dependent on imports of intermediate goods and parts. Other disadvantages include heavy remittances abroad (the US oil company, ESSO, with an invested capital of Rs 30 *crores* took away Rs 83 *crores* as remittances of profit in 1968–70), an adverse effect on balance of payments and the use of the myth of Indianization of foreign-controlled firms as a smokescreen to soften the resistance of the people of the Third World (Datt and Sundharam, 1995: 292–3).

Foreign trade

Britain was India's main trading partner before 1947 and accounted for 34 per cent of India's exports and 30 per cent of India's imports (Datt and Sundharam, 1995: 653), although during the Second World War these percentages declined. After independence, other countries such as the US, USSR, West Germany, Japan and members of the OPEC became important trading partners. Indian economists Datt and Sundharam (1995: 638–9) remark that 'this spatial or geographical diversification has helped India to go for diversification of industries along with specialisation in certain goods, and secure new markets for her products'.

After independence, the colonial pattern of trade had to be changed to suit the needs of India's programme of development. Having adopted the capital goods-led industrialization model of development as indicated above, machinery and equipment had to be imported that could not be produced at home. These are known as developmental imports. For instance, imported capital goods required for the setting up of the steel plants, the locomotives factory at Chittaranjan and the hydro-electric projects. India also had to import raw materials and intermediate goods to utilize properly the productive capacity created in the country. These are known as maintenance imports. As discussed above, India also had to import foodgrains and consumer goods. In the late 1940s, the foreign trade of India showed an excess of imports over exports. During the first five-year plan period, the annual average value of imports was Rs 730 *crores* and that of exports was Rs 622 *crores*. The average annual trade deficit was around Rs 108 *crores* (Datt and Sundharam, 1995: 639). The trade deficit was largely due to programmes of industrialization which gathered momentum and pushed up the imports of capital goods. This situation did not change for many years and in fact led to a foreign exchange crisis during the second plan period. During the third plan period the defence needs of the country also increased following the war with China in 1962 and added to the import bill. In order to deal with the balance-of-payments problems, India had to borrow extensively from other countries and international institutions. In June 1966, the Indian rupee was devalued by 36.5 per cent (Datt and Sundharam, 1995: 640). The intention was to boost exports. However, the immediate effect of the devaluation of the rupee was a further increase of the trade deficit as imports could not be curtailed, partly because the country was hit by a drought and partly because the government had adopted a policy of liberalizing imports in the case of fifty-nine industries. Moreover, the devaluation of the Indian rupee did not lead to a sufficient growth in exports to balance the import bill. It was only in 1972–73 that the country achieved a favourable balance of trade following a curtailment of imports and vigorous export promotion. Unfortunately for India, the hike in oil prices which started in October 1973 and which seriously affected world trade increased the value of its imports considerably. However, India experienced an export boom in the mid-1970s and this helped to maintain a favourable balance of trade and balance of payments.

In the 1980s, India began to liberalize its economy very cautiously under Rajiv Gandhi, the process of which has been discussed in Chapter 4. By the late 1980s/early 1990s it was public knowledge that Indian was facing a balance-of-payments crisis. The Indian government, therefore, had to approach the IMF and the World Bank for assistance. A new era was dawning, in which the Indian government as well as the Indian public began to debate the pros and cons of globalization. Initially, the reforms that were carried out did not benefit the poorest sections of Indian society (as discussed in Chapter 4) and, by the late 1990s, even though there was enthusiasm for economic liberalization, especially within the business community, the government continued to be cautious.

A World Bank policy research report comments that since 1980 there has been unprecedented global integration. The first wave of modern globalization took place from 1870 to 1914 and flows of goods, capital and labour all increased dramatically. However, protectionism slowed down global growth. A second wave of globalization occurred from 1950 to 1980 that focused on integration among rich countries. Europe, North America and Japan concentrated on restoring trade relations through a series of multilateral trade liberalizations under the auspices of the GATT (World Bank, 2002).

The most recent wave of globalization that started around 1980 has been spurred by technological advance in transport and communications technologies and by the choice of large developing countries to improve their investment climates and to open up to foreign trade and investment. For the first time, poor countries have been able to harness the potential of their abundant labour to break into global markets for manufactured goods and services. Manufactures rose from less than a quarter of developing country exports in 1980 to more than 80 per cent by 1998. Countries that strongly increased their participation in global trade and investment include Brazil, China, Hungary, India and Mexico. The growth rates of the 'more globalized' developing countries now substantially exceed those of the rich countries. However, 'while the new globalizers are beginning to catch up, much of the rest of the developing world – with about 2 billion people – is becoming marginalized. Their aggregate growth rate was actually negative in the 1990s' (World Bank, 2002: 5).

As a result of the policies of globalization followed by India after joining the WTO in 1995, its exports increased by US$4.1 billion in 1994–95, and by $5.5 billion in 1995–96, touching the level of $31.8 billion as against $26.3 billion in the previous year. But during 1996–97, Indian exports increased merely by 4.1 per cent, reaching $33.5 billion. During 1997–98 they increased by barely $1.5 billion and during 1998–99, they declined by $1.35 billion. Critics feared that the new policies had developed a dependency syndrome and the Indian economy's fortunes were being determined by the international market (Datt and Sundharam, 2001: 770; *Economic Survey 1997–1998*: 78–9; *Economic Survey 1998–1999*: 76–7).

However, according to the Indian government, India's balance of payments in 1999–2000 was manageable. The *Economic Survey 2000–2001* states that 'the current account deficit in 1999–2000 was contained to 0.9 per cent of the GDP, despite an unfavourable international trade and financial backdrop'. India's oil import bill went up mainly because of oil price hikes, but exports and remittances also went up 'reflecting sharp increases in software service exports and private transfers' (*Economic Survey 2000–2001*). However, the survey also stated that the oil import bill may lead to the current account deficit widening in 2000–01 because of the tripling of international oil prices. The government did not expect non-oil imports to grow or exports to decline. Between 2000 and 2003 India's exports grew by 32 per cent (*Economic Survey 2003–2004*: 104); its share of world trade also increased slightly from 0.7 per cent to 0.8 per cent. According to union commerce minister, Kamal Nath, export values in 2003–04 stood at $63 billion and, he suggested, would rise to $75 billion in 2004–05. India's export target for 2005–06 is $88 billion (*The Statesman*, 13 December 2004) and $150 billion for 2008–09 (*Economic Survey 2004–2005*).

India and GATT/WTO

GATT was established in 1948 to promote free trade and reduce trade barriers. It aimed to stimulate international trade by bringing about the reduction of tariff barriers and also non-tariff restrictions on imports imposed by member states. By the late 1980s, however, world trade had undergone a structural change since the establishment of GATT. The share of agriculture in world trade had declined drastically (from 46 per cent to 13 per cent) and the share of the service sector in the GDP of developed countries was rapidly increasing. Thus, the developed countries took the initiative of bringing the service sector into trade negotiations. But differences between member states made it difficult to reach an agreement. The differences were highlighted at the Uruguay Round of Negotiations/eighth round of GATT. The differences affected the following areas: agriculture, textiles, trade-related intellectual property rights (TRIPS) and anti-dumping measures. In the end, India and 117 other nations signed the Dunkel Act in April 1994, based on the proposals of Arthur Dunkel, director-general of GATT.

On tariffs, India promised to reduce the basic duty by 30 per cent. However, on anti-dumping measures and export subsidies India did not really benefit. Its share of world trade as regards certain commodities like rice, tea and iron ore is relatively high and it did not qualify for exemptions. There were other serious concerns relating to TRIPS and its effects on agriculture and pharmaceuticals. As regards the patent regime and pharmaceuticals and drugs many Indians feel that in a poor country, life-saving drugs and other basic medicines should be available at affordable and low prices. This can be achieved only through price control. The Indian Patent Act of 1970 helped to keep prices down. It had two objectives: to develop a prosperous indigenous pharmaceuticals industry and to provide low-cost access medicines for the Indian population. It, therefore, satisfied both suppliers and consumers. The GATT and WTO agreements, on the other hand, challenge the right of states to control the prices of drugs. TRIPS obligations are heavily biased towards protecting pharmaceutical industries (George, 2004). There is, therefore, a genuine fear in India that drug prices in India will increase. Multinationals are able to make big profits in other countries, but so far have not been able to in India. Critics of the WTO urge the government to be very cautious (Datt and Sundharam, 2001: 764–5).

As regards agriculture, an American company has been granted a patent right for neem – traditionally used by mothers and grandmothers in India as a remedy – as a pesticide. Basmati rice, which was a universal variety in India, has been patented as Kasmati and Texmati. The next item that may be patented is the tulsi (basil) plant. These are a few cases of biopiracy of India's herbal wealth and to prevent huge losses India will have to undertake huge documentation about its use. Vandana Shiva, an eminent Indian ecofeminist, asserted in her BBC Reith Lecture in 2000 that the 'wealth of the poor is being violently appropriated through new and clever means like patents on biodiversity and indigenous knowledge'. She pointed out that patents and intellectual property rights are supposed to be granted for novel inventions and not for rice varieties such as basmati which is grown in the valley in which she was born in Himachal Pradesh in India or for pesticides derived from neem. Addressing a wider issue, Vanadana Shiva argued that 'instead of recognizing that commercial interests build on nature and on the contribution of other cultures, global law has enshrined the patriarchal myth of creation to create new property rights to life forms just as colonialism used the myth of discovery as the basis of the take over of the land of others as colonies' (BBC Reith Lectures, 2000). However, it is not just India that is affected by TRIPS. Biggs notes that most developing countries have weak patent laws, especially in relation to food and drugs. Many countries deliberately do not allow medicines or food to be patented because they are so fundamental to any society's needs (Biggs, 1998: 133). As members of the WTO, however, they now have to strengthen their patent laws. India had to amend its Patent Act to introduce product patents before the WTO deadline of 31 December 2004.

But the Indian government also has to address the concerns of the Indian citizens. In late December 2004, the government issued an ordinance on the amendment to the Patents Act, to bring the country under a product patents regime in food, drugs, chemicals and embedded software. However, seeking to allay fears that the new patent regime would result in an increase in drug prices, the commerce and industry minister, Mr Kamal Nath, said that 'since 97 per cent of the drugs would be off patent, the shift from process to product patent would not have any impact on prices of life saving and essential drugs'. In order to safeguard public health the Indian government has reserved the right to revoke a patent as well as allow pre-grant opposition (*The Statesman*, 28 December 2004: 10). The ordinance was replaced by the Patents (Amendment) Bill 2005 (*Economic News*, 1 April 2005), which prevents domestic companies copying branded drugs. Multinationals such as GlaxoSmithKline are relieved, but NGOs including Médecins sans Frontières argue that India's obligations under WTO rules to grant twenty-year patents on pharmaceutical products would jeopardize its role as the largest exporter of generic drugs to developing countries, notably anti-retroviral treatments to combat HIV/Aids (*Financial Times*, 23 March 2005).

India also has other concerns. The main provisions of the trade-related investment measures (TRIMS) ensure that governments shall not discriminate against foreign capital. Indians feel that these militate against their goal of self-reliance. The phasing out of the Multifibre Arrangement (1974–94) will also affect India (and Indian textiles exports) by ending quotas.[1] Quotas were originally introduced to limit access to western markets but in reality guaranteed access. Countries that export textiles, like India, Pakistan, China and Sri Lanka, will now have to compete with one another, which will benefit China and possibly India (*The Statesman*, 7 March 2005). Access to western markets is an issue most developing countries are concerned about and India is no exception. So long as developed countries deny developing states access to their markets and pursue protectionist policies, there is no free trade. The Indian government asserts that 'despite revival of world trade, exports of developing countries like India continue to be threatened by the emerging protectionist sentiments in some sectors in the guise of technical standards, environmental and social concerns' (*Economic Survey 2000–2001*).

Restrictions on labour mobility is yet another concern. In future WTO meetings India, along with other developing countries, has to address issues relating to labour mobility and insist on appropriate safeguards. India should take up at the WTO issues of legal migration, exploitation of foreign workers, their conditions of employment, workers' remittances, work permits, unemployment benefit and so on.

Emerging opportunities in the twenty-first century

In January 2004 an Indian business magazine commented that 'Indeed, 2003 has been the best year [India has] had in a long, long while' (*Business Today*, January 2004). It was, of course, referring to the performance of the Indian economy. The Indian economy performed very well in 2003; at the end of the year it was estimated that the economy was growing at 7 per cent (per annum), with agriculture growing at 8 per cent, industry at over 6 per cent and services also at 8 per cent (NDTV, *The Year of the Bull*, 31 December 2003). Thus, all three sectors of the economy contributed to this overall good performance. By the end of the fiscal year 2003–04 the economy had registered a growth rate of 8.5 per cent, with the growth rates of the agricultural and allied sector, the industrial sector and the services sector at 9.6 per cent, 6.6 per cent and 9.1 per cent respectively (*Economic Survey 2004–2005*). Good growth rates are important for all developing economies. However, it is not just growth rates but also new business/economic opportunities that excite business analysts. After pursuing import substitution industrialization for several decades India is finally opening its doors to foreign investors and indeed to foreign competition. Indian companies are getting prepared to face stiff competition both at home and abroad and some are beginning to do extremely well. For Indians with disposable incomes 'consumer choice' has become a factor (and a fact of life) that is shaping lifestyles. There is no doubt that the Indian market is booming. According to a report published by *Business Today* (4 January 2004) corporate earnings in the first half of the 2003–04 fiscal year (for a sample of 3,287 companies across industries), increased by 43 per cent. Consumer spending has gone up; a survey reveals that in 2002 spending by upper- and middle-class families shot up by 12 per cent and the percentage of income spent on basic food and groceries fell for the first time in five years, whereas the share of income spent on clothing, personal care and 'eating out' rose significantly (*India Today*, 9 June 2003). Even sectors that some analysts describe as 'beleaguered', such as consumer goods and the automotive industry have seen their sales and profits go up. Exports in the first half of 2003–04 increased by 12 per cent and the Sensex (the Indian stock exchange) 'has been on a roll'; at last count in 2003, the bellwether index had gained 1,939 points, or 57 per cent, over the previous year's closing (*Business Today*, 4 January 2004). On the last day of 2004 the Sensex closed at a record high of 6,602 (NDTV).

The result, it is claimed, is that 'there are more takers than ever for India's growth story. Be it manufacturing companies that are beating a path to the country to source products, be it buyers of information technology products and services or simply back office operations, or foreign institutional investors, who made a net investment of more than Rs 30,000 *crores* this year alone' (*Business Today*, 4 January 2004: 43). Business analysts are very optimistic about India's future.

The opening up of the Indian economy as well as its good performance in recent years has attracted foreign investors. Taiwanese industrialist and businessman, Kuen Yao Lee (president of BENQ) wants BENQ to capture the two big emerging markets of China and India. His comments summarize the changes taking place in India: 'there are more cars ... people are getting so global. They are concerned about what is happening outside the country. Many global companies have R&D centres, call centres, and software centres in India. International banks have their back offices here. The knowledge workers are global, not just for India.' The emerging 'new Indian middle-class' is a potential and lucrative market for the mobile phones that he produces as well as IT products. He notes: 'there is a new mobile generation here ... a mobile phone is an important lifestyle product' (*Business Today*, 4 January 2004).

But it is definitely a two-way process. Not only is India opening up to foreign companies, 'the made-in-India badge is now a very visible player in the global supermarket' (*India Today*, 1 December 2003: 22). Indian companies have fought hard to survive and today there are sixteen companies whose exports net over Rs 1,000 *crores*, fifteen whose export goods are worth over Rs 500 *crores* and 150 companies which earn over Rs 100 *crores* in foreign exchange. The number of Indian companies on Forbes Best list of under US$1 billion companies increased from ten in 2001 to eighteen in 2003. TATA Sons' exports brought in Rs 9,658 *crores* in 2002. Their products include automobiles/commercial vehicles, software, finished leather goods, packaged tea and steel (*India Today*, 1 December 2003). A fifth of TATA group sales of $14.25 billion were earned from overseas markets in 2004 (*Financial Times*, 23 March 2005). Doctors in the US and UK are prescribing medicine produced by Indian companies Ranbaxy, Dr Reddy's, Orchid and Wockhardt claims *India Today*. WalMart alone buys towels worth over Rs 100 *crores* a year from India. Other global buyers include Tommy Hilfiger, J. C. Penny, Target and K Mart. It is estimated that by 2006, the top ten retailers in the world are likely to buy goods worth $20 billion from India and Mexico. Daimler, Chrysler, Volvo, Benz and others source auto parts worth $1.5 billion from India (*India Today*, 1 December 2003). And that is not all. Indian companies are now taking over foreign businesses. The trend began with TATA Tea's acquisition of Tetley. The number of foreign acquisitions increased from forty-nine in 2003 to sixty in 2004 (*India Today*, 4 July 2005).

Will growth be sustained?

The Indian economy is the fastest growing economy in the world after China. The government thinks that there is a 'feelgood factor' in the country. It is leading to more consumption, which is good news for those who want to sell their products in the Indian market. Furthermore, with the availability of credit, liquidity is no longer such an important factor. The key to domestic consumption staying buoyant is low interest rates. Indian middle classes are buying more houses, automobiles and consumer goods and spending more on travel (*India Today*, 2 February 2004). Even if interest rates go up it will not have a significant impact as a momentum has been achieved. Some analysts feel that interest rates will not go up in the near future. However, they may be wrong. At the time of writing, a lot of foreign institutional investors and non-resident Indians are investing in India because India offers a higher rate of return, be it debt or equity. Once the bigger economies – particularly the US – revive, there will be less money flowing into India, which may prompt Indian banks to increase interest rates (*Business Today*, 4 January 2004).

Another important question was whether India's GDP would grow by 7.5 per cent in 2004–05? Good monsoons had led to a bumper harvest and it was estimated that agricultural production would increase by 20 per cent. However, the dependence of Indian agriculture on the monsoons meant that deficient rainfall could check growth rates and they could plummet to 4 per cent. The manufacturing and services sectors would also have had to perform well. And indeed in 2004 the poor performance of agriculture had to be compensated by manufacturing, which continued to perform well (*Fortune India*, 31 December 2004; *The Statesman*, 1 January 2005). In an interdependent world these sectors of India's economy are affected by the health of the US economy, which, after a downward turn, began to revive in 2005. As demand revives in the US, India can export more products and services. 'The playground for Indian industry is the globe today' says Sunil Sinha, consultant at NCAER, implying that there are wider growth opportunities for industry to tap (*Business Today*, 4 January 2004). The *Economic Survey 2004–2005* asserts that the performance of the Indian economy in 2004–05 exceeded expectations formed at the beginning of the year. The economy was likely to grow by 6.9 per cent and had maintained the growth momentum in spite of a deficient south-west monsoon, hardening international prices of oil and steel and its first recorded experience of tsunami which caused extensive damage to life and property in Andaman and Nicobar Islands and 2,260 kilometres of coastline in Tamil Nadu, Kerala, Andhra Pradesh and Pondicherry. In early 2006, the union finance minister, Mr P. Chidambaram, said that in all respects 2005 had been a good year. India's GDP growth in the first half of 2005–06 had been 8.1 per cent and the overall growth for the full year was expected to be over 7.5 per cent.[2]

Economic reforms

The performance of the Indian economy and the emerging opportunities, however, should be considered in the context of economic liberalization, an issue that has become important since the 1990s. As discussed in Chapter 4, reforms were introduced in June 1991 following a balance-of-payments crisis that compelled the government of India to apply to the IMF for a loan. The reforms were similar to reforms other developing countries were implementing. They 'aimed at reducing the extent of government controls over various aspects of the domestic economy, increasing the role of the private sector, redirecting scarce public sector resources to areas where the private sector is unlikely to enter, and opening up the economy to trade and foreign investment' (Cassen and Joshi, 1995: 13).

International business opinion welcomed these reforms and generally urged a much faster pace of implementation, especially in view of the changes taking place in other countries. However, within India, 'while there was widespread support for the elimination of bureaucratic controls over domestic producers, there are differences on such issues as the speed at which protection to domestic industry should be reduced, the extent to which domestic industry can be subjected to foreign competition without being freed from the currently prevalent rigidities in the domestic labour market, the extent to which privatization should be pursued' and so on (Cassen and Joshi, 1995: 13).

An important feature of India's reform programme is that it is gradualist – it has not embarked on a rapid restructuring of the economy or 'shock therapy'. Advocates of a faster pace of reform both within and outside the country are not satisfied with this approach. However, the difference between India and many other countries is that the reforms were not a response to a prolonged economic crisis or a collapse of the economic system. Growth rates were not bad in the 1980s and as a result the necessity of radical restructuring was never felt. Indians recognized the need for reforms even before the balance-of-payments crisis in the early 1990s and its impact on economic performance. They recognized that the system of controls, with a heavy dependence on the public sector and a highly protected inward-oriented type of industrialization, could not deliver rapid growth in an increasingly competitive world environment. The sustained superior performance of the East Asian countries led to the feeling that India's performance should improve. Several initiatives were taken to mitigate the rigours of the control regime, lower direct tax rates, expand the role of the private sector, and liberalize licensing controls on both trade and foreign investment. However, these changes were marginal rather than fundamental in nature.

The reforms of the 1990s were more comprehensive and also based on the recognition that India needs to integrate with the global economy through trade, investment, and technology flows. The Indian government also realized that it needed to create conditions which would give Indian entrepreneurs an environment broadly comparable to that in other developing countries, and that this would have to take place rapidly. British Indian steel industrialist L. N. Mittal feels that the economic reforms will benefit Indian entrepreneurs. As a young businessman he had had to move to Indonesia to expand his family business as it was not possible to expand in India as the rules were too 'restrictive' (NDTV, *Walk the Talk*, 19 December 2004).

Economic liberalization and the removal of MRTP and FERA restrictions have benefited the top Indian industrial houses whose assets have grown dramatically in recent years. The top five industrial houses are Birla, Tata, Reliance, Singhania and Thapar; others include Modi, Bajaj, Mafatlal, Hindustan Lever and Mahindra and Mahindra. Most are household names and produce a range of consumer products from tea, textiles and soap to vehicles and automobiles.

However, the government has to take some controversial decisions (disinvestment of the oil companies and other public-sector undertakings, for example) and has been soft-pedalling. It has to take into account political and social constraints. In early 2004, with general elections around the corner, the BJP was being cautious. However, the results of a poll conducted by *Business Today* indicated that executives in the six metro cities, Delhi, Mumbai, Kolkata, Chennai, Bangalore and Hyderabad, thought that reforms/disinvestment would resume in 2005. According to Tarun Das of D-G/CII, 'Industry is strongly confident that reforms will continue, despite 2004 being an election year' (*Business Today*, 4 January 2004: 17). In February 2006 the union finance minister, Mr P. Chidambaram, confirmed that the Indian government would sell certain public-sector companies in spite of the stiff opposition from various quarters.[3] The United Nations Conference on Trade and Development (UNCTAD) is also positive about India. According to a study commissioned by UNCTAD of changes in regulations affecting FDI inflows during the 1990s there has been a shift in developing countries from state-directed, inward-looking economic strategies to an acceptance of markets and integration into the world economy. China, India and Vietnam stood out as the most active liberalizers over the course of the decade (UNCTAD, 2002).

The growth of business processing outsourcing (BPO)

One of the emerging opportunities in the twenty-first century is new call centres in Indian metros such as Delhi, Bangalore and Mumbai. American and European companies are setting up their 'back offices' in India. However, it is not a completely new development. American Express first outsourced work to India in 1994, and it currently has 4,000 employees there, handling financial accounting, data management, information analysis and control, administration, recruiting and staffing and payroll services. Citibank employs 3,000 people in Mumbai and Chennai. It is worth noting that these are coveted jobs and usually go to well-qualified graduates and postgraduates. Various UK banks have also outsourced to India: HSBC, Barclays, Standard Chartered Bank and most recently Norwich Union, which announced on 2 December 2003 that it will 'sack British workers and move thousands of jobs to India' (*Daily Express*, 3 December 2003). HSBC first outsourced to India in 2000 and now has more than 2,000 employees in Bangalore and Hyderabad who deal with accounting transactions and transaction processing. However, angry union chiefs have warned that 200,000 jobs in finance will be lost to the UK over five years as more companies follow Norwich Union's example. Meanwhile, researchers at Deloittes estimate that 2 million out of 13 million insurance and banking jobs in the western world could move to India by 2008 (at the Indian end it is estimated that BPO will generate 1.5 million jobs by 2010). The British government is not particularly sympathetic to the plight of the sacked British workers and Tony Blair feels that 'that is the way the world is today' (*Daily Express*, 3 December 2003). George Monbiot points out that Britain's industrialization was secured by destroying the manufacturing capacity of India. Now, he writes, 'the jobs we stole 300 years ago are returning to India'. The irony is that Indian workers can take away British jobs because the East India Company and the colonial authorities obliged Indians to speak English, adopt British working practices and surrender their labour to multinational corporations. He asserts that 'there is nothing new about multinational corporations forcing workers in distant parts of the world to undercut each other. What is new is the extent to which the labour forces of the poor nations are also beginning to threaten the security of our middle classes' (Monbiot, 2003).

Some of the companies are unaffected by public opinion in the UK, although others have subsequently become more cautious about retrenching workers. However, the advantages of relocating are obvious. Norwich Union's parent firm Aviva argues that costs in India are 40 per cent lower than in the UK and relocating to India would help it provide 24-hour services. Average call-centre salaries in the UK are £12,500 a year compared with £1,200 in India. Aviva, which employs 33,000 workers in Britain, already has 1,200 workers in Delhi and Bangalore. Its experience there has been 'positive'. In September 2004 Aviva announced that it was transferring 950 call-centre jobs to India and Sri Lanka, and that it would have 7,000 staff working in the subcontinent by 2007 (*Daily Express*, 3 December 2003; *Guardian*, 11 October 2004).

Indian executives explain that cost effectiveness is the only survival mantra in these competitive times and that there is little governments can do about it. However, cost effectiveness is not the only factor – skills and talent are also important. That is why companies like GE, Intel, Cisco and Google have set up engineering centres in India. In a free market, companies that choose not to take advantage of cheap and skilled labour wherever it is available could lose out. The *Times of India* claims that India is the most preferred outsourcing destination in the world (*Times of India Online*, 15 February, 2005) and Kobayashi-Hillary, author of *Outsourcing to India: The Offshore Advantage* (2005), agrees.

However, there is also a downside to India's BPO success. According to a Delhi-based psychiatrist, call-centre workers often suffer from depression, anxiety disorders, substance abuse and relationship-related problems. Working night shifts, the constant use of listening devices, the monotonous nature of the work and assuming a false/foreign identity leads to these problems. A call-centre worker comments that he has lost weight in seven months, suffered severe hair loss, smoked and drank too much and rarely met his family: 'It's also the monotony of work and boredom that sometimes makes me feel suicidal' (Srinirasan and Banerjee 2004: 63). Sometimes they are also abused by customers abroad for 'taking away our jobs' and/or ostracized by local people and neighbours. Moreover, there aren't any real career prospects. On the other hand, these are well-paid jobs by Indian standards. Not many graduates earn Rs 7,000 to 16,000 per month and there are often other perks such as training trips to the US (*Business Today*, 4 January 2004).

Indian investment in the UK

The British media often fails to mention that Indian companies are also investing in the UK and creating jobs. According to British government sources, the UK attracts around 60 per cent of Indian investment into Europe.[4] The IT/software sector currently accounts for half of all investment from India into the UK. Indian firms that are investing in the UK include Infosys Technologies (software), Tata Tetley GB (tea), ITC Infotech (IT), TATA Consultancy Services (IT). In a joint declaration signed on 20 September 2004, prime ministers Tony Blair and Manmohan Singh noted that bilateral trade between the two countries grew by over 20 per cent in 2003 and stated: 'we want this rapid growth to continue. But the real partnership lies in the strength of investment in both directions.' According to Amit Mitra of FICCI, 'over 450 Indian companies are in the UK and view it as a gateway to Europe' (*Times of India Online*, 8 October 2004). Indian companies created 646 jobs with twenty-eight projects in Britain in the financial year 2003–04. India and China were among the top ten inward investors in Britain according to the British department of trade and industry (*Times of India Online*, 14 October 2004).

Employment opportunities

New employment opportunities are a boon for the Indian people as unemployment is a major issue in India and one of the key issues in electoral politics. In the Indian context, economic growth will not benefit all the people in the country unless it is creates more jobs. According to the 2001 census 40 per cent of the population is in the working age group. The economic reforms and disinvestment have if anything had an adverse effect on jobs. The loss of jobs in the public sector is not being compensated for by new jobs in the private sector. Moreover, the private sector has created jobs in mainly the services sector that employs skilled labour. For the unskilled workers to gain, the manufacturing sector will have to undergo a services-like boom. That, however, currently seems unlikely (*Business India*, 8–21 December 2003).

It is estimated that employment in the organized sector is not even growing at 1 per cent. The tenth five-year plan target of creating 10 million new jobs each year seems to be unachievable. In the year 1999–2000 the organized sector's total contribution to employment was only 8 per cent, of which the private sector's contribution was only 2.5 per cent. The remaining 92 per cent came from the unorganized sector. The Planning Commission has, therefore, focused on the unorganized sector to achieve its target. However, employment opportunities in the unorganized sector are unlikely to grow at the rate that they must grow to meet those targets. Some analysts feel that small and medium enterprises (SMEs) appear to be the only hope for growth and employment-generation. However, the opportunities and threats to the SME sector in the context of globalization have not received adequate academic attention.

The problem of unemployment has been compounded by the poor quality of basic education in India. As a result, India cannot produce ordinary products like clocks on a large-scale and at competitive rates for export to other countries. China, on the other hand, has been able to do this because of better basic education in China. In 1992, the adult literacy rate in India was 50 per cent, whereas in China it was 80 per cent. (Dreze and Sen, 1999). It is, however, encouraging to note that the adult literacy rate in India went up to 61.3 per cent in 2002, although the corresponding rate for China was much higher at 90.9 per cent (UNDP, *Human Development Report 2003*).

Foreign investment and domestic infrastructure

India requires more investment. China has been the largest recipient of FDI among the developing economies of Asia. Its share in total FDI of these economies increased from 43 per cent in 1996 to almost 46 per cent in 2001. India has been less successful in attracting FDI than China and has marginally improved its share in total FDI inflows of developing economies of Asia from 2.7 per cent in 1996 to 3.3 per cent in 2001. A sharp rise in volume of FDI inflows in the Indian economy in 2001–02 indicated its growing attractiveness as an investment destination, the Indian government's economic survey claims (*Economic Survey 2002–2003*: 120). India received US$3.9 billion in FDI in 2003 and the $5 billion target for 2004 was achieved.[5] Indians, however, are aware of the reasons for uncertainty: high tariff rates, rigid labour policies, poor infrastructure and bureaucratic problems (*Business Today*, 4 January 2004). The American consul-general based in Kolkata interviewed by the present author on 2 January 2004 also felt that American investment in India was low and that this was recognized by the US administration and American business. During a debate in the Rajya Sabha on 20 August 2001, the then planning minister, Arun Shourie, was asked why India had received only $17 billion in FDI in a decade when China had attracted $323 billion. Shourie stated that the reason was that the Chinese government is 'market savvy, quick in decision-making and better still in executing decisions' (*The Statesman*, 21 August 2001).

Some analysts think that foreign institutional investors (FII) could be the next big story for India. Since 2000, net FII inflow into India has steadily grown. Foreign investment was allowed in the Indian stockmarket for the first time in 1993–94 and FII net inflow was around US$1.6 billion (less than 1 per cent of the total market capitalization), by 2003 FIIs had invested around $6.8 billion. According to most recent estimates, FII investment has increased dramatically since May 2003 by 856 per cent. However, compared with other Asian countries such as Taiwan, India is 'underowned by FIIs' (*Business Today*, 4 January 2004).

According to a Bank of Japan survey, India is the fifth most attractive investment destination after China, Thailand, the US and Vietnam. Goldman Sachs even predicts that by 2050 India will be the second global economic power after China and that the US will occupy third place. It all sounds very positive for India, however, the fact remains that even a small country is more attractive to potential investors because of its fast pace of economic reforms, good infrastructure and the total absence of bureaucratic delays. Feedback received from potential foreign investors indicate that India's vast market-place and skilled workforce do not compensate for poor infrastructure and a slow pace of economic reforms as well as a corrupt bureaucracy. Indian businessmen and analysts also agree with these views (*Fortune India*, 31 December 2003: 8). The union budget (2003–04) addressed some of these concerns. One of the highlights of the budget is a major thrust to infrastructure projects.

Former finance minister Yashwant Sinha emphasized that there is simply no alternative to providing quality roads, railroads, ports, airports, reliable and reasonably priced power supply, safe drinking water and sanitation. He said that without these, India could not take advantage of the opportunities now offered by technology and competition. In the developing infrastructure, there is a need to encourage public-private partnership so that public funds are leveraged and the quality of service delivery improved, thus yielding better value for money.[6] The Indian government is investing in the improvement of infrastructure like airport development in the metros with a view to attracting foreign investors. However, cynics point out that four out of ten proposals are not implemented and that more time is needed to achieve targets. At the end of 2004 the president of FICCI, O. S. Kanwar, was optimistic about the future of the Indian economy. He asserted that 'there is a buoyancy in the Indian economy. Foreign direct investment has touched $5 billion. All this augurs well for the country.' However, he also acknowledges that Indians need to 'improve the country's global rating' (*The Statesman*, 31 December 2004).

Table 5.1 *India's major trading partners, 2000–04*
(Percentage share in total trade (exports + imports)

	Country	2000–01	2001–02	2002–03	2002–03	2003–04 April–February
1	USA	13.0	12.2	13.4	13.4	11.6
2	UK	5.7	5.0	4.6	4.7	4.4
3	Belgium	4.6	4.4	4.7	4.7	4.1
4	Germany	3.9	4.0	4.0	3.9	3.9
5	Japan	3.8	3.8	3.2	3.3	3.1
6	Switzerland	3.8	3.4	2.4	2.3	2.7
7	Hong Kong	3.7	3.2	3.1	3.1	3.4
8	UAE	3.4	3.6	3.8	3.8	5.0
9	China	2.5	3.1	4.2	4.1	4.9
10	Singapore	2.5	2.4	2.5	2.5	2.9
11	Malaysia	1.9	2.0	1.9	2.0	2.1
	Total (1 to 11)	48.6	47.2	47.9	47.8	48.1

Source: Government of India, *Economic Survey 2003–2004*.

Promoting exports

Unlike many countries in East and Southeast Asia, exports have never been India's strong point and neither has the Indian government been in favour of basing economic growth on export promotion. However, it is now becoming more important and India has to compete with other developing countries. India's main trading partner is the USA. Other important trading partners include the UK, Germany, Belgium, Japan, United Arab Emirates (UAE) and Switzerland (see Table 5.1). However, China is becoming an important trading partner and so are some South Asian countries such as Nepal, although trade with Pakistan remains depressed.

While India's exports to China, in US$ value, increased by 67 per cent, imports from China grew by 32 per cent in April–October 2002. Trade between India and China continued to grow in 2003 and 2004. Thus, in 2003–04 China emerged as India's highest trading partner after the USA and UAE, overtaking the UK and Belgium. The two countries' shares of exports to industrial and developing countries are broadly comparable. However, China's exports to developing countries in Asia constitute around 33 per cent of its total exports as compared with a share of about 24 per cent for India. Developing countries in Africa and the Middle East absorb a larger share of Indian exports. In order to realize India's strong export potential reforms have been introduced and include the withdrawal of quantitative restrictions, reduction and rationalization of tariffs, liberalization in the trade and payments regime and improved access to export incentives, besides a realistic and market-based exchange rate. The focus of these reforms has been on 'liberalization, openness, transparency and globalization with a basic thrust on outward orientation focusing on export promotion activity and improving competitiveness of Indian industry to meet global market requirements' (*Economic Survey 2002–2003*: 110–20).

The lifting of the ban by the US on steel imports from other countries in 2004 was good news for the industry across the globe, including in India. The Indian steel industry had been suffering from excess capacity for nearly a decade and was facing a crisis. The result of the lifting of the ban is raised prices of both steel products and exports. The Indian steel industry is seeing new opportunities in Europe, Japan and South Korea, an indirect result of the lifting of the ban that will promote steel exports of these countries to the US (*Fortune India*, 31 December 2003: 12). This is an example of the interdependent world in which we live, that is beginning to affect countries like India that are opening up their economies. However, it is also worth noting that Indian companies are often not able to meet the stringent US standards and rising freight rates. The Asian market is therefore very important for Indian companies and almost 50 per cent of India's steel exports of 4 million tonnes per annum are exported to China.

The signing of the South Asian Free Trade Agreement (SAFTA) in the first week of January 2004 has created new opportunities for Indian business. The objectives of the agreement were to promote and enhance mutual trade and economic co-operation among the states of South Asia.[7] Trade with the South Asian Association for Regional Co-operation (SAARC) countries constituted 3 per cent of India's total trade. In 2003–04 the Association of Southeast Asian Nations (ASEAN) + 3 (China, Japan and Korea) countries emerged as India's dominant trading partners, accounting for 19.7 per cent of India's total merchandise trade, while the EU accounted for 19 per cent and North America for 12.8 per cent. The India-ASEAN Framework Agreement on Comprehensive Economic Co-operation will lead to more trade between India and the ASEAN region (*Economic Survey 2003–2004*: 114).

Redistribution and not 'trickle down'

However, the real challenge will be to redistribute the benefits of growth. It is estimated that 260 million people (26 per cent of the population) still live below the poverty line. Over the years the Indian government has succeeded in bringing the percentage of people living in poverty down (it was 55 per cent in 1973–74), however, many people in India do not believe in the 'trickle-down' theory. The focus will have to be on 'the poor'. Both the union budget of 2004 and the social charter adopted by the twelfth SAARC summit refer to poverty alleviation. The former Indian prime minister, Vajpayee, had pledged $100 million for poverty reduction. Moreover the benefits of growth have been felt mainly in the urban areas, but unfortunately the majority of Indians live in the villages. Rural development, therefore, has to be given priority, but without causing damage to the environment. Compared with other Asian countries outside South Asia, India's GDP per capita is still very low – lower, for example, than China's. The reason is that China started the development process at least a decade earlier and their investment in development has been much higher. South Asia is one of the poorest regions in the world in terms of per capita GDP. The other issue that needs to be addressed is human development as experiences in other parts of South Asia have shown that if human development is neglected economic growth will not be sustained.

The president of India, A. P. J. Abdul Kalam, comments that 'we should take cognisance of the fact that India, though the largest democracy in the world is still a developing country even after five decades of independence. This situation needs to be changed and India must become a developed country.' He feels that technology will play a pivotal role in achieving this goal. Five areas have been identified, based on India's core competence, for integrated action: (1) agriculture and agro-food processing; (2) education and healthcare; (3) information and communication technology; (4) infrastructure, including electric power; (5) strategic industries and critical technology (Abdul Kalam, 2004). In November 2004, the government of India announced that all villages in India will be electrified. That is a significant step forward that will lead to more progress, especially in the rural sector. India is also emerging as a knowledge society. It already has a large pool of scientists, engineers, technologists, technicians and farmers. Developed countries such as the UK are beginning to 'fear' Indian competition, notwithstanding the agreements that have been signed between the two countries, for example the New Delhi Declaration of January 2002. Tony Blair, the prime minister of the United Kingdom pointed out on 14 April 2005 that 'China and India already each produce 2 million graduates a year, compared with 250,000 in the UK. China is forecast to become the world's second largest economy within a decade; India the third largest within three decades.' He also emphasized that to succeed in the future 'economies will need to be fundamentally knowledge-based, flexible and adaptable and globally networked to a wholly new degree' (Blair, 2005). However, India needs more investment in all sectors especially infrastructure and education, and also has to sustain the political will to forge ahead.

Notes

1 The rules of the Multifibre Arrangement governed the bilateral negotiations of countries importing and exporting clothing and textiles. It allowed importing countries to apply selective quantitative restrictions (quotas) when an increase in imports of particular products caused, or threatened to cause, serious damage to their own industry. According to the WTO the arrangement was a major departure from

the basic GATT rules and particularly the principle of non-discrimination. It was replaced by the WTO Agreement on Textiles and Clothing on 1 January 1995, which sets out a transitional process for the ultimate removal of these quotas.
2 Available at http://southasia.oneworld.net/article/view/125504/1/32?Printable Version=enabled.
3 Available at http://southasia.oneworld.net/article/view/125504/1/32?Printable Version=enabled.
4 Available at www.britishhighcommission.gov.uk.
5 Available at www.thehindubusinessline.com/2005/10/01/stories/2005100100460700.htm.
6 Available at www.economywatch.com/budget/union-budget-2003-04.htm.
7 SAARC website available at www.saarc.org.

References

Aiyar, S., 2003, 'Made in India', *India Today*, 1 December.
Bandyopadhyaya, J., 1982, *North Over South: A Non-Western Perspective of International Relations*, The Harvester Press, Brighton.
Baylis, J. and Smith, S., 1997, *The Globalization of World Politics*, Oxford University Press, Oxford.
Beynon, J. and Dunkerley, D., 2000, *Globalization: The Reader*, The Athlone Press, London.
Biggs, S., 1998, 'The biodiversity convention and global sustainable development' in Kiely, R. and Marfleet, P. (ed.), *Globalisation and the Third World*, Routledge, London and New York.
Bose, S. and Jalal, A., 1998, *Modern South Asia*, Routledge, London and New York.
Blair, T., 2005, 'Labour Party: the party of wealth creation', 14 April, available at www.labour.org.uk.
Cassen, R. and Joshi, V. (eds), 1995, *India: The Future of Reforms*, Oxford University Press, Delhi, Bombay, Calcutta, Madras.
Datt, R. and Sundharam, K. P. M., 1995 and 2001, *Indian Economy*, S. Chand and Co., New Delhi.
Dreze, J. and Sen, A., 1999, *Economic Development and Social Opportunity*, Oxford University Press, New Delhi.
George, J., 2004, 'The drugs sector', *The Statesman*, 18 December.
Giddens, A., 1990, *The Consequences of Modernity*, Polity Press, Cambridge.
Gupta, A., 2004, 'Ten questions for 2004', *Business Today*, 4 January.
Held, D., McGrew, A., Goldblatt, D. and Perraton, J., 1999, *Global Transformations: Politics, Economics and Culture*, Polity Press, Cambridge and Stanford University Press, Stanford.
Hirst, P. and Thompson, G., 1996, *Globalization in Question: The International Economy and the Possibilities of Governance*, Polity Press, Cambridge.
Hoogvelt, A., 1997, *Globalisation and the Postcolonial World*, Macmillan, Basingstoke.
Kalam, A. P. J. Abdul, 2004, *Envisioning an Empowered Nation*, Tata McGraw-Hill Publishing Company, New Delhi.
Kiely, R. and Marfleet, P., 1998, *Globalisation and the Third World,* Routledge, London and New York.
Kobayashi-Hillary, M., 2005, *Outsourcing to India* (second edn), Springer-Verlag, Berlin, Heidelberg New York.
Lal, D., 1999, *India in the World Economy*, Oxford University Press, Oxford.

Malhoutra, J., 1999, 'Globalisation and interdependence', Statement by Member of Parliament on October 26, in the Second Committee (Economic and Financial) of the United Nations, available at www.indianembassy.org/policy/trade/eco_fin_oct_26(1)_99.html.
Michalet, C. A., 1982, 'From international trade to world economy: A new paradigm' in Makler, H. et al., *The New International Economy*, Sage, London.
Monbiot, G., 2003, 'The flight to India', *Guardian*, 21 October.
Robertson, R., 1992, *Globalization: Social Theory and Global Culture*, Sage, London.
Rothermund, D., 1993, *An Economic History of India*, Routledge, London and New York.
Sahai, S., 2000, 'GATT/WTO and the TRIPS agreement: a South Asian perspective', *South Asia Economic Journal*, 1: 2.
Shiva, V., 2000, 'Poverty and globalisation', BBC Reith Lectures, available at http://news.bbc.co.uk/hi/english/static/events/reith_2000/lecture5.stm.
Singh, V. B., 1965, *Economic History of India 1857–1956*, Allied Publishers Private, Bombay, New Delhi, Calcutta, London, New York.
Spero, J. E., 1985, *The Politics of International Economic Relations*, George Allen and Unwin, London.
Srinivasan, P. and Banerjee, S. 'The high cost of working', *Business Today*, 4 January 2004.
Stein, B., 1998, *A History of India*, Blackwell, Oxford.
Stubbs, R. and Underhill, G. R. D., 1994, *Political Economy and the Changing Global Order*, Macmillan, Basingstoke.
Swamy, D. S., 1994, *The Political Economy of Industrialisation: From Self-reliance to Globalisation*, Sage, New Delhi, Thousand Oaks and London.
Tooze, R., 1997, 'International political economy in an age of globalization' in Baylis, J. and Smith, S., *The Globalization of World Politics*, Oxford University Press, Oxford.
UNCTAD, 'A decade of FDI liberalization: the evidence', available at www.unctad.org.
UNDP, Human Development Reports, available at www.hdr.undp.org/statistics/data/cty/cty_f_IND.html.
Washbrook, D., 1990, 'South Asia, the world system and world capitalism' in Bose, S. (ed.) *South Asia and World Capitalism*, Oxford University Press, Oxford.
World Bank, 2002, *Globalization, Growth and Poverty*, A World Bank Policy Research Report, January.

6 Alternative approaches to 'development'

This chapter explores the argument that 'development' is much more than economic growth and involves a process of democratization that promotes the welfare of the people. Chapter 2 focused on the Indian constitution and political system and argued that, although British colonial rule led to the end of feudalism and to modernization in the area of government and politics, the British Indian state was not a democratic state. The democratization of Indian politics began with the birth of the Indian National Congress in 1885. The Indian nationalist movement that mobilized the masses was awe-inspiring, especially under Mahatma Gandhi's leadership, and influenced people all over the world, especially in other developing countries (for example on the African continent) struggling for freedom from colonial rule. Jawaharlal Nehru's famous speech delivered on the 14 August 1947 at midnight marked the birth of a new nation-state: 'Long years ago we made a tryst with destiny, and now the time comes when we shall redeem our pledge ... At the stroke of the midnight hour, when the world sleeps, India will awake to life and freedom. A moment comes, which comes but rarely in history, when we step out from the old to the new, when an age ends, and when the soul of a nation, long suppressed, finds utterance.'[1]

The adoption of a new constitution and the establishment of a republic was a great achievement. It gave rise to great hopes about the future of India and its people; a nation that had fought for and won its freedom from 'colonial exploitation and oppression'. The Westminster model of government adopted by the founding fathers has served India well but unfortunately did not lead to the empowerment of all sections of the society. Coupled with economic doctrines that did not lead to rapid economic growth or eradicate poverty, the framework for the democratization of Indian society and politics seemed to have failed to deliver, leaving the door wide open for opposition to the state and its policies from many different quarters and for many different reasons. This chapter will examine the Gandhian approach to development, and also some academic critiques of the Indian state, as well as some social movements that are striving to promote the welfare and empowerment of disadvantaged people in Indian society. The Indian government is keen to show the international community that it is responding (and is responsive and indeed receptive) to new ideas and concerns including those of the international community often expressed in declarations adopted by international institutions such as the United Nations and at world summits such as in Rio in 1992.

Globalization, it would appear, has facilitated global governance at one level by intensifying interactions between subnational, national, transnational and international actors, some of whom are governmental while others are non-governmental. A global network of actors has emerged. These actors have contributed to a pool of ideas and resources which have informed attempts to set standards in critical areas without erasing cultural diversity, for example environmental protection. In India industrial pollution is causing damage to historical monuments and environmental legislation may help to preserve cultural heritage such as the Taj Mahal. Implementation of UNESCO conventions could have prevented the destruction of Buddha's statues in Bamiyan, Afghanistan (Lewis, 2000: 148–9). However, it is not just the intensification of interactions between actors but the commitment to a set of core values that can improve global governance. The report of the Commission on Global Governance has identified some 'neighbourhood values' that all humanity could uphold. They are respect for life and its corollary non-violence, liberty, justice and equality, mutual respect, caring and integrity. It states that 'these provide a foundation for transforming a global neighbourhood based on economic exchange and improved communications into a universal moral community in which people are bound together by more than proximity, interest or identity' (United Nations, 1995: 48–9).

In June 1997, the UN General Assembly adopted the Agenda for Development. It states that 'development is a multidimensional undertaking to achieve a higher quality of life for all people. Economic development, social development and environmental protection are interdependent and mutually reinforcing components of sustainable development' (UN, 1997). These ideas were well received by global social movements dealing with development and related issues and also tie in well with Gandhi's values and beliefs.

The Gandhian approach to development focuses on the villages of India. Gandhi wanted village communities to be self-sufficient. He had certain ideas on how India should be organized politically, and the approach that should be taken towards development. The approach is bottom up. Corbridge and Harriss (2000: 26) write:

> like most members of the Constituent Assembly, Nehru's understanding of democracy and government had been shaped by the Raj and Westminster, and by the limited experiments in democracy that were signalled by the reforms of 1909, 1919 and 1935. An alternative understanding of what democracy might mean had been promoted by Gandhi and some of his followers, who sought a distinctively 'Indian'

form of government. The alternative was founded on a view of the centrality of the village in Indian society, and on hostility to the idea of the modern state, partly because it was seen as a western concept.

Directly elected village councils or *panchayats* form the core of this system. Above them there would be a hierarchy of indirectly elected bodies. At the apex there would be a national *panchayat* with limited functions. Although Gandhi's ideas were not adopted by the newly independent state and the new constitution did not give much importance to *panchayats* (merely stating in Part IV, Article 40, dealing with the Directive Principles of State Policy, that village panchayats should be organized as units of self-government), the 73rd Amendment to the Indian constitution adopted in 1993 has given them importance as units of self government and has increased their powers (Pylee, 1994: 366).

Corbridge and Harriss (2000: 27) note that 'the realities of power, in the context of Partition and its consequences in terms of internal and external security, as well as of their whole experience of government, made Nehru and Patel and others resolutely hostile to panchayati democracy as to other Gandhian ideas'. Although Gandhi's ideas were appreciated by some, on the whole Congress leaders did not subscribe to them in their totality. Austin argues that 'the [Constituent] Assembly's adoption of a democratic, centralized, parliamentary constitution meant that members believed that to achieve the object of social revolution India must become a modern state' (cited in Corbridge and Harriss, 2000: 27). The irony is that Gandhi was a revolutionary and therefore his ideas were about bringing about social change, especially the emancipation of the downtrodden. His relentless campaign to remove the practice of untouchability from the caste-ridden Indian society is well known. He was a devout Hindu but did not believe in the practice of untouchability and promoted the interests of the lower castes whom he called Harijans. Some social reformers found him a touch patronizing but Gandhi sincerely tried to root out this evil. It is worth noting that the fundamental right dealing with the Right to Equality also abolishes untouchability (Article 17) and its practise in any form is made an offence punishable under the law. Pylee (1994: 81) asserts that 'no article in the Constitution was adopted with such unanimity and so great an acclamation and enthusiasm as this article. It was the only one which had the special distinction of having been adopted with cries of "Mahatma Gandhi ki jai" [long live Mahatma Gandhi].' The Untouchability (Offences) Act came into force in June 1955. The then home minister of India, G. B. Pant, argued 'this cancer of untouchability has entered into the very vitals of our society. It is not only a blot on the Hindu religion, but it has created intolerance, sectionalism and fissiparous tendencies' (Pylee, 1994: 82).

Gandhi gave priority to rural (as opposed to urban) development and the reform of agriculture. The reforms suggested included land reforms and the abolition of moneylending. The latter often led to the exploitation of poor farmers by moneylenders. Credit facilities were required. Gandhi's views on industries are distinctive. He believed that agricultural development should be complemented by the rehabilitation, development and expansion of cottage industries. His promotion of spinning and weaving is almost legendary. He wrote: 'I do regard the spinning-wheel as a gateway to my spiritual salvation, but I recommend it to others only as a powerful weapon for the attainment of *swaraj* and the amelioration of the economic condition of the country' (cited in Chatterjee, 1993: 108). The manufacturing of *khadi* (cloth woven by hand using handspun yarn only) was almost as important as the production of rice and wheat. Gandhi put emphasis on self-sufficiency. Every village should be self-sufficient and produce enough food and cloth to meet the needs of the villagers. He believed the state has an important role to play in achieving these objectives, however, he was not in favour of state intervention. Chatterjee (1993: 115) explains that 'what he was suggesting in fact was that the national state should formally use its legislative powers to abdicate its presumed responsibility of promoting development and thus clear the ground for popular non-state agencies to take up the work of revitalizing the village economies'.

The term that is often used to describe goods produced in India as opposed to foreign (made and even inspired) goods is *swadeshi*. Boycotting foreign goods was a method used by the Indian freedom fighters during the freedom struggle in the first half of the twentieth century to show opposition to foreign rule and support for self-rule and indigenous industry. Even today there are supporters of *swadeshi* in India who are sceptical about foreign investment and products and argue that it will lead to an erosion of sovereignty. The Indian brand is important to them. Gandhi put emphasis on *swadeshi*. However, as Sethi (1983) explains, 'swadeshi was not narrow nationalism: it implied an extended link between the villages, the nation and the global system. It was not a limited economic concept. It at once meant the autonomy of the individual and of institutions and of the maximum self-reliance of the nation' (cited in Datt and Sundharam, 2001: 159). There was another dimension to *swadeshi*. It nurtured forms of technology that were seen to be appropriate to the needs of the majority of the people. It also promoted the dignity of labour. For Gandhi, the winning and maintenance of freedom was impossible without such a work ethic (Hardiman, 2003: 78).

Conflict between the village and the city?

Gandhi perceived a conflict between village industries and capital-intensive industries based on a high degree of urbanization. His approach to development as discussed above was a grass-roots approach. He focused on the villages and the villagers and wanted to improve the economic conditions of the Indian villages. However, India's modernizers adopted a different approach, as explained in Chapter 4. An Indian academic comments that 'the twin compulsions of reconstructing the economy and achieving rapid economic development after

Independence, prompted India's rulers to adopt a model of development based on the experience of the West: the implicit emphasis was on capital-intensive industrialization and urbanization. Over time a distinct bias became apparent towards urban settlements in general and big cities in particular' (cited in Datt and Sundharam, 2001: 159)

India has been urbanizing rapidly and this process is unlikely to be reversed as it is a global trend. However, the growth of megacities creates problems that have to be tackled at various levels (Dutt, 2000), an issue that has been discussed elsewhere. One of the factors responsible for rural–urban migration or migration from the villages to the cities is the lack of economic opportunities in the rural areas. After India became independent, the Indian leaders concentrated on the development of modern industries and village industries were not given much importance. On the contrary, villages were encouraged to supply cheap raw materials and semi-finished products to the urban organized sector. They included diary products such as milk and agricultural products such as vegetables, oil seeds, cotton and foodgrains. At the beginning of the twentieth century village industries accounted for about 40 per cent of the labour force. By the middle of the twentieth century this had decreased to 10 per cent and by the end of the twentieth century it was about 2 per cent (Datt and Sundharam, 2001: 159). But even in the twenty-first century more than half of the total population of India still lives in the villages. This is the reason Gandhi's ideas are worth revisiting especially since most of the people living in the villages live in poverty.

However, it is also important to note that Gandhi was not against the development of large-scale industries. The Gandhian Plan, brought out in 1944 by Acharya S. N. Agarwala and re-affirmed in 1948, recognized the need for and the importance of certain selected basic and key industries in India, especially defence industries, hydro-electric and thermal power generation, mining and metallurgy, machinery and machine tools, heavy engineering and heavy chemicals. However, these key industries were to be owned and managed by the state – in other words, they would be in the public sector – and they should not hinder the growth of cottage industries.

Gandhi was not against machinery but was against the use of machinery for the exploitation of labour by a few capitalists. He was in favour of machinery and modern amenities when they lightened the burden of the villagers without displacing human labour. As India is a country with a large population and high unemployment rates, the Indian government recognizes the need to retain labour-intensive methods of work that provide an income and livelihood for a large number of people. For example, cleaners in the city of Mumbai were against the introduction of mechanical street sweepers in the 1980s as they would lead to large-scale redundancies.

After independence, Gandhi and his economic ideas were forgotten. Instead, Indian planning on the model of the Russian experience of socialism and state control of the economy was introduced. However, in the mid-1970s when the country was in the grip of an economic crisis, political parties and the Planning Commission began to think of the Gandhian model as a possible alternative to the Nehru model of growth. The Janata government (1977–79) tried to adopt some of Gandhi's ideas. Its Industrial Policy Statement (1977) emphasized that 'the main thrust of the new industrial policy will be on effective promotion of cottage and small industries widely dispersed in rural areas and small towns. It is the policy of the government that whatever can be produced by small and cottage industries must only be so produced' (Datt and Sundharam, 2001: 168). However, when the Congress returned to power in 1980, the Janata industrial policy was scrapped.

The Gandhian model of growth calls for employment-oriented planning to replace production-oriented planning. The problem of unemployment has to be tackled if poverty and inequality are to be reduced. India has a population of more than 1 billion and high unemployment rates compared with the developed world. The Janata government recognized this problem in the 1970s, however, even in the twenty-first century the Indian government has to deal with this issue. The focus has to be on job creation and not simply on economic growth.

Another Gandhian idea is that instead of job creation in industry and in urban areas, the agricultural sector and rural areas can provide employment for more people if there is more investment there. There is scope for enlarging employment in three main areas: (1) agriculture, including animal husbandry, compost-making, sanitation and gobar (bio)gas; (2) rural works such as irrigation projects, soil conservation, land reclamation, afforestation and so on; and (3) rural or cottage industries.

The Gandhian model of growth is in favour of small-scale and cottage industries and against large-scale industries producing consumer goods. As we have seen, Gandhi believed that concentration of economic power in the hands of a few was wrong and that the promotion of small-scale and cottage industries would lead to a more equitable distribution of wealth, but that key industries should be owned and managed by the government. In 1919 on Gandhi's initiative a prize of Rs 5,000 was offered for the best design for a spinning wheel. After the selection of a design, funds were raised by Gandhian activists to manufacture and distribute wheels. Thread was supplied to handloom weavers to produce *khadi* and stores called *khadi bhandars* were opened to sell it. They also stocked other Indian-made products and nationalist literature and became a symbol of the nationalist spirit. The Indian National Congress decided in 1920 during its Nagpur session to encourage *khadi* and the first *khadi* production centre was established at Katiawad in Gujarat. The All-India Spinners Association was founded in 1925 by Gandhi. *Khadi* was not however able to compete with mill-made cloth in terms of price. Nonetheless the Indian government continued to support it. In 1955 the Khadi and Village Industries Commission Act was passed and in 1957 the Khadi and Village Industries Commission came into existence. Critics comment that *khadi* has been kept alive because of its great symbolic importance. It had become, in Gandhi's words, the 'livery of freedom'. In strictly economic terms, the production of khadi did not provide a good example of self-sufficiency (Hardiman, 2003: 78–9).[2]

However, Gandhi was not primarily an economist. He was guided by his ethical principles. Hardiman (2003: 5) writes that 'it is hardly adequate ... to see Gandhi merely as a backward-looking representative of a "traditional" culture that was being destroyed inexorably by the forces of modernity. Although a few of his admirers may have been and continue to be driven by a nostalgia for a romanticized past, the majority have been and are moved by a strong desire to evolve a better world in the light of existing realities.' Gandhi did not want Indians to blindly ape the Europeans. He did not believe that western culture was superior and was against materialism and what he regarded as the 'amoral pursuit of knowledge'. At the same time, he adopted some of the values of the European enlightenment, such as the doctrines of human rights, egalitarianism and democracy. He also drew upon Indian values in certain areas and as a result his thought is considered to be highly eclectic.

Gandhi was born in Porbunder, Gujarat and had strong family values. He also had professional ambitions and trained to be a barrister in England. His experience of racial discrimination against him, mainly in South Africa, eventually turned him into a political activist, struggling against apartheid in South Africa before fighting the injustices of British colonial rule in India. In 1915 he returned to India and soon became the undisputed leader of the Indian national movement and was extremely successful in mobilizing the masses, the middle classes and the peasantry as well as the working classes. In 1920 he launched the first non-co-operation movement against British rule. It was a *satyagraha*, a form of passive resistance. This was followed in later years by two more powerful confrontations with the British, the civil disobedience movement of 1930–34 and the 'Quit India' movement of 1942. Hardiman (2003: 2) explains that, from the start, Gandhi 'refused to accept the inferior status imposed on Indians by a racist ruling class and resolutely fought the various restrictions that had been imposed on his fellows there. In the process, he developed the new technique of civil resistance now universally known as satyagraha, deploying it to powerful effect against the white rulers in South Africa and later, opponents in India.'

The word *satya* means truth in Hindi and other north Indian languages that have their roots in Sanskrit. For the common man in north India it is not an esoteric term. *Agraha* means to hold. Gandhi was a deeply religious man and defined truth in terms of the almighty, i.e. God. His *satya* stood for sincerity, honesty, faithfulness, purity and virtuousness. It also implied acting according to one's conscience. It is for this reason that Gandhi is better known for his ethical principles than for his economic ideas. Gandhi was a revolutionary, but not one who believed in the use of violent methods to achieve one's objectives. For him, non-violence was part of his doctrine of truth. He was inspired and influenced by various protests in India and elsewhere but also by the ideas of Henry David

Thoreau and Leo Tolstoy. He was also conscious of the fact that the battle may not be won by the use of force as the 'enemy'/oppressors were physically more powerful and had the power to inflict great damage. Gandhi's belief in non-violence is well known . He even suspended the non-co-operation movement of 1920–22 when it turned violent in the affair of Chauri Chaura in which a police station was burnt down and twenty-two Indian constables killed by an angry mob. Gandhi wanted to win over his enemies and opponents to his point of view and would not condone the use of force against them. He wanted to pit his moral power against the brute power of his enemies and made a distinction between passive resistance and *satyagraha*. He argued that 'passive resistance may be a political weapon based on expediency; satyagraha is a spiritual weapon. Passive resistance is a weapon of the weak; it is only a man who is morally and spiritually strong who can practise satyagraha. Passive resistance does not entirely ignore the possibility of violence ... satyagraha will not tolerate violence in word or deed' (Gandhi cited in Agarwal, 1981: 330). The civil disobedience movement that he launched in 1930 and the famous Dandi march gave him an opportunity to practise his ideas. There is a tradition of non-violence or *ahimsa* in Indian culture that also influenced Gandhi to some extent. Buddhism and Jainism preach non-violence; Jains believing that one should not kill any living being. However, Gandhi's approach to *ahimsa* was slightly different. Hardiman (2003: 58) writes that 'the general thrust of Gandhi's injunction was that ahimsa involved qualities of respect and sympathy for the opponent, freedom from anger, and a desire for peace'.

Gandhi was a champion of the downtrodden and as such he influenced all kinds of people, activists and movements throughout the world: civil-rights movements, peace movements, women's movements and national liberation movements. Hardiman (2003: xii) summarizes his contribution in the following words: 'He forged a method of resistance that sought to build bridges with an opponent, while at the same time refusing to accept injustice. He directed a powerful spotlight on the injustices that ran through his own society, such as the practice of untouchability and the exploitation of low-caste and "tribal" groups by the high castes and he fought these abuses with great energy and commitment.'

Gandhi's efforts to end untouchability in Indian society have already been commented on in Chapter 2. It led to the passage of the Untouchability (Offences) Act in 1955. Although Gandhi was himself not from a low caste (he was a *buniya;* a trading class) like Ambedkar, his efforts gave an impetus to the Dalit and Adivasi (tribal) movements. The importance of social movements in the modern world and in modern India should not be underestimated. Social movements are not a new phenomenon and many of them started during colonial times and influenced the founders of modern India and the framers of the Indian constitution. Even the Indian nationalist movement was a social movement that attempted to mobilize the Indian masses, unite the nation and bring about social and political change. The history of the Indian nationalist movement often eclipses the histories of other movements, although both Indian and foreign scholars have taken an interest in these and some of their histories are well documented. The main argument that this chapter puts forward about them is that their leaders were often inspired by western values but also that they became a source of inspiration for other leaders and movements in other parts of the world. Globalization in more contemporary times, by intensifying interaction at all levels, the local, national and international/global, has made it possible for these movements to publicize their causes more widely and even influence the international agenda. The discussion of the Dalit and Adivasi movements will be followed by comments on other movements inspired by Gandhian ideas both in India and in other countries.

The Dalit movement

Just as the Indian nation was an 'imagined community', various tribes and castes too were imagined collectives. The British colonial state labelled them (quite arbitrarily) on the basis of their social status. Low-caste groups were defined initially as the 'depressed classes' and, from 1909, the 'Untouchables' because high-caste groups considered physical contact with them to be polluting. Adivasis or tribals were similarly treated and both groups were classified as 'Hindus' as opposed to Muslims, Christians and so on. Once they had been given a political identity, political leaders sought to represent them. Even leaders of the Indian nationalist movement wanted to champion their cause. Initially, Gandhi was not opposed to the caste system, however, in later years he became a strong critic of the system of the early twentieth century, which he felt was the very antithesis of *varnashram*, the classical division between the Brahmins, Kshatriyas, Vaishyas and Shudras. He was completely opposed to untouchability and during the non-co-operation movement of 1921–22 he called on Hindus to 'remove the sin of untouchability', otherwise there would be no *swaraj*, even in a hundred years. Sanatanist Hindus accused Gandhi of being corrupted by Christian propaganda, but he argued that Hinduism was not a text- (scripture) based religion, but one that was rooted in moral precepts, and texts that conflicted with morality could be discounted. Gandhi was not simply interested in expressing his views about untouchability but was also an activist *par excellence*. He extended his support to various protests launched by various groups of Untouchables who felt that they were victims of social discrimination. For example, he supported their right to enter temples. Upper-caste Hindus sometimes argued that Gandhi was going against their religious traditions, but he argued in return that they were trying to hold on to their social privileges. Gandhi was also a social reformer and his objective was to reform Hindu society and not simply to gain political concessions from the ruling classes. He also wanted to keep the Hindu community united.

However, educated leaders of the Dalits considered his approach to be too gradualist. In the 1920s Ambedkar emerged as a powerful young leader of the Dalits of Maharashtra and although he praised Gandhi for his efforts to abolish untouchability, he felt that a far more radical stance was needed. He also wanted Gandhi to focus on their civil rather than their religious rights. However, Ambedkar was in favour of separate electorates for the Untouchables and Gandhi was not as he wanted to unite the Hindu community. In 1932, Ramsay MacDonald announced his decision known as the Communal Award, on 16 August, that granted separate electorates to the Untouchables. Agarwal comments that the award recognized the Harijans as a minority. Separate seats were allotted to them and 'they exercized two votes each, one in the general constituency and the other in special constituencies ... this was deliberately done to alienate Harijans from the Hindus' (Agarwal, 1981: 217). Gandhi informed him that he would begin a fast to death if the decision was not reversed. On 20 September 1932, Gandhi began his fast and succeeded in mobilizing Hindu leaders who agreed to negotiate with the leaders of the Untouchables. The negotiations led to the Poona Pact and was signed on 26 September and later ratified by the Hindu Mahasabha and accepted by the British government. It was based on an agreement between Gandhi and Ambedkar to retain joint electorates but double the number of reserved seats for the Untouchables, or Harijans as Gandhi preferred to call them. It led to as many as 149 seats being reserved for them against the 71 allotted by the Communal Award. This has now become a tradition in India and, as discussed in Chapter 2, the Indian constitution has specified special provisions relating to the SCs and STs, including the reservation of seats for them in the Lok Sabha.

Gandhi's efforts to promote Harijans and their rights, religious and civil are well documented by Hardiman. He also explores the relationship between Gandhi and the more radical Ambedkar. They did not always see eye to eye on how best to promote the interests of the Harijans. For example, Ambedkar supported conversion to other religions such as Christianity, Islam and Sikhism and himself converted to Buddhism. Gandhi, on the other hand, wanted to keep the Hindu community, including the Harijans, united. He launched the Harijan movement all over India; on his initiative the All-India Anti-Untouchability League was renamed the Harijan Sevak Sangh. However, despite all these efforts, the majority of Dalits throughout India remained unaware of these campaigns. The communities that were influenced by Ambedkar's ideas included the Mahar Community of Maharashtra and educated Dalits and industrial workers in some of the larger cities. The Vankar Community of Ahmedabad and the Valmikis of Delhi supported Gandhi. The work of the Harijan Sevak Sangh had a higher profile in the rural areas than in the urban centres. However, the Dalits were often reluctant to assert their rights as they feared the village elites (Hardiman, 2003: 133–4).

Eventually, when Gandhi realized that it was not easy to bring about rapid reform and change in Indian society, he began to support the banning of the practice of untouchability. He also accepted that the empowerment of the Dalits had to be given more importance and agreed with Ambedkar that this was an important political (and not just social) issue, that had to be resolved. Unfortunately, even after fifty-eight years of independence the Dalits continue to be victims of exploitation and oppression. The Indian government's policy of positive discrimination – i.e. reservation of places in schools and colleges, government posts and seats in the parliament and state legislatures for Dalits and other special provisions such as scholarships – have benefited only a small minority. The majority of the Dalits continue to live in poverty. The police fail to protect them and politicians use them. The English-language Indian media regularly publishes reports on the abuse and exploitation of this class of people in various parts of the country. However, Dalits have continued their struggle for social justice and political representation. They have even deployed *satyagraha* to good effect.

Representatives of the Dalits attended the World Conference Against Racism, Racial Discrimination, Xenophobia and Related Intolerance held in Durban, South Africa between 31 August and 7 September, 2001. It was a controversial step as it equated caste with race and highlighted the social problems in India and the government's inability and even lack of enthusiasm to do anything about them. The government of India, however, does not wish to 'internationalize' the issue. Soon after the Durban conference members of the Dalit community adopted the Bhopal Declaration in January 2002 (see Figure 6.1). They categorically stated that they believed in Babasaheb Dr. B. R. Ambedkar's ideal of social democracy and his prophecy in the declaration that 'a democratic form of government presupposes a democratic form of society' and that 'the formal framework of democracy is of no value and would indeed be a misfit if there was no social democracy'. They also endorsed 'the ideals of civil society enshrined in the Constitution of India, particularly its Preamble' that the Indian state is committed to justice, liberty, equality and fraternity. The declaration refers to both UN charters and declarations and the Indian constitution, to basic human rights and Indian social movements. It reflects an awareness of global ethics and the opportunity that the age of globalization has given Dalits to publicize their grievances. It also notes that Ambedkar's successors have unfortunately failed to carry forward his emancipatory movement.

Expressing the hope that India will no longer remain an exception to the global norm of progress, equality, justice, peace and social harmony, the conference rededicated itself to work in unison to achieving the basic rights of Dalits. It also adopted a twenty-one-point action agenda for the twenty-first century that demanded cultivable land for the Dalits, living wages for Dalit agricultural labourers, better working conditions and welfare measures, the restoration of the rights of tribals over forests and forest produce and the compensation and rehabilitation of Dalits displaced due to the construction of dams and development

Box 6.1 An extract from the Bhopal Declaration

Recognizing that the tenets established by the Universal Declaration of Human Rights and various other charters of the United Nations which our nation has acceded to also emphasize the same principles,

Recognizing also the tribals' legitimate and historical rights over forest and forest-produce,

Acknowledging the role of tribal communities, particularly tribal women, [in] the protection and conservation of the country's rich biodiversity and natural resources as well as its culture and civilization,

Acknowledging also the need to ensure that SCs and STs are given due representation in all bodies of decision making,

Recalling the struggles that Babasaheb had waged for the emancipation of his people and the historic rights he had won for them,

Mindful of the fact that even after fifty-four years of Independence, the Dalit community is denied of its basic human rights and is also at the receiving end of the most brutal and oppressive forms of discrimination and exclusion,

Reaffirming that concerted action by society as a whole – especially co-ordination among the political leadership, officials and grassroots activists – is necessary for the over-all development of the most oppressed of India,

Bearing in mind the responsibility to take forward our struggle at this critical juncture in spite of the fact that most political formations are reluctant to pursue any policy favourable to the Dalits,

Recognizing that the social consensus over the Dalit cause – reluctantly agreed upon at the time of independence – has by and large broken down,

Convinced that informed and democratic discourse at all levels is essential to re-negotiate a new consensus over redeeming the pledges of the founding fathers of the Republic to do justice to Dalits,

Convinced also that the national psyche and public discourse in the country accepts uncritically the rigid hierarchy and discrimination caused by caste and thereby denies that caste is a major source of prejudice and brutal violence ...

Recognizing the need for Dalits to make common cause with other liberation and human rights movements in and outside the country,

Conscious of the hurdles that caste-Hindu society – and its tentacles in government, media, voluntary sector, etc. – is likely to hurl at any serious movement that challenges the entrenched system of discrimination and exclusion,

Noting that women – especially Dalit women – represent the most oppressed sections of our society, and that they face multiple forms of discrimination, including caste-based, religious and patriarchal ideology and practices,

Welcoming the winds of change the world over that are conducive to inclusion, Equal Opportunity, Diversity, Democratization and Civil Society, and against discrimination, stereotype, stigma, exclusion and caste society.

(*Source:* www.indiatogether.org/dalit/events/bhopal.htm)

projects, the right to a standard of living adequate for the health and well-being of women and men equally, effective measures to deal with atrocities against Dalit women, the recognition of SC and ST women as a distinct category among women (and accordingly make segregated data on women available in census reports) and national- and state-level plans for mainstreaming SC and ST women in developmental programmes among other things. The chief minister of Madhya Pradesh, Digvijay Singh, also accepted the agenda and promised to implement it.

The Adivasi movement

Gandhi also fought for the rights of the Adivasis (tribal groups) who were later classified by the Indian constitution as Scheduled Tribes. The term Adivasi means 'original inhabitants' and most of these groups lived in the north-east of the country, in the new state of Jharkhand and surrounding areas in Bengal, Orissa and Bastar, and in a tribal belt stretching across the Indian states of Rajasthan, Gujarat, Madhya Pradesh and Maharashtra. The British had subjugated them and denied them their rights to their land and forest resources, in order to allow the commercial exploitation of the forests. The Adivasis were encouraged by the British to practise settled and intensive agriculture but were ruthlessly exploited by landlords, usurers and liquor dealers who were protected by the colonial and princely states. Members of the Indian nationalist movement took up the cause of the Adivasis and during the non-co-operation movement of 1920–22 Gandhi attempted to assimilate the Adivasis into the nationalist movement. Some Adivasi movements drew inspiration from his ideas and tenets. It should be noted, however, that Gandhi's primary objective was to achieve the goals of the nationalist movement and, being an astute political leader, he understood that he had to support exploited and oppressed groups in order to win their support for the (urban middle-class-led) nationalist movement, and for it therefore to be successful. However, these disparate groups did not always adhere to Gandhi's principles. For example, tribals in some areas launched 'forest *satyagrahas*' that sometimes turned violent. In later years, some Adivasis even joined the Naxalite movement (that started in the 1960s), which used violent methods to achieve its objectives.

The Government of India Act of 1935 discriminated against the Adivasis by denying them political representation. They were considered to be too politically immature to deserve any electoral representation. English missionaries like Elwin felt that Gandhi was not taking a great deal of interest in the Adivasi issue. In 1938 an Adivasi Mahasabha was formed in Jharkhand to press for constitutional rights for the Adivasis of the region. Many had converted to Christianity and some of them were involved in this organization. As Gandhi did not want them to start a separatist movement in later years he began to give them more importance. However, the Gandhian approach to Adivasis tended to focus on their education into citizenship rather than on their rights. Even today the Adivasis continue to be displaced, marginalized and exploited. Chapter 3 comments on the identity politics of tribal groups in India and their relationship with the Indian state. It is worth noting here that although leaders like Gandhi wanted to assimilate them, they have continued to maintain a distinctive identity of their own that has even led to the creation of new states within the Indian union, such as Jharkhand. The exploitation of tribal groups by high-caste farmers who often seize their land, commercial companies who want access to their forest wealth and bureaucrats who want to build large dams, mine minerals and build tourist resorts and wildlife reserves in the forests and hills where they live has continued even after many years of independence.

It has already been noted that Gandhi gave more importance to the Dalits and the Dalit movement than to the Adivasi movement. However, above all, Gandhi remained true to his principles. Gandhi also believed that everyone had a right to practise any religion they chose to follow and that the state should not concern itself with religious education; in fact that religion should be separate from the state. Hardiman (2003: 157) writes that 'Gandhi's religious tolerance was reinforced by secularist doctrines that had emerged in Europe in the years after the religious wars of the post-Reformation period. The latter was formulated most clearly by John Locke, who argued that the state should not seek to adjudicate within the sphere of private belief – this was a matter for the subjective conscience of the individual.' It is well known that Gandhi and other Congress leaders were against the partition of India and tried to promote Hindu-Muslim unity. Although the Muslim League had been formed as early as 1906 to represent Indian Muslims and assert their rights, the Congress concluded the Lucknow Pact with them in 1916 and accepted the principle that the minorities should be given adequate separate representation in the elected bodies. In 1919 Gandhi also extended his support to the *khilafat* movement to preserve the institution of the *khalifa*. He wanted to demonstrate his goodwill towards the Muslim community. However, not all Muslims in India supported the movement. In *Hind Swaraj* Gandhi wrote: 'India cannot cease to be one nation because people belonging to different religions live in it ... If the Hindus believe that India should be peopled only by Hindus, they are living in dreamland. The Hindus, the Mohamedans, the Parsis and the Christians who have made India their country are fellow countrymen, and they have to live in unity, if only for their own interest' (Gandhi, 1948).[3] Chapter 1 makes it very clear that the Indian subcontinent was frequently invaded by foreign groups who brought with them their beliefs and religious, cultural and social practices and often settled in the subcontinent and contributed to the social, cultural and religious diversity that we find in India today.

Gandhi was assassinated in 1948 by Hindu extremist Nathuram Godse. Many right-wing Hindus were opposed to the partition of India and felt that Gandhi and the Congress had 'betrayed' the Hindus by allowing it to happen. Of course, it was primarily the British who had accepted the two-nation theory of the Muslim League and noting the enmity between the two communities, decided that the Hindus and Muslims were two separate nations. Gandhi did try to win the support of the right-wing Hindus. In April 1915 he attended the inaugural meeting of the Hindu Mahasabha at Hardwar. The Hindu Mahasabha's constituency comprised of high-caste Hindu businessmen and professionals in Uttar Pradesh. Gandhi maintained close relations with Madan Mohan Malaviya, the founder of the Benaras Hindu University and influential member of the Hindu Mahasabha. However, Gandhi did not give unqualified support to their agenda. Furthermore, he increasingly began to see that the problem of Muslim alienation from the Congress was caused as much by the intolerance of many Hindus as by Islamic fundamentalism. It is not necessary to discuss the politics of Hindu right-wing organizations here; the history of the Hindu right has been well documented (Jaffrelot, 1996). However, it is necessary to point out that Gandhi's approach, despite its limitations, was very different from theirs. Many Hindus did not believe in non-violence and *satyagraha* and did not agree with Gandhi's reading of the *Bhagavadgita*. They argued that the later enjoined violence in defence of one's faith. Some of his critics felt that Gandhi was inspired more by Jesus Christ and Christianity than by Hindu *dharma*, which insists that violence is often a matter of religious duty. In recent years, the rise of the BJP has coincided with the liberalization of the Indian economy. The Hindu right felt encouraged to think in terms of a global Hindu movement by appealing to the sentiments of its supporters and sympathizers residing abroad. Yet Gandhi remains the 'father of the nation' and the good performance of the Congress in the elections of 2004 and the swearing in of a Congress-led government shows that the protest vote is still very strong in India. It is, therefore, necessary to emphasize that Gandhi's ideas were powerful and although his main objective was to end British rule in India, his ideas influenced social movements even after his death and even outside India. In other words he has left a global legacy.

Other social movements

The *bhoodan* and *gramdan* movements were both inspired by Gandhian ideals. They are associated with Vinobha Bhave and Jayaprakash Narayan and their work formed a part of the overall *sarvodaya* movement (compassion through service). Its main aim was to promote work for public welfare by *lok sevaks* (servants of the people) who were trained in Gandhian institutions. The *bhoodan* movement involved giving land to the poor, and landowners were encouraged to join. The *gramdan* movement involved a process of democratization of village governance, aiming to bring all land in a village under the control of the village community and encouraging village self-sufficiency. It was, therefore, not based on the principle of ownership of private property, and many villages joined the movement. However, its achievements were limited (for example, the redistribution of a million acres of land that benefited over 200,000 families) and mainly symbolic, and due to a variety of reasons it waned (Wolpert, 1993: 359).

Three other movements are worth mentioning: the Jayaprakash Narayan movement to bring about social, political and economic change in India, the Chipko *andolan* (movement) which opposed the cutting down of trees for commercial purposes and the Naramada *bachao andolan* (Save the Naramada movement) to prevent the construction of the Narmada dam that would have displaced thousands of local people and had an adverse impact on the environment. The Jayaprakash Narayan movement was launched in the early 1970s against the corruption of Indira Gandhi's government. Students were mobilized to campaign against corrupt politicians. The movement also attacked blackmarketeering, profiteering and hoarding by capitalists that led to price rises. Other issues included land reform and unemployment. On 5 June 1974 Jayaprakash Narayan addressed a public meeting in Patna and declared: 'after 27 years of freedom, people of this country are wracked by hunger, rising prices and corruption … oppressed by every kind of injustice … it is a Total Revolution we want, nothing less!'[4] The movement started in Gujarat in 1974 and was sponsored by the *nav nirman* (new wave) *andolan*, which succeeded in discrediting the Congress administration of Chimanlal Patel, who was forced to resign. The movement then spread to Bihar. Unfortunately it led to violence, including clashes with the police and even Jayaprakash Narayan himself was injured. Indira Gandhi responded by imposing a state of emergency on 26 June 1975 and arresting the movement's leaders. Gandhi lost the general elections of 1977 and the period of emergency came to an end. For a short period of time Jayaprakash Narayan got the opportunity to promote his policies and programmes, and worked for a genuine devolution of power at village level. Under his guidance several parties united to form the Janata Party, and his goals were incorporated in its manifesto. The party won the general elections of 1977.

The Chipko *andolan* was a protest against the forest policy of the government in the Uttaranchal region of the northern state of Uttar Pradesh. It was started and led by Gandhian activists. India has considerable forest wealth, upon which the rural people of India depend for subsistence. Forests provide food, fuel and fodder and also stabilize soil and water resources. The commercial felling of forests and the nexus between corrupt politicians and businessmen and industrialists has led to the exploitation of forest resources and disregard for the rights of the people who depend on them for their livelihood. Although the Chipko movement started in the 1970s, there is a long history of protest in this region against the government's forest policy. The word 'chipko' means to hug and the activists by using the Gandhian method of *satyagraha* and non-violent resistance sought to end the destruction of forests by putting their own bodies between the trees and the contractor's axe. The movement achieved a major victory in 1980 when a fifteen-year ban on green felling was announced by the government of Indira Gandhi. The movement has spread to Himachal Pradesh, Karnataka,

Rajasthan, Bihar and Central India. It has also generated pressure for a natural resources policy which is more sensitive to people's needs and ecological requirements. Prominent Chipko leaders include Sunderlal Bahuguna, a Gandhian activist and philosopher. Another significant feature of the movement was that many of the activists were women. The activists wanted to promote the conservation and sustainable use of forest wealth for local benefit, and even the United Nations Environment Programme has noted its achievements.[5]

The Narmada *bachao andolan* that began in the late 1970s and early 1980s was another civil disobedience movement against the construction of the Narmada dam. The dam (and the Sardar Sarovar lake that would be created) will lead to the displacement of between 100,000 and 250,000 people in about 450 villages. The dam will affect mainly farmers and Adivasis but will also submerge some old and historic temples. The bulk of the finance for the construction of the dam was to come from the World Bank and the Japanese government. The movement was driven by the belief that modern developmental projects supported by the state ignore the economic needs as well as the civil rights of the rural poor. The only way to counter such tyranny is, therefore, through non-violent mass resistance. The two main leaders of the movement were Medha Patkar and Baba Amte, a Gandhian social worker, both of whom have also used fasting as a weapon with some success. In the 1990s, the author Arundhuti Roy also joined the movement. The World Bank set up a commission of enquiry and as its report was highly critical of the whole project, the bank withdrew its financial support in 1993. However, the government of Gujarat did not give up the project and resorted to ruthless repression to crush the movement. The organization that had been set up to represent the movement then challenged the legality of the project in the Supreme Court of India in 1994. It was accepted that there had been various irregularities in the implementation of the project but eventually the ruling did not stop the construction of the dam. This is what the state government of Gujarat had hoped for. Jayal has used the Narmada Valley projects to explore the relationship between state, society and democracy in relation to the achievement of specific goals of social transformation, namely, development. He concludes that the lack of autonomy of the state from powerful classes and its autonomy from marginalized groups may be seen as a factor contributing to its capacity to evade its proclaimed commitment to social justice and equity (Jayal, 2001).

Jogdand and Michael (2003: 7) argue that one of the negative consequences of globalization is environmental degradation. They write that 'much environmental damage has assumed global dimensions. Acid rain, global warming and deforestation have adversely affected the whole ecosystem of the earth and can only be solved on a global level'. These kinds of concerns led to the Stockholm Conference of 1972 and the Conference on the Environment and Development in Rio in 1991, both held under the auspices of the UN. They established a link between development and the environment and emphasized the importance of

sustainable development (Thomas, 1992). Environmental movements in India have, therefore, become an important part of global social movements.

Gandhi's main objective was to end British rule in India and therefore, his views and opinions on other struggles in other parts of the world may or may not be worth noting. However, his participation in the anti-apartheid movement is worth noting, as it was there that, for the first time, he used his technique of non-violent resistance. In 1945, the fifth Pan-African Congress endorsed Gandhian passive resistance as the preferred method for resistance to colonialism in Africa, however, after the Sharpeville massacre of 1960 many Africans, including leaders of the African National Congress, lost their faith in non-violence. Nevertheless, African leaders such as Nelson Mandela continued to be passionate admirers of Gandhi, whom he saw as a champion of the rights of the colonized and racially oppressed. Another black leader who was particularly impressed by the way in which Gandhi had channelled his anger at injustice into a constructive and creative non-violent engagement was Martin Luther King. Gandhi would not have aspired for sainthood, yet millions of Indians, as well as others, called him the Mahatma, the Great Soul. The reasons for this elevation of a mere mortal are not difficult to understand. Palkhivala writes that 'the Mahatma dealt with problems which are timeless and universal, because they spring from enduring weaknesses of human nature and human society. Since the solutions he found for them were based on eternal verities his influence and his relevance are also timeless and universal' (Palkhivala, 1984: 280).

There are many kinds of social movements in India and the whole of the South Asian region. The Adivasi and Dalit movements have already been discussed. There is also a women's movement, a human rights movement, a labour movement, a peace movement, a fair trade and development movement and finally an environment movement. The Chipko movement and the Narmada Bachao movement are two of the most high-profile environmental movements. The human rights movement addresses issues such as child labour in India, the women's movement addresses women's concerns, including dowry deaths, although it is not a homogenous movement. The peace movement looks into Indo-Pak relations while the labour movement covers trade union movements. The fair trade and development movement is interested in mass mobilization against the WTO as well as the impact of globalization, neo-liberal economic reforms and multinational corporations on the Indian economy and more specifically, on the poor. Finally, there is also a gay, lesbian, bisexual, transgender movement.[6] However, not all of them are inspired by Gandhi's ideas. Some of them, such as the gay and lesbian movement, are opposed to his advocacy of sexual abstinence. Parajuli argues that the emergence of new social movements coincides with the declining hegemony of the development discourse both in the developed and developing worlds. New social movements in the west reject the idea of linear progress and view modernity as a theory that is more exclusive than inclusive. The development discourse articulates a relation of domination-subordination between the developed and developing worlds. In India it has also led to the subordination of women, Dalits, tribals and minority populations (Parajuli, 2001; Pieterse, 2001).

Social movements try to bring about or resist social change. They try to influence the holders of economic and political power through mass mobilization. Camilleri and Falk argue that their mode of political action closely resembles Michel Foucault's conception of power. Instead of the 'traditional notion of state-centred power, of which "sovereignty" is the logical expression (that is power located at the centre of the state, "centred on the sole functioning of the law and on the sole functioning of prohibition"), Foucault postulates the dispersal of power within the social order, in other words a plurality of power woven into the whole fabric of society' (Camilleri and Falk, 1992: 221). Social movements in India are not new but are getting an impetus from the transnationalization of issues. They are influencing both domestic and foreign policy and this is reflected in the proliferation of political parties, and the growing pluralism that one finds in Indian politics in contemporary times. They are also demanding social justice. Collectively, social movements have become a force to reckon with.

Notes

1 Available at www.fordham.edu/halsall/mod/1947nehru1.htm.
2 Available at www.kric.org.in/v4/KHADI2.ASP.
3 Available at www.mkgandhi.org.swarajya.coverpage.htm.
4 Available at www.liberalsindia.com/freedomfirst/ff452-01.html.
5 Available at www.iisd.org/50comm/commdb/desc/d07.html.
6 Available at www.lib.berkeley.edu/SSEAL/SouthAsia/movements.html.

References

Agarwal, R. C., 1981, *Constitutional History of India and National Movement*, S. Chand and Co., New Delhi.
Attenborough, Richard (dir.), 1982, *Gandhi*, film, Sony Pictures.
Camilleri, J. A. and Falk, J., 1992, *The End of Sovereignty?*, Edward Elgar, Aldershot.
Chatterjee, P., 1993, *Nationalist Thought and the Colonial World*, Zed Books, London.
Corbridge, S., and Harriss, J., 2000, *Reinventing India*, Polity Press, Cambridge.
Datt, R. and Sundharam, K. P. M., 2001, *Indian Economy*, S. Chand and Co., New Delhi.
Gandhi, M. K., 1948, *Hind Swaraj and Indian Home Rule*, Navjivan Publishing House, Ahmedabad.
Hardiman, D., 2003, *Gandhi in His Time and Ours: The Global Legacy of His Ideas*, Hurst & Co., London.
Jaffrelot, C., 1996, *The Hindu Nationalist Movement and Indian Politics*, Hurst and Co., London.
Jayal, N. G., 2001, *Democracy in India*, Oxford University Press, Oxford and New Delhi.
Jayal, N. G., 2001, *Democracy and the State*, Oxford University Press, Oxford and New Delhi.

Jogdand, P. G. and Michael, S. M., 2003, *Globalization and Social Movements*, Rawat Publications, Jaipur and New Delhi.

Lewis, J., 2000, 'Afghanistan: the wounds of war' in Dutt, S., *UNESCO and a Just World Order*, NOVA, New York.

Nanda, B. R., 1974, *Gokhale, Gandhi and the Nehrus*, George Allen and Unwin, London.

Palkhivala, N. A., 1984, *We the People: India the Largest Democracy*, Strand Book Stall, Bombay.

Parajuli, P., 2001, 'Power and knowledge in development discourse: New social movements and the state in India' in Jayal, N. G. (ed.), *Democracy in India*, Oxford University Press, Oxford.

Pieterse, J. N., 2001, *Development Theory: Deconstructions/Reconstructions*, Sage, London, Thousand Oaks, CA, New Delhi.

Pylee, M.V., 1994, *India's Constitution*, S. Chand and Co., 1994.

Rahnema, M. and Bawtree, V., 2001, *The Post-Development Reader*, Zed Books, London and New Jersey.

Sethi, J. D., 1983, 'Gandhi betrayed', *Indian Express*, 6 October.

Thomas, C., 1992, *The Environment in International Relations*, Royal Institute of International Affairs, London.

United Nations, 1995, *Our Global Neighbourhood: Report of the Commission on Global Governance*, United Nations, New York.

United Nations, 1997, *An Agenda for Development*, United Nations, New York.

Vasquez, John A., 1990, *Classics of International Relations*, Prentice Hall, New Jersey.

Vincent, R. J., 1986, reprinted 1991, *Human Rights and International Relations*, Cambridge University Press, Cambridge.

Wolpert, S., 1993, *A New History of India*, Oxford University Press, Oxford.

7 A nation on the move: the Indian diaspora

The Indian diaspora is the third largest diaspora in the world according to some estimates (Bhat et al., 2002). People of Indian origin are found in five continents and in many countries such as Mauritius, where they are the single largest ethnic group, Fiji, Surinam, Trinidad and Tobago, Guyana and Nepal, where they form a substantial proportion of the host country's population, and in the United Arab Emirates, Qatar, Oman, Bahrain, Malaysia, Sri Lanka and Kuwait where they have a significant presence. According to the Report of the High Level Committee on the Indian Diaspora (RHLCID) published in 2002 the Indian diaspora today numbers over 20 million. This committee was set up by the Indian government in September 2000 under the chairmanship of MP L. M. Singhvi, former high commissioner to the UK, who has spent many years dealing with the Indian diaspora (Khan, 2002). It had been one of the BJP's election commitments that it would set up a committee on the Indian diaspora to study the needs and expectations of Indians living abroad. It wanted the Indian diaspora to invest in India, although there are ideological reasons also for this commitment; the BJP's concept of the Indian nation encompassed all Indians, or at any rate all Hindus, living all over the world and in many different countries. It has long embraced 'ethnic' rather than 'civic' nationalism. This committee submitted its report to the prime minister on 8 January 2002. A significant feature of it was the recommendation relating to dual citizenship, an issue raised over a decade ago by non-resident Indians (NRIs), soon after the launch of economic reforms in India. However, Singhvi noted that 'dual citizenship does not mean dual allegiance ... it will be permitted only for members of the Indian diaspora who satisfy the conditions and criteria laid down in the legislation to be enacted to amend the relevant sections of the Citizenship Act, 1955' (Khan, 2002).

International migration from the Indian subcontinent

Castles and Miller argue that 'international migration is not an invention of the late twentieth century, nor even of modernity in its twin guises of capitalism and colonialism. Migrations have been part of human history from the earliest times' (Castles and Miller, 1993: 3). The large-scale emigration of Indians took place mainly in the nineteenth and twentieth centuries, although migration from the Indian subcontinent started centuries ago. It has been noted in Chapters 1 and 5 that trade with other countries in other parts of the world was brisk in ancient India. Permanent settlements of Indian traders sprung up along the coast of East Africa and elsewhere. Indian traders, manufacturers and clove cultivators were concentrated in Zanzibar Island. They were both Hindus (mainly Vaishyas) and Muslims (Ismailis and Bohras). Apart from traders, Indian missionaries also went abroad. For example, Buddha's disciples went to neighbouring countries to spread Buddhism and settled there. Emperor Ashoka (268–39 BCE) embraced Buddhism and sent monks to central and eastern Asia to spread the gospel of Buddha. King Kanishka (first century AD) was another champion of Buddhism. During his rule, Buddhism spread to southern India, eastern Iran, Central Asia, China, Greece, Kandahar (now in Afghanistan), Southeast Asia and Indonesia (Narayan, n.d.). India's cultural influence on countries in Southeast Asia has also been noted in Chapter 1. Java was colonized by the Hindus between the first and seventh century. The Javanese were converted to Hinduism, Hindu kingdoms were formed, and an elaborate Hindu culture developed by the tenth century. Narayan argues that 'the people of Java came to share with the Indians their religions, languages, art and architecture, their cultural mores, and legal and political ethos and forms. This area was exposed to the "heaviest Indianization". The majority of the people of Bali island still practice Hinduism.' In Indochina the kingdoms of Fu-nan, Champa, Kambujadesa (Kampuchea), Angkor and Laos were also greatly influenced by Indian culture and civilization.

However, mass migration of people from the Indian subcontinent began only in the nineteenth century. Narayan, as well as the RHLCID, notes that the nineteenth and early part of the twentieth centuries witnessed unprecedented emigration of indentured and other labourers, traders, professionals and employees of the British government to the British, French, Dutch and Portuguese colonies in Asia, Africa, Latin America and the Caribbean. According to Peach, South Asian migration overseas has two main periods of direct outflow, and a third period of secondary movement. The first period was dominated by the indenture movement and extends from 1834 to 1920. Indenture replaced slavery; after slavery was abolished indentured labour was needed to work on plantations. Indians migrated in large numbers to Mauritius, British Guiana (Guyana), Natal (South Africa), Trinidad and Fiji among other places. Appleyard asserts that 'in the latter half of the nineteenth century, slaves were replaced by indentured workers as the main source of plantation labour. Indenture (or the "coolie system") involved recruitment of large groups of workers, sometimes by force, and their transportation to another area for work. British colonial authorities recruited over 30 million people from the Indian sub-continent' (Appleyard cited in Castles and Miller, 1993: 49). However, not all the migrants were indentured labour – some were railway builders and administrators. Some of the migration was free-market migration. Doctors, lawyers and traders migrated to areas where South Asian communities were settled.

The second phase of migration began after the Second World War and involved migration to developed countries such as the United Kingdom, United States of America, Canada, Australia and New Zealand, some European countries and various countries in the Middle East. Peach also identifies a third phase of migration and characterizes it as 'secondary migration, often forced, of the descendants of the first phase of migration'. The best-known example of this is the South Asians expelled from East Africa in the 1970s. He also mentions expulsions or repatriations from Burma and Sri Lanka and political flights of South Asians from Surinam and Fiji (Peach, 1994: 38).

There are push-and-pull factors that affect migration, especially voluntary migration. One of the factors affecting emigration from the Indian subcontinent after the Second World War was the upheavals of the 1947 partition. Thousands of people affected by partition left India and permanently settled abroad. However, the migrants were mainly economic. The most important single destination for South Asians living in the developed world is the United Kingdom. Of the 1.5 million living in Europe in the early 1990s, 1.2 million lived in the UK (Peach, 1994). Post-war labour shortage in the UK and the Commonwealth membership of the successor states of British India encouraged migration to the UK from these countries. Prior to the enactment of the British 1962 Commonwealth Immigrants Act, Indians had the right of entry and settlement in the UK. Peach (1994: 49) argues, however, that 'the movement to Britain should not be seen as a fortuitous outcome of a historical colonial tie. The British demand for labour was a particular example of a general Western European phenomenon'. These countries needed and attracted immigrant labour often from former colonies. According to Peach, migration from India (and Pakistan) peaked in 1965–74 and from Bangladesh in 1980–84. It is interesting to note, however, that by the end of the twentieth century, British born Indians outnumbered those born outside the UK, whether in India or elsewhere such as East Africa.

The United Kingdom

The RHLCID states that two-thirds of the Indian community in the fifteen member European Union (EU),[1] the largest economic entity in the world, lives in the UK, where they constitute the single largest ethnic minority group. From 'humble origins in the industrial and retail sectors, the Indian community has risen to become one of the highest earning and best-educated groups in the UK' (Government of India ((hereafter GI)), 2002: xix). Indians have been successful in various sectors of the economy such as business, information technology, health, the media and entertainment. There are several eminent British industrialists of Indian origin, including Lakshmi Mittal, the Hinduja brothers and Lord

Swaraj Paul. There are people of Indian origin in the British parliament, in both the House of Commons and the House of Lords. Lord Dholakia was the first British Indian chairman of the Liberal Democrat Party, the first Indian to occupy the top post in a mainstream political party. Indians have risen to high positions in the mainstream British media, including the BBC, the *Daily Telegraph* and the *Financial Times*. The contribution of people of Indian origin is increasingly recognized in mainstream British society. The Indian community has also formed a number of social, cultural and political organizations; trusts and charities have been set up by wealthy British Indian philanthropists to fund projects on health, education or other infrastructure in their home state and villages in India. During national crises and natural calamities in India, the community organizations raise generous contributions for relief and rehabilitation of the victims. The contributions of British Indians to the humanitarian assistance given to the people of Gujarat during the Gujarat earthquake in January 2001 is an example of these humanitarian activities.

The RHLCID states that the Indian community in the UK occupies a unique position, enriching British culture, society and politics, and contributing to making the UK a genuinely multicultural society. The report does not dwell on the problems experienced by the Indian community, although it does acknowledge that Indians have experienced racism. However, on the whole, Indians are considered a disciplined and model community with the lowest crime rates among all immigrant groups. The RHLCID asserts that the Indian communities' educational achievements and success in the political and economic fields in the UK and elsewhere 'have guaranteed that old stereotypes about India have faded and have been replaced by a new image of India as a dynamic nation' (GI, 2002: xix). It is unclear what the old stereotypes were, moreover, references to a new image of India as a dynamic nation is not much more than a promotion of the BJP's 'India Shining' campaign slogan of 2004 that highlights the (mainly economic) achievements of certain Indian communities. Even the editor of *Outlook* comments that 'since the news media is made up of people comprising India Shining, it did not submit the dubious slogan to the scrutiny and scepticism it deserved' (Mehta, 2004: 34). The Indian government also commends the efforts of British Indians in promoting bilateral relations between Britain and India, and clearly feels that the British Indian community has an interest in investing in India's future.

The United States of America

Another country in which Indians have done remarkably well is in the USA. The RHLCID notes that 'at 1.7 million and 0.6% of the total US population of 280 million, the Indian community enjoys the distinction of being one of the highest earning, best educated and fastest growing ethnic groups … their high levels of literacy, economic success, knowledge of English and experience with democracy in their home country has eased their transition in the land of their adoption' (GI: xx). Indian Americans are pursuing careers in the following high-profile occupations and sectors: medicine, engineering, law, information technology, international finance, management, higher education, mainstream and ethnic journalism, writing, films and music. They also work in real estate, retailing and agriculture and as taxi operators, factory workers and news-stand workers. Many Indian Americans are entrepreneurs. Restaurants, shops, motels and petrol stations in some of the large American cities such as New York are owned and run by Indians (Daniels, 1995). The RHLCID is very positive about the Indian community in the US and states that it reflects the diversity of India. It does not mention the ABCDs or the 'American-born confused *desis*' (people of Indian origin) but instead emphasizes that the first-generation Indian immigrants have successfully transmitted 'some of their attachment to their culture and traditions to the second generation' (GI: xx). Although it cannot be denied that Indians in the US do often promote Indian culture, the mingling of different cultures has led to a hybridization that many other studies highlight. The growth of hybrid cultures is not limited to the US alone, but is found in many other countries such as the UK. Caglar argues that 'designations of settlers in European societies now mark their identities as hyphenated: German-Turks, British-Pakistanis, French-Algerians. Such hyphenations, familiar from the US context, have gained prominence in European minority discourses as much as in the scholarly discourses of European anthropologists and sociologists' (Caglar, 1997: 171). Creolization and hybridization are concepts used in the critiques of cultures as homogeneous, bounded, continuous and incommensurable wholes. Anthias too argues that 'hybridity (and diaspora) has been central to the debate about cultural globalization, and has functioned to celebrate it. Such a cultural globalization has been seen as a challenge to ethnic essentialisms and absolutisms.' Moreover, a distinction needs to be made between transethnic and transnational. She argues that the concept of diaspora 'neglects the aspects of ethnicity that are exclusionary, for the commonality constructed by racism is different, and indeed may be transethnic rather than transnational' (Anthias, 2001: 632).

The RHLCID also fails to address two other issues: first the integration of new immigrants, often female, into British or American society, and second, the problems faced by new immigrants who have lost their jobs and fear that they will lose their right to live in the USA/UK. On the 7 September 2004, BBC television's *Newsnight* reported that hundreds of Indian doctors are stranded in Britain without jobs. Britain needs foreign doctors and the British government would like Indian doctors to apply. However, according to John Hutton, minister for health, they want specialists and consultants and not junior doctors. Junior Indian doctors however have got the wrong message and are taking the Professional and Linguistic Assessment Board (PLAB) examination (an examination they must pass if they wish to work in Britain) in large numbers. There is also evidence that they are being exploited, for example targeted by private landlords and housed in substandard accommodation. Many Indian software engineers had similar problems in the US a few years ago when they lost their jobs and were stranded with their families and without the green cards necessary for permanent residence (*India Today*, 2 July 2001). As the present author had the opportunity to work for a voluntary organization in the mid-1990s that was set up with the aim of helping new women immigrants from the Indian subcontinent integrate into British society and promote multiculturalism, the lessons learnt from the Multicultural Women's Association of Slough (MCWAS) will be discussed towards the end of this chapter in order to highlight some of the issues relating to women, culture and migration in developed western countries.

The RHLCID focuses mainly on the established Indian community, and states that 'for the first time, India has a constituency in the US with real influence and status. The Indian community in the United States constitutes an invaluable asset in strengthening India's relationship with the world's only superpower.' In Canada, Indians constitute 2.8 per cent of the total population of 30 million (GI, 2002: 185). They have a strong presence in the fields of medicine, academia, management and engineering. In general the Indian Canadians are a prosperous and well-educated community. Some of them maintain close personal ties with politicians in India and want India to be strong and play a role in the world commensurate with its importance.

The Gulf and West Asia

The Indian government is cognisant of the problems faced by Indian workers in the Gulf. Large-scale labour migration to the Gulf and West Asian countries occurred during the 1970s and 1980s on account of the oil and economic boom and acute labour shortages. Narayan notes that while there were only 14,000 Indians in the Gulf in 1948, their population had risen to 40,000 by 1971. The Indian government notes that currently there are more than 3 million Indian workers in the Gulf and West Asia/North Africa (*Year End Review 2004*). More than half are from the Indian state of Kerala. Zachariah argues that 'migration has been the single most dynamic factor in the otherwise dreary development scenario of Kerala during the last quarter' of the twentieth century. It has 'contributed more to poverty alleviation and reduction in unemployment in Kerala than any other factor' (Zachariah, 2001: 64). As Kerala has become so dependent on migration and remittances, policies on migration should form an essential part of the state's planning process. This is particularly important since there is evidence to suggest that emigration is declining. In the past there was a demand for unskilled labour from the state for the construction industries of the Gulf countries, but this demand has declined. Kerala workers therefore have to acquire new skills and be able to compete with workers from other Indian states and other parts of Asia to get jobs not just in the Gulf but also in other countries.

About 70 per cent of the Indian population in the Gulf and West Asia consists of semi-skilled and unskilled workers, 20–30 per cent consists of Indian professionals and while-collar workers (doctors, engineers, architects, chartered accountants and bankers), and a small fraction is composed of domestic help. The contributions of these workers to the Indian economy is recognized by the RHLCID and the Indian government. The former notes that 'remittances to India from the Gulf, long recognized as a significant contribution to India's balance of payments, are mostly made by Indian workers in the first category' (GI, 2002: xiii), i.e., semi-skilled and unskilled workers. The first Gulf War hit Indian workers and India hard. Following Operation Desert Storm, the number of Indians in Iraq was reduced to a handful. The Indian community in Libya has also shrunk, mainly due to an economic slowdown, from almost 40,000 in the mid-1980s to about 12,000 in 2000–01. However, on a visit to Dubai in December–January 2003–04, the present author noted the presence of Indian workers and businesses in the city. Although it is not always easy to distinguish Indians from Pakistanis or Bangladeshis, it may be safely concluded that large numbers of South Asians are employed by the airport authorities, hotels and the tourism industry, shops and businesses. Shops run by Indians sell Indian products including medicines/drugs and pharmaceutical products, computers and software. Indian professionals such as accountants earn high salaries but semi-skilled workers too appeared to be content and hotel workers commented that Dubai was a safe city to live in. However, the Indian media frequently reports that some Indian workers in Dubai are unhappy and even suicidal (*The Statesman*, 18 December 2004).

Most of the Gulf countries do not grant citizenship to Indian workers, regardless of their employment category. The high turnover because of the nature of job contracts and personal and family commitments has ensured that the Indian population in the Gulf has retained active familial and economic links with India. Indian schools have also been established in several Gulf countries for educating the children of the Indian workers. The Indian government is aware that 'the conditions of employment and emoluments vary greatly between the various categories of employees. While professionals are allowed to bring their families with them (even here there are many restrictions), labourers are not. The latter category is prone to exploitation both in the Gulf countries and at home' (GI, 2002: xiv). They are often exploited by recruiting agents, forced to live in substandard accommodation and work well beyond the legal eight hours per day. Some employers withhold employees' salaries and return passages, deduct fees from their salaries and take away their passports on arrival. Moreover, they may not have access to medical facilities. They are 'at the mercy of their employers, reinforced by laws requiring local official sanction for a change of job, or for an exit permit to return to India' (GI, 2002: xiv). Women recruited as housemaids and domestic workers are often ill-treated. Pettman argues that 'the growing feminisation of migrant labour flows from South and Southeast Asian states ... is part of globalisation processes ... more and more women are on the move, from rural to urban areas, to EPZs, and across state borders'. Unfortunately, as women, they are 'bearers of sex and signifiers of cultural difference' and are often 'vulnerable to exploitation, unwelcome advances, or actual violence. This is especially where they are seen to be "out of place", beyond protection or control of family, male kin or community' (Pettman, 1998: 393). According to the RHLCID and, as previously mentioned, also the Indian media, Indian workers in the Gulf are often unhappy and depressed and many even commit suicide. Some are used by drug smugglers, leading to their execution under local laws. The problems faced by Indian workers in the Gulf and Middle East are similar to the problems faced by Filipino workers working abroad (Pettman, 1998). On their return to India, Indian workers are often harassed and exploited by the customs authorities at airports. White-collar workers are more concerned about higher education for their children in India and investment incentives.

The committee visited the Gulf countries in 2000–01 and met the representatives of the migrant Indian workers. Their report states that the Indian population in the Gulf is an important contributor to India's economy and the Indian government should give priority to their welfare. The representatives of the migrant Indian workers suggested several measures for safeguarding their interests. These include the institution of effective measures by the ministry of labour to prevent malpractices by recruiting agents in India; negotiation of a 'standard labour export agreement' with all the Gulf countries prescribing a minimum wage, free housing, medical care, limits on daily working hours, overtime allowance rates, return air tickets and compensation for on-the-job death or injury; setting-up of agencies by the state governments to advise prospective Indian workers about their rights and obligations; frequent visits by the consular officers in the Indian Missions in the Gulf countries to the labour camps; and regular consultations by the Indian welfare/consular officers with their counterparts in the respective Labour Ministry of the host country (GI, 2002).

The RHLCID has noted that the protector of migrants in the Indian ministry of labour is charged with the function of protecting the interests of India's overseas blue-collar workers. The committee also undertook an examination of state-level initiatives and noted that 'Kerala had taken commendable initiatives to safeguard the interests of its overseas blue-collar workers' (GI, 2002: xv). The report also notes that the Conference of Welfare Officers of Indian Missions/Posts in the Gulf countries held in New Delhi in October 2001 had come up with useful recommendations, including: the supervision of contracts and improvement of recruitment procedures; expansion of the provision for setting up welfare funds by Indian missions abroad as well as the provision of legal assistance; arrangements for accident insurance cover; provision of a death allowance and assistance for skills upgradation to ensure better remuneration of Indian workers abroad. The committee noted that several additional measures were being considered by the government of India, including the establishment of a Central Manpower Export Promotion Council; an Overseas Workers'

Welfare Fund to help stranded and disabled workers; and special insurance for Indian workers abroad through the New India Assurance Company to cover premature repatriation due to harassment, unemployment benefits, rehabilitation packages and medical benefits.

The committee was of the view that certain measures should be implemented as soon as possible. These included the setting up of a welfare fund for repatriated workers and workers in distress; the negotiation of a standard labour export agreement with the host countries; tightening supervision of both the employment contracts and conditions of India's overseas workers by the Indian missions; launching the aforementioned insurance schemes expeditiously; establishing mechanisms for the provision of legal assistance locally, and instituting training programmes for human development and skills upgradation. The committee recommended that appropriate legislative and administrative measures should be taken to ensure that the concerns of the Indian overseas workers are fully and satisfactorily addressed.

The Caribbean: Trinidad and Tobago, Guyana, Suriname, Central and South America

The Indian diaspora in the Caribbean and Latin American countries numbers over 1.1 million, the former accounting for around 1 million. People of Indian origin constitute over 40 per cent, 51 per cent and 35 per cent of the total populations of the former British colonies of Trinidad and Tobago, Guyana and the Dutch colony of Suriname respectively (GI, 2002). These Indians went to the Caribbean as indentured labour, and after more than a century of toil and struggle in a hostile and discriminatory environment, have attained both economic status and political eminence. The RHLCID also comments that while the relatively small number of Indians in the rest of Central and Latin America have acculturated and intermarried, retaining only symbolic attachments to their Indian origin, most of the Indian migrants in the Caribbean have retained significant elements of their cultural heritage, having resisted attempts to convert them to Christianity at considerable economic and social cost to themselves. On the basis of this information, it may be argued that where there are large, cohesive immigrant communities which have identities based on religion, culture and place of origin, they will resist conversion and assimilation. Where immigrant communities are small and fragmented, conversion and assimilation will take place. It is interesting to note that the committee did not show any preference for assimilation. On the contrary its report appreciates the Indian community's desire to maintain its distinctive identity. It observes that 'their social exclusivity and aloofness has set them apart from the indigenous populations, except in Jamaica where inter-racial marriages have taken place. They have built a large number of temples and mosques and set up their own cultural and religious associations' (GI, 2002: xxi). However, other sources have highlighted that ethnic and cultural differences have led to tensions between the Asian and Caribbean communities of Trinidad and Tobago (NDTV, 25 December 2004). The

RHLCID notes with pride that a large number of Surinamese Indians and other people of Indian origin in the Caribbean have emigrated to Canada, the US and the Netherlands where they have better opportunities; and finally that prominent political and other distinguished personalities from the region include Basdeo Panday, currently prime minister for a second term in Trinidad & Tobago, Cheddi Jagan, the first Indo-Guyanese president, Bharat Jagdeo, his successor, J. Lachmon in Suriname, the famous writer Sir V. S. Naipaul and the former secretary-general of the Commonwealth, Sridath Ramphal.

Africa

Indians began to migrate to Africa centuries ago, first as slaves and then as indentured labour. The latter were mainly from the provinces of Bihar, Eastern Uttar Pradesh, Tamil Nadu and Andhra Pradesh. The next wave of migrants were free migrants. Indian labour was used to build railways in East Africa and also in plantations, dockyards, coal-mines and for domestic work. Over time the Indian community became prosperous and rivalry began between them and the white population in the area of trade and commerce. In South Africa they faced the racial discrimination against which Gandhi began a movement in the late nineteenth century. At present there are over 700,000 people of Indian origin in Mauritius, comprising around 60 per cent of the population. Around 30 per cent of Reunion's population is also of Indian origin. There are also large numbers of people of Indian origin in countries such as Kenya, Uganda, Tanzania, Zambia, Zimbabwe and Nigeria. In the early 1960s there were 360,000 people of Indian origin in East Africa. However, after some of these countries became independent in the 1960s they began to discriminate against and even expel Asians. In 1972 President Idi Amin expelled all Ugandan citizens of Asian origin. At present there are around 100,000 people of Indian origin in Kenya, 90,000 in Tanzania and 12,000 in Uganda (GI, 2002: 94). Large numbers of East African Asians migrated to Britain in the 1960s and 1970s; their investment in and contribution to the British economy is worth noting as they brought with them capital as well as skills.

Southeast Asia

India's interactions with Southeast Asia since ancient times have been noted elsewhere in this book. The RHLCID notes that 'its imprint is visible even today in the language and literature, religion and philosophy, art and architecture, of the whole of Indo-China, Myanmar and South-East Asia' (GI, 2002: xxii). However, large-scale migration took place only in the nineteenth and twentieth centuries. Some of these migrants were indentured labour while others were traders, clerks, bureaucrats and professionals. The report comments that 'thousands of Indians were mobilized to fight in the Indian National Army (INA) [formed by Subhash Chandra Bose] in Malaya and to contribute to the cause of Indian independence'.

After independence Indians continued to migrate to Thailand, Malaysia, Singapore, Brunei and Indonesia in search of employment. According to the RHLCID the size of the Indian population in the various countries of Southeast Asia are as follows: 7,600 in Brunei, 55,000 in Indonesia, 1.67 million in Malaysia, possibly 2.9 million in Myanmar, 38,500 in the Philippines, 307,000 in Singapore, 85,000 in Thailand and a very small number in Cambodia, Laos and Vietnam. Economic growth created job opportunities that attracted the Indian migrants and which ranged from blue-collar jobs in the construction and hospitality industries to employment with Indian companies, international (mainly UN) organizations, multinationals, banks, consultancies and financial institutions and recently the IT sector. However, economic decline, instability and conflict has left some Indian communities impoverished such as in Myanmar and has also led to their flight to more prosperous regions. The RHLCID notes that in Singapore, one of the most prosperous states in the region, Indians 'are represented at the highest levels of the civil services, judiciary, business and politics' (GI, 2002: xxii). They are on the whole integrated well with the local population but are culturally very active, and have preserved their traditions and maintained links with India. Other studies have also attempted to analyze the problems faced by Indian communities in countries like Malaysia where they have been marginalized. Chakraborti (2004: 217) argues that 'the Malaysian Indians belong to the poorest groups in the plantation villages and among the urban poor. The socio-economic position of the Indians lag behind the other ethnic groups and inadequate policy attention has been accorded to this group in the government's development efforts.'

The Asia-Pacific region

Indian communities are to be found in several countries of the Asia-Pacific region. There are both people of Indian origin and non-resident Indians (Indian citizens living abroad) living in Australia and New Zealand. There are close to 200,000 Indians/ people of Indian origin living in Australia, 55,000 in New Zealand and 50,000 in Hong Kong (GI, 2002). Many Indo-Fijians fled to Australia and New Zealand following the coup in 1987. Migration to Australia from the Indian sub-continent increased after the restrictive immigration policy was relaxed in 1966. Many Anglo-Indian families migrated to Australia. The film *36 Chowringhee Lane*, directed by Aparna Sen and starring Jennifer Kendall, wife of famous Indian film star Shashi Kapoor, is a story about an elderly Anglo-Indian school teacher living alone in Calcutta. She is urged by her relatives who have migrated to Australia to join them but she is reluctant to leave the city she knows so well. Apart from Anglo-Indians, all kinds of Indian professionals such as engineers, doctors, accountants and IT specialists also migrated to Australia and New Zealand. There are also about 10,000 Indian students in Australian universities. There are also Indian traders, taxi drivers and restaurant owners, often with their own associations. In Hong Kong, the Indian community is quite diverse, ranging from wealthy businessmen to labourers. The RHLCID remarks that the links of the Indian community in Hong Kong with India are basically cultural and not adequately commercial. The Indian communities in Japan, Taiwan and South Korea are quite small but relatively wealthy and include prosperous Sindhi business families and diamond merchants. The Indian community in the region has on the whole integrated well with the local population but is also culturally very active and has preserved its traditions and maintained family and cultural links with India.

The RHLCID has clearly avoided political controversies. However, it has not ignored the plight of the Indo-Fijians. It notes that 'the history of the still 340,000 strong Indian community in Fiji has been quite tragic. From the days of indentured labour, to the post independence phase when jealousy of their economic status and political activism prompted several anti-Indian coups, the Indian community has been at the receiving end' (GI, 2002: xxiii–iv). The people of Indian origin have maintained a separate identity based on ethnic origins. However, the indigenous Fijian population has shown hostility towards them and have attempted to prevent them from wielding political power. Castles and Miller too note that 'a number of post-colonial interethnic conflicts (for example, hostility against Asians in Africa, against Chinese in Southeast Asia, against Indians in Fiji) have their roots in the divisions brought about by indenture' (Castles and Miller, 1993: 49). The report expresses the opinion that 'the future of the Indian Diaspora in Fiji is rather bleak' (GI, 2002: xxiv). Many Indo-Fijians are planning to migrate again to any developed country that is willing to accept them.

The Indian diaspora has played an important role in promoting India's relations with several countries, mobilizing political support on issues of vital concern to India in countries like the US and the UK, and in India's economic growth and development and during national crises. The Indian media, too, is waking up to the fact that overseas Indians are doing very well. *India Today* noted in its Republic Day special issue on 26 January 2004 that 'a new tribe of British Indian is making its mark in every sector, be it business, politics, media or entertainment. And testifying to this success are their growing numbers in *The Times*' Who's Who.' The article mentions spice girl/entrepreneur Meena Pathak who has also been awarded an OBE, Krishnan Guru Murthy, Channel 4 news presenter, consultant psychiatrist Raj Persaud and Arun Sain, chief executive of Vodafone group and one of the UK's highest paid executives (Bhasi, 2004: 25–6).

The Indian Diaspora and the government of India

On 21 August 2001, 'in recognition and appreciation of the constructive economic, political and philanthropic role played by the Indian Diaspora and its achievements' (GI, 2002: xxvii), the High Level Committee on the Indian Diaspora made two interim recommendations to the government of India. The first was that an annual '*Pravasi Bharatiya Divas*' (Overseas Indian Day) should be observed in India and abroad on 9 January every year (a symbolic date as Gandhi returned to India from South Africa on this day); the second was that '*Pravasi Bharatiya Samman* Awards' should be awarded to eminent PIOs (persons of Indian origin) and NRIs. On 22 December, 2003, the Indian parliament passed a bill to grant dual citizenship to the people of Indian origin belonging to sixteen specified countries, mainly in North America and western Europe, as well as Indian citizens who choose to acquire citizenship of any of these countries at a later date. The bill received the president's assent on 7 January 2004. Accordingly, the first *Pravasi Bharatiya Divas* was held in 2003, and the second in 2004. The overseas Indians who attended were delighted that the Indian government had delivered on its promises of dual citizenship for *pravasis* (overseas Indians) in the sixteen select countries, compulsory insurance schemes to protect workers in the Gulf, and the reservation of seats in academic institutions for resident children of Gulf and Southeast Asian NRIs. However, the Indian media was critical on account of the poor organizational skills demonstrated by the Indian government which offended many invitees (Khan, 2004: 20–3).

The RHLCID notes the contributions made by the Indian diaspora and makes recommendations for strengthening ties with it, addressing their concerns and tapping their expertise in the economic rejuvenation of India as well as encouraging them to invest in India. The committee noted (and, indeed, it is common knowledge) that the Chinese diaspora's investment in China is far greater than the Indian diaspora's investment in India. The Chinese Diaspora contributes about 70 per cent of all inward foreign investment into China. Ethnicity is not the only factor that has prompted them to invest in their country of origin. The Chinese government launched economic reforms in 1978, invested in physical and social infrastructure, offered special tax incentives, and gave assurances for fast-track clearances of investment proposals. The committee therefore strongly recommended to the government of India that, if it wished to increase FDI inflows both from its diaspora and other investors, it needed to invest heavily in infrastructure, both social and physical, create a conducive operating environment for conducting business through administrative reforms, and implement the so-called second generation reforms to increase the dynamism of the Indian economy.

The Indian diaspora's presence in their countries of settlement has catalyzed demand for Indian goods and services, ranging from food and fashion to the Indian entertainment industry. This is corroborated by the personal experiences and observations of many other writers and NRIs. For example, Roy writes about the 'Indianization' of Houston, Texas. She cites veteran Bharatnatyam and Kuchipudi danseuse, Rathna Kumar who comments that thirty years ago the city had only a handful of Indians 'struggling to create an identity and a market of their own'. Today Houston has an Indian population of about 100,000 and the city is full of Indian stores and its Little India in Hillcroft has become a tourist attraction (Roy, 2004). Similarly in the United Kingdom, Leicester's Belgrave Road also combines commerce with culture. Moreover, members of India's diaspora, who are employed by the top consultancies and multinational firms can facilitate access to the top management, support India's trade and FDI initiatives, and help in increasing its share of products outsourced by large multinational corporations. Indian professionals, traders and businessmen can provide useful insights for market penetration strategies and use their networks for the entry of new products and services from India.

The contributions made by Indian doctors and medical practitioners, both at home and abroad, are also important. Indian medical institutions train thousands of doctors, many of whom emigrate and make a significant contribution to the countries in which they settle. However, NRIs have also invested in hospitals and clinics and in the provision of health care and medical services in India. In the 1970s the Indian government became concerned about a 'brain drain'. It realized that some of India's best scientific and engineering talent was emigrating to the USA and even offered them incentives to return (Lall, 2001: 147–8). Research and development opportunities offered by major multinationals in other countries (for example Nortel in Canada) were also attracting India scientists and engineers. The emigration of Indian engineers increased significantly in the wake of America's IT-led economic boom in the 1990s, 'to which Indian IT professionals have made a visible, high-profile and widely recognized contribution' (GI, 2002: xxxiii). However, according to a report entitled *Trends in International Migration* Guyana is the biggest net exporter of skilled staff followed by Jamaica and Haiti. The percentage of their graduates living in Organization for Economic Co-operation and Development (OECD) countries is 83 per cent, 81.9 per cent and 78.5 per cent respectively. Emigration of highly skilled workers from Asia is moderate in comparison. Only 3 per cent of known Indian and Chinese graduates live in the OECD countries (Turner, 2005).

The Indian government has for many years has ignored the Indian communities living outside India. Many Indian nationalists argued that, as these people had voluntarily left their country of origin, they should not be given (or allowed to retain) Indian nationality but should adopt the nationality of the country in which they were permanently settled. The Indian government was also reluctant to grant dual citizenship to overseas Indians because it felt that this could undermine India's security. For example, separatists are not loyal to the Indian state and often operate from across the border or even from distant lands. The Khalistan movement was one such movement. However, economic interests have motivated the Indian government to grant dual citizenship to certain categories of NRIs, and also to take an interest in the welfare of Indian blue-collar workers in the Gulf. The RHLCID emphasizes that NRIs want to invest in India, and that they have strong cultural and family ties with the country and its people. In self-interest, the Indian government has emphasized ethnicity and culture, and praises Indian communities that have maintained their cultural traditions and values, as well as individuals who have done well in various fields. In reality, Indians living abroad often have hyphenated or hybrid identities, such as British-Asian or Indian-American. Moreover, the emphasis on cultural differences can be divisive and even promote racism inadvertently. The present author's research on South Asian women and multiculturalism in Britain in the 1990s revealed many problems that immigrants faced, and also the fuzziness surrounding the concept (Dutt, 1996). Kazancigil writes that multiculturalism is a democratic policy response for coping with cultural and social diversity in society. It 'embodies the ideal of reconciling respect for diversity with concerns for societal cohesion and the promotion of universally shared values and norms' (Kazancigil, 1996: 6–7). Countries such as Australia, Canada and Sweden have officially adopted multiculturalism. However, other academics argue that multiculturalism 'currently means no single thing, that is, it represents no single view of, or strategy for, contemporary complex societies' (Vertovec, 1996: 51).

There are many problems with multiculturalism. Firstly, as Anthias and Yuval-Davis point out, the notion of multiculturalism assumes that cultural collectivities are static, with fixed boundaries and no space for growth and change. It is also simplistic to assume that members of minority collectivities are homogeneous, and that all members of a specific cultural collectivity are equally committed to that culture (Anthias and Yuval-Davies, 1992). Issues of identity cannot be reduced to identification with the cultural/ethnic group. Moreover, studies of South Asian women's ethnic identity have shown that their construction of their ethnic and gender identities is complex and located in specific contexts (Woollett et al., 1994). The construction of identities, therefore, is not unproblematic. Identities are not 'given' but are constructed and can, therefore, be deconstructed and reconstructed. There is a growing body of literature on this (Krause and Renwick, 1996). I also would like to argue that many women (and also men) do not like to be stereotyped. This is one reason why the Multicultural Women's Association of Slough (MCWAS) did not appeal to young South Asian women born and brought up in the UK. Moreover, such a construction of cultural/minority collectivities could not explain internal power conflicts and interest difference within them, along the lines of class and gender and of both a political and cultural nature (Patel, 1991). In Slough, for example, some members of the Indian Women's Association formed a new organization in the 1990s, a break-away group called the Eastern Women's Cultural Organization. The desire to control the organization was one reason why this split occurred. Other researchers have written about similar cases in other cities in the UK. For example, in Coventry in the 1980s, proposals for a community centre for Muslims revealed the extent to which the community was divided (Ellis, 1991). The study also found that local authority officers tend to attribute a cohesiveness to ethnic minority 'communities', which they would not expect to find among indigenous whites. They also tend to assume that a small number of 'leaders' speak for the entire community.

Second, feminist critics of multiculturalism such as Sahgal and Yuval-Davis argue that both black and white anti-racists and multiculturalists have allied themselves with the traditional male leaders of minority communities who often have a rigidly patriarchal view of the role of women. So, while fundamentalist leaderships have been the main beneficiaries of the adoption of multiculturalist norms, women from minority communities have had to conceal their oppression in order to uphold the honour of the family and the community (Sahgal and Yuval-Davis, 1992). If multiculturalism is reduced to preserving the 'traditions and cultures' of different ethnic minorities, it diverts attention from the promotion of women's rights. Kandiyoti argues that 'wherever women continue to serve as boundary markers between different national, ethnic and religious collectivities, their emergence as full-fledged citizens will be jeopardised'. It is therefore necessary to construct identity which allows for difference and diversity without making women its hostages (Kandiyoti, 1991: 435). Moreover, the postmodern emphasis on difference and identity (that encompasses hybridity and diaspora) has shifted the earlier focus on social inequality and exclusion as a result of material conditions to the cultural bases of racist subordinations, inequalities and exclusions (Anthias, 2001). In other words, the postmodern discourse has become hegemonic within the social sciences. In any case, western governments are not always eager to promote multiculturalism. A report produced in 2000 by the commission, chaired by Lord Bhikhu Parekh, entitled *The Future of Multi-ethnic Britain: The Parekh Report*, was not particularly well received by the British government. While Parekh called for the empowerment of the marginalized, a spokesperson for the British prime minister, Toy Blair, said that the government was disappointed that the commission had allowed the whole debate to be 'skewed' in the way they had (*India Today*, 20 November 2000).

Notes

1 It should be noted that since the 1 May 2004, the EU has twenty-five member states.

References

Anthias, F., 2001, 'New hybridities, old concepts: the limits of "culture"', *Ethnic and Racial Studies*, 24: 4.
Anthias, F. and Yuval-Davis, N., 1992, *Racialized Boundaries*, Routledge, London.
Ballard, R. (ed.), 1994, *Desh Pardesh: The South Asian Presence in Britain*, Hurst and Co., London.
BBC4, 2004, *From Raj to Rhondda: How Asian Doctors Saved the NHS*, 14 November.
BBC4, 2004, *Coolies: How Britain Reinvented Slavery – The Story of Enforced Indian Labour*, 17 September.
Bhasi, I., 2004, 'Rising to conquer', *India Today*, 26 January.

Bhat, C. S., Laxmi Narayan, K. and Sahoo, S., 2002, 'Indian diaspora: a brief overview', *Employment News*, 27: 38, 21–2 December.
Brah, A., 1996, *Cartographies of Diaspora: Contesting Identities*, Routledge, London.
Channel 4, 2004, *The Great British Asian Invasion*, 7 October.
Brown, J. M. and Foot, R. (eds), 1994, *Migration: Asian Experience*, Macmillan, Basingstoke.
Caglar, A. S., 1997, 'Hyphenated identities and the limits of "culture"' in Modood, T. and Werbner, P. (eds), *The Politics of Multiculturalism in the New Europe*, Zed Books, London and New York.
Cashmore, E. E., with Banton, M., 1994, *Dictionary of Race and Ethnic Relations*, Routledge, London.
Castles, S. and Miller, M., 1993, *The Age of Migration*, Macmillan, Basingstoke.
Chakraborti, T., 2004, 'Minority underclassed: negating a sociological truism in Malaysia' in Ghosh, L. and Chatterjee, R. (eds), *Indian Diaspora in Asian and Pacific Regions: Culture, People, Interactions*, Rawat Publications, Jaipur and New Delhi.
Daniels, R., 1995, 'The Indian diaspora in the United States' in Van der Veer, P., *Nation and Migration: The Politics of Space in the South Asian Diaspora*, Pennsylvania University Press, Philadelphia.
Dhume, S., 2002 'From Bangalore to Silicon Valley and back: how the Indian diaspora in the U.S. is changing India', in Ayres, A. and Oldenburg, P. (eds), *India Briefing*, M. E. Sharpe, New York and London.
Dutt, S., 1996, 'Women and multiculturalism in Slough, East Berkshire', conference paper presented at the Annual Conference of the British Association of South Asian Studies (BASAS), University of Bradford, April.
Ellis, J., 1991, *Meeting Community Needs*, Centre for Research in Ethnic Relations, University of Warwick.
Government of India, 2002, *Report of the High Level Committee on the Indian Diaspora*, New Delhi, available at http://indiandiaspora.nic.in/contents.htm.
India Today (International), 2004, 'The OBIs: A generation of overseas-born Indians that dares to dream', 19 January.
Kandiyoti, Deniz, 1991, 'Identity and its discontents: women and the nation', *Millennium: Journal of International Studies*, 20: 3.
Kazancigil, A., 1996, in Inglis, C., *Multiculturalism: New Policy Responses to Diversity*, UNESCO Policy Paper 4, UNESCO.
Khan, N. H., 2002, 'Dual citizenship', *India Today*, 21 January.
Khan, N. H., 2004, 'Pravasi Bharatiya Divas 2004', *India Today*, 26 January.
Krause, J. and Renwick, N. (eds), 1996, *Identities in International Relations*, Macmillan, Basingstoke.
Lall, M. C., 2001, *India's Missed Opportunity*, Ashgate, Aldershot.
Mehta, V., 2004, 'You can't buy the people of India', *Outlook*, 24 May.
Modood, T. and Werbner, P., 1997, *The Politics of Multiculturalism in the New Europe*, Zed Books, London and New York.
Narayan, K. L., 'Indian diaspora: a demographic perspective', Centre for Study of Indian Diaspora, University of Hyderabad, Hyderabad, India, n.d.
NDTV, 2004, *Indian Rhythms – Island Stories: A Taste of Chutney*, 25 December.
Patel, P., 1991, 'Multiculturalism: the myth and the reality', *Women: A Cultural Review*, 2: 3.
Peach, C., 1994, 'Three phases of South Asian emigration' in Brown, J. M. and Foot, R. (eds), *Migration: Asian Experience*, Macmillan, Basingstoke.
Pettman, J. J., 1998, 'Women on the move: globalisation and labour migration from South and Southeast Asian States', *Global Society*, 12: 3.
Roy, R., 2004, 'Diaspora dandy', *The Statesman*, 18 December.

Sahgal, G. and Yuval-Davis, N., 1992, 'Fundamentalism, multiculturalism and women in Britain' in Sahgal, G. and Yuval-Davis, N. (eds), *Refusing Holy Orders: Women and Fundamentalism in Britain*, Virago Press, London.

Turner, D., 2005, 'Graduate brain drain threatens poorest nations, says OECD', *Financial Times*, 23 March.

Van der Veer, P. (ed.), 1995, *Nation and Migration: The Politics of Space in the South Asian Diaspora*, Pennsylvania University Press, Philadelphia.

Vertovec, Steven, 1996, 'Multiculturalism, culturalism and public incorporation', *Ethnic and Racial Studies*, 19:1 (January).

Woollett, A., et al., 1994, 'Asian women's ethnic identity: the impact of gender and context in the accounts of women bringing up children in East London' in Kum Kum Bhavani and Phoenix, Anne (eds), *Shifting Identities Shifting Racisms: A Feminism and Psychology Reader*, Sage, London.

Zachariah, K. C., 2001, 'Social, economic and demographic consequences of migration on Kerala', *International Migration, Quarterly Review*, 39: 2.

8 India's foreign policy and global politics

This chapter argues that India's foreign policy post-independence was based on idealism as well as realism and the desire to function as an autonomous actor in world politics after centuries of colonial rule. Events proved that states had to deal with diverse issues, some involving the management of bilateral relations and others involving international relations and multilateralism. Moreover, India was a developing state, not a major power, and had to contend with asymmetrical relations with the west, notwithstanding the nonaligned movement (NAM). In more recent years, the Indian government has acknowledged that Indian foreign policy has to take into account the fact that we live in an interdependent world, and that globalization affects India.

One of the aims of this chapter is to discuss the domestic, international and ideological factors that have affected India's foreign policy. Domestic factors include political leaders and political parties, public opinion and issues such as economic development and growth, ethnic conflict and humanitarian crises. International factors include bilateral relations with neighbouring states and superpowers, as well as issues relating to national and international security, foreign trade and investment, migration, multinational corporations and defence (Kapur, 2002). Many nationalists and old-fashioned Indian academics and politicians make two claims about India's foreign policy goals: first, that they are based on a national consensus (for example, the UPA government's *Year End Review 2004*), and second, that they have remained the same since Nehru's time. Such academics and analysts either do not want to adopt a critical stance or genuinely believe that the state is a monolithic entity. It is worth examining these claims, especially in the light of what other foreign policy analysts have to say. A review of the literature on Indian foreign policy indicates that there are a variety of perspectives, an examination of which serves to enrich the debate.

As a leading member of the Indian National Congress and the first prime minister of India, Nehru was bound to play an important role in the formulation of India's foreign policy. However, his elitist background, pride in India and identity as an Indian, his desire to modernize India and his internationalist outlook also influenced India's foreign policy. Nehru's rationalism has already been referred to in Chapter 4. He believed that progress was the development and spread of science and industry – the progressive universalization of reason. This development and spread of science and industry led to the creation of a single world, one marked by increasing commonalities and interdependence. He argued that 'the world has become internationalized ... no nation is really independent, they are all interdependent' (Seth, 1993: 461). Nehru equated internationalism with progress and rejected narrow nationalism. He once said: 'I do not want our country to be a victim of that narrow nationalism which is now to be found in almost all countries of Europe and Africa'. The oppressed had a right to national independence. Where nationalism was self-consciously anti-imperialist and internationalist, it was an essential part of the progress of history. In his opinion 'the British Empire and real internationalism are as poles apart, and it is not through that empire that we can march to internationalism' (Seth, 1993: 462). He categorically stated that 'there can be no real internationalism unless the component parts are entirely free ... Thus though we must look forward to an international order, we can only reach it by achieving national independence first' (Seth, 1993: 462). Nehru's internationalism was not an international order maintained by the major powers, but based on the sovereign equality of all nation-states, a principle recognized by the UN in theory. Although Nehru is considered to be the chief architect of India's foreign policy, he has himself documented the Indian National Congress's policies on India's involvement in international affairs and events in his book, *The Discovery of India*. Many Indian writers argue that few Indians were experienced in international affairs, and so the conduct of India's international relations after independence was left to Nehru's judgement. But this may well be due to the fact that Nehru was internationally respected, and had a high status in international society that other political leaders did not have.

Commenting on India's foreign policy in the evolving global order after the end of the Cold War, Muchkund Dubey, professor of South Asian studies and former foreign secretary, writes that 'the primary purpose of any country's foreign policy is to promote its national interest – to ensure its security, safeguard its sovereignty, contribute to its growth and prosperity, and generally enhance its stature, influence, and role in the comity of nations' (Dubey, 1993: 117). Although Dubey makes a general statement about a country's foreign policy, he is obviously implying that this statement applies to India. Kegley and Wittkopf point out that, 'according to realist theorizing, the primary goal of states' foreign policies is to ensure their survival. From this viewpoint, strategic calculations about national security are the primary determinants of policymakers' choices. Domestic politics and the process of policy making itself are of secondary concern' (Kegley and Wittkopf, 1999: 53). However, as we shall see later, defining India's national interest may not be such a simple task. Dubey's statement appears to be based on realist principles relating to national security, but he voices normative concerns, too, when he writes that 'a country's foreign policy should also be able to serve the broader purpose of promoting peace, disarmament, and development and of establishing a stable, fair and equitable global order. This latter purpose may at times appear to conflict with the former, but in the medium and long run it too is likely to serve the country's national interest' (Dubey, 1993: 117).

The subject of war and peace often gives rise to controversy, for example, that India's defence expenditure is high and is considered by many (e.g. peace movements; the authors of *Human Development in South Asia 2001*) to be wasteful in view of the mass poverty in the country. In Bandyopadhyaya's view, 'there is no escape from the conclusion that, given the economic compulsions and the constitutional and political set-up, the only rational stance for our diplomacy can be one of avoidance of war to the best of our ability. Peace is a minimum precondition for our economic development' (Bandyopadhyaya, 1991: 63). However, after several wars with Pakistan and one with China India is not prepared significantly to reduce defence spending, although it also gives importance to confidence-building measures in South Asia. It is interesting to note that, although India is a relatively new modern nation-state, themes such as war and peace are not foreign concepts or western importations. Ancient Indian writers such as Kautilya wrote about inter-state relations. Jha explains that, in Nehru's view, two aspects of India's foreign policy – the 'positive aspect of peace' and the desire to promote 'a larger degree of cooperation among nations' – were directly traceable to the influence of India's past thinking, i.e. its cultural and philosophical heritage, on the formulation of foreign policy. Discussing war and peace, he writes that even the *Bhagavadgita*, which is apparently a plea to engage in war, in fact recommends non-violence as a way of life and prescribes war only as a last resort. This is also evident from the role of Krishna as an emissary of the Pandavas.[1] He goes time and again to the Kauravas to counsel them to see reason and to avoid war. He also counsels patience to the five Pandavas and tells them to ask for what is due to them in a proper and friendly way. It is only when all efforts to secure justice through peaceful negotiation fail that Krishna exhorts the Pandavas to wage war (Jha, 1989: 45). In fact, part IV of the Indian constitution dealing with the Directive Principles of State Policy asserts that the state shall endeavour to secure (a) the promotion of international peace and security; (b) the maintenance of just and honourable relations between nations; and (c) respect for international law and the settlement of international disputes by arbitration (Article 51, Constitution of India). These principles are clearly based on the UN Charter also. Article 33 of the UN Charter says that 'the parties to any dispute, the continuance of which is likely to endanger the maintenance of international peace and security, shall, first of all, seek a solution by negotiation, enquiry, mediation, conciliation, arbitration, judicial settlement, resort to regional agencies or arrangements, or other peaceful means of their own choice' (www.un.org). Article 42 asserts that 'should the Security Council consider that measures provided for in Article 41 would be inadequate, it may take such action by air, sea, or land forces as may be necessary to maintain or restore international peace and security' (www.un.org). India is a founder-member of the UN and its specialized agencies. Professor M. S. Rajan writes that 'support to, and strengthening of, the world organization is an important goal of India's policy'. India has faith in the UN and its purposes and principles, however, like many other member-states, it too has at times been disappointed and frustrated with the functioning of the organization, its limitations and the constraints under which it operates (Rajan, 1998: 102).

In Rajan's opinion, 'since the geopolitical bases of India's role in foreign relations have largely remained constant, so also have the goals of policy since Nehru's time'. These were and still are the pursuit of nonalignment; maintenance of world peace; peaceful settlement of disputes; peaceful coexistence of nations of diverse social/political/economic systems; opposition to the remnants of colonialism and neo-colonialism; promotion of its own economic development (and that of other Third World countries); and support to and strengthening of international organizations – the UN in particular. Rajan also argues that these goals are based on a broad national consensus and reflect, not merely 'official policy' but the 'foreign policy of the people of India' as claimed by a former minister, N.D. Tiwari (Rajan, 1998: 75).

However, India's foreign policy post-independence was not based on Indian thought on international relations (apart from Nehru's ideas), but shaped by global politics. Soon after India became an independent state, the Cold War started. America's policy of the containment of communism affected all parts of the world. Countries that were not in the Soviet bloc were often under pressure to join a military alliance led by the American superpower for strategic reasons. In 1949, NATO came into existence and was followed by the Baghdad Pact, the Central Treaty Organization (CENTO) and the South East Asian Treaty Organization (SEATO). India's response to the Cold War was a kind of internationalism, co-founding the NAM in the 1950s together with Yugoslavia, Indonesia, Egypt and Ghana.

Nonalignment

Most scholars agree that nonalignment is one of the main goals of India's foreign policy and Rajan holds that it is also the means by which other goals are sought to be achieved. Thakur, too, expresses the opinion that the only conceptual underpinning Indian foreign policy has is to be found in non-alignment (Thakur, 1994: 14). For India, 'nonalignment not only meant maintenance of independence, sovereignty and equality in foreign policy and relations; it also meant ... opposition to division of the international community into blocs/groups of any kind – political, economic or ideological' (Rajan, 1998: 76). India was opposed to Great Power hegemony, the cold war between superpowers and the co-option of other countries into this war, and the stationing of foreign military forces or bases or facilities on Indian territory, since they impinge on India's freedom of policy/action; and in favour of peaceful co-existence of nations of different political, economic and social systems (Rajan, 1998: 76). Outlining the principles on which India's foreign policy was to be based, Nehru said in a radio broadcast on 7 September 1946 that

> We shall take full part in international conferences as a free nation with our own policy and not merely as a satellite of another nation ... we propose, as far as possible, to keep away from the power politics of groups, aligned against one another, which have led in the past to world wars and which may again lead to disasters on an even vaster scale. (cited in Thakur, 1995: 25)

Nehru also made references to anti-racialism and the desire for friendly relations with Britain, the Commonwealth, the US, China and the Soviet Union (Thakur, 1994: 25). Kapur holds that the principles and ideologies that underpinned Nehru's broad thinking stemmed from two sources; anti-imperialism and socialism. The first flowed from the long history and tradition of the Congress Party's struggle for independence. The second stemmed from a variety of influences which were essentially Fabian in character, though during his youth he was also attracted to Marxism. Kapur opines that the framework Nehru designed for India's foreign policy essentially mirrored these influences, the concrete manifestations of which were anti-colonialism and non-alignment. Such a policy, which constituted the two pillars of India's foreign policy, was almost universally accepted by Indian public opinion and by the mainstream (Kapur, 1994: 181).

Emphasizing the importance of nonalignment, the then prime minister, Indira Gandhi, told the Colombo Nonaligned Summit Conference (1976) that 'in a fast changing world, nonalignment remains the bulwark of an ever-widening area of peace, a shield against external pressures and a catalyst of a new world economic order based on equality and justice' (Rajan, 1998: 76). Thakur holds that nonalignment was the result of a common sense approach to India's foreign policy after independence. It combined pragmatism with prudence. It was pragmatic in recognizing the need to establish mutually beneficial relations with as wide a circle of countries as possible in order to reduce political and economic dependence on a narrow range of benefactors and protectors. It was prudent in rejecting ideological blinkers, averting domestic divisiveness, and, by incorporating an ever-expanding number of newly independent countries into a growing movement, enlarging the areas of the world insulated from the chill of the Cold War in a rigidly bipolar world (Thakur, 1994: 14). Indeed Indira Gandhi pointed out that nonalignment was the only practical policy for the preservation of the newly won independence of many countries. For them the choice between one military bloc or another seemed irrelevant and unreal. Their choice was 'between independence and dependence, between progressing through cooperation and perishing through confrontation' (Rajan, 1998: 76).

However, in another speech delivered in the same year in Mauritius, Indira Gandhi argued that the policy had indigenous roots. She said that 'nonalignment is the translation in international affairs of the Gandhian concept of tolerance, for it connotes constant efforts towards peaceful co-existence and cooperation' (Rajan, 1998: 76). Bandyopadhyaya, too, stresses that Nehru and other Indian policy-makers were 'profoundly influenced by the nonviolent national movement led by Mahatma Gandhi, as well as by the modern Indian tradition of idealist political thinking in general' (Bandyopadhyaya, 1991: 71). Thus, the policy of nonalignment was not meant to serve India's interests only but 'was, from the beginning, conceived as also serving the interests of world peace' (Rajan, 1998: 76). India was one of the co-founders of the NAM, the roots of which may be traced to personal friendships between Egypt's Gamal Abdul Nasser, India's Jawaharlal Nehru and Yugoslavia's Josip Broz Tito. The states which were invited to the first NAM conference in Belgrade in 1961 were expected to adhere to the following:

i an independent policy based on peaceful coexistence and nonalignment
ii a consistent support for national liberation movements
iii non-membership in multilateral military alliances involving great-power conflicts
iv a refusal to permit the lease of military bases in the context of great-power rivalry
v non-membership in bilateral or regional defence arrangements made in the context of great power conflicts (Thakur, 1994: 16–17).

Thakur writes that 'NAM's origins unquestionably lay in a reflexive antipathy by the new states towards attempts at assimilating their identity into the Cold War rivalry'. The three co-founders of the movement were united in their opposition to great power alliances: Egypt to the Baghdad Pact, India to the Baghdad Pact and SEATO, and Yugoslavia to the Warsaw Pact. In 1970, five additional principles were adopted by the NAM to which India already subscribed. They were: i) strengthening the United Nations, and the role of the nonaligned countries within the organization; ii) anticolonialism and antiracialism; iii) peaceful settlement of disputes; iv) arms control and disarmament; v) economic independence and cooperation on the basis of equality and mutual benefits (Thakur, 1994).

However, nonalignment obviously did not preclude a special relationship with one of the superpowers, the Soviet Union. Describing India's relations with the Soviet Union, Dutt writes that 'the political relationship was buttressed by a close economic relationship and an even closer defence link'. India could rely on the Soviet Union to supply arms and often paid in Indian rupees, thus saving scarce foreign exchange. It was also able to obtain the technology to manufacture arms indigenously from the Soviets (Dutt, 1999: 65). Hewitt explains that, although Soviet aid did not match US and western aid in terms of value, it was less conditional, and had a high military component. Also, the Soviets acknowledged India's influence in the nonaligned and Third World. They were also keen to show that they were on the side of poor, ex-colonial nations and committed to their industrial development (Hewitt, 1997). Many Third World countries felt that they had an ideological affinity with the Soviets and Thakur writes that 'for about its first thirty years the nonaligned movement seemed to be in a relationship of political sympathy with the Soviet Union and a reflexive antipathy towards the United States' (Thakur, 1994: 27). However, the Cold War offered the Third World an opportunity to obtain aid from both the superpowers; they sensed that both of them wanted to increase their spheres of influence and gain allies. Kapur holds that India was the first developing country to benefit from the Cold War situation. It obtained concessionary aid from the two, competing and opposed blocs that dominated the international system.

National security and regional hegemony

However, the question is: did the policy of nonalignment protect and promote every aspect of India's national interest? If it did not, what were India's other main foreign policy goals and concerns? According to Kapur, with the death of Nehru, the exalted image that the world had of India began to fade, although there were other reasons also including events which occurred before his death. India's priorities too seemed to have changed. India's military action in December 1961 to 'free' Goa from the Portuguese was criticized by many world leaders who felt that it was not only unnecessary but also that by resorting to violence, India was not practising what it preached, i.e., the effectiveness of peaceful methods. Second, India's humiliating defeat in the war with China in 1962, a country with which it has a border dispute, and the external assistance it received from the US, Britain and France, exposed its weakness and inability to safeguard its vital interests. The Indo-Pak War of 1965 also exposed how badly India was managing its bilateral relations with Pakistan. Finally, the Bangladesh War of Liberation in 1971 proved that India was 'now considered a full-blooded regional power with hegemonic designs of her own – a state of affairs that disqualifies a nation from playing the type of role that Nehru had defined' (Kapur, 1994: 130–3).

A number of factors were therefore responsible for the new emphasis on national security rather than on international issues and participation in world politics. There were also changes in the global environment. By the mid-1960s, most of the colonies in Africa had achieved their political independence, so India's role in this sphere had become redundant. The apartheid issue in South Africa too had been taken over by the African states. With the emergence of an East-West *détente*, the need for mediation had also become less important.

Nehru's successors, Lal Bahadur Shastri, Indira Gandhi and Rajiv Gandhi, tacitly acknowledged this change of priorities and reinforced them. Under Indira Gandhi, India attempted to become militarily strong by investing in research and development, and by buying sophisticated arms abroad. A nuclear programme was initiated and India conducted an underground nuclear explosion in May 1974. The country also launched into the space sector by blasting, in July 1980, India's own satellite launching vehicle, SLV-3, thus placing in orbit an indigenously designed and built thirty-five-kilogram satellite (Kapur, 1994: 134), the forerunner of a series of giant satellite launchers. India's telephone companies and television channels now largely depend on these satellites (*India Today*, 18 August 2003).

On the other hand, it is worth noting that India's relations with its neighbours are supposed to be guided by the *Panchsheel* (five principles) which were incorporated in a treaty between India and China over Tibet in 1954. These five principles are:

- mutual respect for each other's territorial integrity
- mutual non-aggression
- mutual non-interference
- equality and mutual benefit
- peaceful co-existence (Wolpert, 1993: 364).

These principles are compatible with the idea of nonalignment. However, it is questionable whether India could have implemented them and at the same time pursued a policy of regional hegemony. In fact, India's relations with almost all its neighbours in South Asia gradually deteriorated. This was partly due to India's bad management of bilateral relations. However, Professor Muni explains that 'there has emerged a powerful school of thought in India's policymaking and strategic community which prefers to take neighbourhood relations in its stride and rejects the need to stretch policy efforts to cultivate reluctant and defiant neighbours beyond a limit' (Muni, 1993: 189). Yet India cannot afford to be arrogant or, worse still, complacent. In Muni's opinion, Indian policy has to address the task of building a stable, secure, and cooperative neighbourhood in three specific issue areas: relations with the Great Powers, bilateral relations, internal conflict and turbulence in South Asia and regional development (Muni, 1993: 191).

Relations between India and Pakistan are a good example of regional dynamics and since the terrorist attacks on the World Trade Centre in New York and other sites in the US on 9/11, and especially 13/12 (the terrorist attacks on the Indian parliament in 2001) – have become an aspect of global security. India and Pakistan have always felt threatened by each other, and the Kashmir issue has led to several wars. The Kargil War in 1999 led to a complete breakdown of trust between the two countries, especially as it came so soon after the Lahore Declaration was signed by the Indian prime minister, Atal Bihari Vajpayee, and the Pakistani prime minister, Nawaz Sharif. The Agra Summit, held in July 2001, failed. President Musharraf insisted that no progress could be made towards normalization of relations with India unless the Kashmir issue was resolved in accordance with the wishes of the people of the state; India, on the other hand, wanted to discuss other bilateral issues such as cross-border terrorism. By the end of the year, the two countries were on the brink of war (Dutt, 2002). Yet, within a few years – in January 2004 – the thirteenth SAARC Summit was held in Islamabad. Did this indicate that the Indian government is prepared to make concessions? Former prime minister Vajpayee did initiate a thaw in relations with Pakistan in 2003 (*India Today*, 9 June 2003), however, speeches made by Indian politicians (including the prime minister in Parliament) and diplomats on various occasions in recent years indicate that India's position has not changed significantly since the Agra Summit. In December 2004 the Indian prime minister, Manmohan Singh, told the Rajya Sabha that confidence-building measures would not make any progress if the flow of terrorists from across the border (meaning Pakistan) goes on 'without any check and without control'. India intended to pursue the path of co-operation and dialogue with Pakistan but would not compromise its 'basic national interests' (*The Statesman*, 22 December 2004).

In December 2004 the Indian foreign secretary, Shyam Saran met his Pakistani counterpart Riaz Khokar in Islamabad. They reviewed progress made on a number of issues such as the control of narcotics, Sir Creek, the Khokrapar-Munnabao rail link and the Srinagar-Muzaffarabad bus service and also exchanged views on the Baglihar project, the problems of fishermen, the re-opening of consulates in Karachi and Mumbai and the issue of prisoners. India and Pakistan have also set up an Indo-Pakistan joint study group to look at preferential trading arrangements and also the possibility of enhancing economic co-operation in other areas.[2] Trade between India and Pakistan is growing. According to the Associated Chambers of Commerce and Industry (Assocham), bilateral trade between these two countries is expected to touch US$10 billion by 2010 from $345 million in 2003–04, provided the execution of the South Asian Free Trade Agreement (SAFTA) is not thwarted by the two countries. About 71.2 per cent of Pakistan's exports to India consists of fruits and nuts, spices, leather, textile yarn, fabrics, made-up articles and raw wool, while 53.7 per cent of India's exports to Pakistan consists of oil meals, drugs and pharmaceuticals, chemicals, dyes/intermediates, coaster chemicals, rubber-manufactured products except footwear, paints/enamels/varnishes, plastic and linoleum products and inorganic/organic agro-chemicals. However, 'to achieve the projected $10 billion-mark by 2010, the two countries will have to diversify the existing trade basket' (*The Statesman*, 21 and 28 December 2004; 5 January 2005).

There are different perspectives within India on India's relations with Pakistan. Bajpai identifies three main perspectives: the hyperrealist, Nehruvian and neo-liberal. The hyperrealists are concerned about India's security and consider Pakistan to be an aggressive state and a serious threat to India. India, therefore, must be militarily prepared to meet the Pakistani threat. The Nehruvians, on the other hand, have more faith in diplomacy, in agreements between the two countries and in confidence-building measures. The neo-liberals believe that states pursue not only military power but also economic well-being. They believe that trade and economic interactions will lead to the improvement of relations between India and Pakistan (Bajpai, 2001).

Nonalignment and post-Cold War relations

Before we proceed to examine India's foreign policy in the twenty-first century, an era in which India is showing more awareness of global trends, we need to ask ourselves how the end of the Cold War has affected India's foreign policy, especially its policy of nonalignment. Rajan asserts that, 'although nonalignment had emerged as a new, additional foreign-policy choice in the years of the cold war and the bipolar world, its continued relevance had little to do with either of the contexts' (1993: 142). The relevance of the policy was reaffirmed by the nonaligned foreign ministers' conference held in Accra in September 1991, and again at the nonaligned summit conference held in Jakarta in September 1992. The NAM continued to highlight the concerns of the southern countries. In April 2000, India's minister of external affairs, Jaswant Singh, asserted at the thirteenth Conference of Foreign Ministers of the Movement of Non-Aligned countries that 'it is necessary for us to rededicate ourselves to the fundamental values and principles of the Movement ... We need to ensure that decisions affecting us are taken with our active and effective participation, and taking full account of our interests and concerns. Such decisions cannot be left to be taken by others in forums where we have no effective voice' (Ministry of External Affairs, Government of India, 2001: 34). Rajan also argues that although the NAM has contributed to the end of bipolarism and the cold war, 'it will be a long time before the demand of NAM for the abolition of all nuclear weapons is accepted. The world is divided between the nuclear haves and the nuclear have-nots' (Rajan, 1993: 143). It is worth pointing out here that India's policy on the issue of nuclear weapons has remained almost unchanged over the decades. India has asserted that it is in favour of the abolition of all nuclear weapons but would not sign the Nuclear Non-proliferation Treaty (1968) because it is discriminatory. On 21 December 2004, prime minister Manmohan Singh told the Rajya Sabha: 'There is no ambiguity about our nuclear policy. India is a nuclear weapon state and we are a responsible nuclear power' (*The Statesman*, 22 December 2004). He added that India was committed to promoting non-discriminatory nuclear disarmament. Chellaney points out that one of the reasons why India had to exercize its nuclear option and conduct nuclear tests in May 1998 is because the costs of remaining a nuclear threshold state were too high (Chellaney, 1998–99). However, ever since China tested the atom bomb in 1964, a nuclear India has been on the Hindu nationalist agenda. In May 1998 L. K. Advani asserted that 'we have always said we are in favour of exercising the nuclear option'. According to an *India Today*–ORG MARG opinion poll, the nation was behind him. Eighty-seven of the respondents approved of India carrying out the nuclear tests (*India Today*, 25 May 1998). Unfortunately for India, the nuclear stalemate between India and Pakistan has eroded the advantage that India had over Pakistan in terms of conventional weapons. A balance of power has emerged in the region which also includes China. However, Paranjpe argues that India rejects the balance-of-power approach to security and 'looks at the world through the conceptual lenses of a cooperative society'. The balance-of-power or deterrence approach is essentially status quo-ist in nature. The Indian policy framework, on the contrary, is rooted in the approach to development – economic, political and social (Paranjpe, 1998: 142).

In Rajan's opinion, 'nonalignment may be said to be only the latest name or label for an old, surviving feature of the sovereign-nation-state system – the struggle of the small/weak states (the overwhelming majority) against the hegemonism of the very small group of Great Powers' (Rajan, 1993: 143). NAM considers itself to be the 'voice of the developing world', 'the main forum representing the interests and aspirations of the developing world'. Its membership has grown from 25 at its inception to 113 today. NAM declares that the end of the Cold War should have led to greater efforts on the part of the international community to deal with economic and social development issues, however, this has not happened. On the contrary, there has been a decline in the resources made available for international development cooperation. The needs of the developing countries continue to be marginalized.[3]

In June 1992, Indian prime minister Narasimha Rao asserted that 'the pursuit of a nonaligned foreign policy is even more relevant today than ever before. Nonalignment basically consists of the espousal of the right of nations to independence and development, regardless of the bloc phenomenon' (Rao, 1993: 143). Paradoxically, the end of the Cold War has made India more dependent on the US and other developed western states. Rajan almost laments that 'now it can obtain military stores only from the United States and other Western states and on the terms and conditions that they lay down' (1993: 144). However, his fears are not justified. Russia remains India's number one supplier of military equipment. Most developing countries are on a path of dependent development. Even the import-substitution strategy created dependence on foreign capital goods – machine tools, plants and technology (Smith, 1996: 145). However, Rajan believes that 'the opening up of India's economy to external economic forces and institutions in the process of merging the hitherto-autonomous economy in the global economy is threatening to erode the economic base of India's nonalignment'. The earlier economic policy was meant to reinforce India's policy of (political) nonalignment *vis-à-vis* the Great Powers. The loan that India took from the IMF in the early 1990s also alarmed many Indians as loans are often associated with indebtedness in the developing world. Both Rajan and Kapur voice the fear that economic liberalization may gravely undermine India's traditional independence in the matter of foreign-policy decision-making. The complacent feeling that India is physically too large and economically too powerful to suffer such a fate might turn out to be a self-deception (Rajan, 1993; Kapur, 2001: 352). Also in Rajan's opinion, India is not playing as active a role as it should in world affairs because of its increasing, if subtle, dependence on the political goodwill of other, advanced, nations. However, this does not mean that US policy towards India is unfavourable. On the contrary, the US has displayed, in recent years, more respect for India's nonalignment and its role as a regional power and as a kind of model for other countries of the Third World (Rajan, 1993).

Globalization and foreign policy

Chris Hill (2003) argues that globalization has not made foreign policy redundant. It has, however, increased the influence of economics on politics. He argues that globalization is not about the spread of universal values primarily, but about the creation of an integrated world capitalist market. His astute observations about foreign policy in the post-1991 period help us to understand how the Indian government is approaching relations with other states and international institutions. He writes that 'much of foreign policy for modern states is about promoting prosperity as much as security, and indeed about blurring the two concepts together' (Hill, 2003: 13). In 2000 the then external affairs minister, Jaswant Singh, declared that 'foreign policy is inextricably linked with trade, commerce, economy. Hence, in today's world the ascendancy of foreign economic policy over foreign political policy'. He also added that the former concerns 'bread and butter' and should benefit 'all the citizens of the land' (Singh, 2000: 57). The UPA government too asserts that its foreign policy recognizes that 'the lines dividing the domestic from external, the political from the economic, are becoming increasingly blurred'.[4] However Hill also recognizes that although 'in some areas of economic and social life governments' role may be extremely limited as they bend the knee before the efficiency of the market principle, but this does not mean that it is non-existent; far from it, in fact. Governments simply become subtle and varied in their strategies for protecting the welfare of their citizens' (Hill, 2003: 14).

Indian foreign policy in the twenty-first century

India's foreign policy for the twenty-first century was summarized by foreign secretary Kanwal Sibal on 23 January 2003 at the Geneva Forum. India faces many challenges, he stated, and they include peace and security in its neighbourhood. For example, 'the combat against international terrorism presents an immense challenge.' India's stance on the events of 9/11 are well known. India sympathized with western countries dealing with the threat posed to their security and the security of their citizens by terrorist groups such as Al Qaeda. Pledging his country's support, Prime Minister Vajpayee declared on 14 September 2001 that India was ready to co-operate with the United States in the investigations into this crime and 'to strengthen our partnership in leading international efforts to ensure that terrorism never succeeds again' (Dutt, 2002). On 13 December 2001, the Indian parliament was attacked by terrorists and the incident almost led to a war with Pakistan. India, for several years now, has openly accused Pakistan of promoting terrorism. In his speech, Kanwal Sibal also explicitly referred to Pakistan. He claimed that 'Pakistan was fully involved in the creation and unleashing of the Taliban on the hapless Afghans. The Al Qaeda networks were built under its nose. Together with Afghanistan, Pakistan became the epicentre of international terrorism. So long as this activity promoted Pakistan's strategic interests and was directed against India, it was ignored by the West. Now we know at what cost' (Sibal, 2003). He went on to add that the forces behind the Taliban and Al Qaeda had not been exterminated, and that they had been displaced from Afghanistan but had re-emerged in the North West Frontier Province and Baluchistan in Pakistan. More fears were expressed about Pakistan's intentions. The speech partly addressed a western audience and played on western fears regarding Islamic fundamentalists, international terrorists, weapons of mass destruction and Pakistan's 'nuclear connection' with North Korea. Sibal acknowledged that in recent years Pakistan had been rewarded for co-operating with the west against terrorism but did not consider it to indicate a real change in policy. He emphasized that 'innocent' Indian citizens had been victimized for the previous two decades. The victims he referred to were either residents of the state of Jammu and Kashmir or Hindu pilgrims travelling through areas bordering Pakistan. Sibal asserted that Pakistan relies on terrorism as a form of proxy war and an instrument of foreign policy: 'This has made terrorism a major security threat and countering it a predominant foreign policy challenge for us.' He also made two other points about Pakistan's relationship with the Taliban. He argued that according to conservative estimates, the extensive cultivation of opium in Afghanistan had provided the Pakistani establishment with between US$90 million and $136 million per annum for at least seven years. He then went on to accuse Pakistan of using this money to 'finance its proxy war in Jammu and Kashmir, equip, train and arm terrorists and infiltrate them into India with weapons and modern communication equipment'. As regards Afghanistan, he emphasized that peace and stability in that country would depend on the economic reconstruction of the country. Second, he argued that peace and stability in Afghanistan is crucial for regional peace and stability. India has provided humanitarian, financial and project assistance to Afghanistan in recent years.

However, Sibal's speech made it very clear that India's foreign policy aims to promote both security and economic interests. He stated:

Energy security, creating favourable conditions for our economic development, coping with the consequences of instability or military conflict in the middle east, the reform of the Security Council, promoting multi-polarity, finding an adequate response to doctrines diluting the principles of sovereignty and seeking to establish the right to intervene, promoting a more equitable equation between the developed and the developing world in the political, economic and technological domains are some of the challenges facing Indian foreign policy. (Sibal, 2003)

The Indian government also gives priority to safeguarding its security interests in its neighbourhood. The Indian government is concerned about the Maoist insurgency in Nepal, the peace process in Sri Lanka, illegal migration from Bangladesh and the advantage that insurgents take of the porous borders between the two countries, as well as the porous borders between India and Bhutan and India and Myanmar. India is trying to promote good and mutually beneficial relations with all of these states to stabilize the region and promote economic projects.

Further afield, India is interested in forging a good relationship with Iran and the Central Asian republics. Iran and India are 'interested in forging a long-term strategic relationship built around energy security and transit arrangements' (Sibal, 2003: 1–2). One of the transnational oil pipelines that India wants to construct is the Iran-Pakistan-India pipeline; the other two are the Myanmar-Bangladesh-India pipeline and the Turkmenistan-Afghanistan-Pakistan-India pipeline (Singh, 2005). India and the Central Asian republics are also 'exploring new avenues of co-operation'. These countries buy Indian drugs and pharmaceuticals and information technology.

India is also concerned about Iraq's future. It was once the source of 30 per cent of India's oil imports and employed about 90,000 Indians, but after the first Gulf War many Indian workers left Iraq. India holds that Iraq should comply with UN resolutions and that sanctions should be lifted for humanitarian considerations if it does. As discussed in Chapter 7, there are also three million Indian expatriates in the Gulf region. The Indian government is concerned that military action in Iraq will lead to more bitterness and violence and create a more unstable and volatile situation.

In an era of economic growth, Indian foreign policy has to give considerable importance to economic factors in international relations. This was highlighted by the minister of external affairs, K. Natwar Singh on 19 January 2005. He asserted that 'as India marches on the path of sustained economic growth, achieving levels of 6-7 per cent of GDP growth per annum, its demand for energy, particularly for oil and gas, continues to soar'. India produces 32 million tonnes of petroleum per annum, but actually requires 113 million tonnes. As India's economy grows in coming years, this gap could increase over the next five to twenty years (Singh, 1995). India is, therefore, underlining the need for 'oil diplomacy'. One of the initiatives taken by the Indian government has been to organize a Round Table of Asian ministers on regional co-operation in the oil economy. It attracted twelve ministers and deputy ministers from Asia's principal producing and consuming nations, and had as its theme 'Stability, Security, Sustainability through Mutual Interdependence'.

East Asia is one of India's foreign policy priorities. The Indian government emphasizes India's Asian identity; it is an Asian country, the second largest both demographically and geographically and 'developments in Asia impinge directly on our security and strategic interests' (Sibal, 2003: 4). The Indian Ocean straddles the most important sea routes that connect the oil producing region of the Gulf with the consumer countries of East Asia. In 2002, Japan, Korea, China and India were the second, fourth, sixth and eighth largest importers of oil in the world. Ensuring the security of sea routes is, therefore, a major priority for all of these countries. However, India would like closer relations with the countries in this region and especially the Asian regional organizations. The Indian government is not happy about the fact that India has been excluded from the Asia-Pacific Economic Co-operation (APEC) and also the Asia-Europe Meeting (ASEM). It has, however, 'a sound framework for meeting the challenges ahead' (Sibal, 2003: 4). India has become a member of the ASEAN regional forum and a summit partner with ASEAN. Sibal asserts that the ASEAN countries have realized the value of engaging India for maintaining greater political, security and economic balance in the region. Special trade and investment arrangements are being made through an India-ASEAN free trade area to be brought about by 2011. Bilateral arrangements are also being made between India and Thailand and India and Singapore, for example. According to P. Prakaspesat, vice chairman of the Federation of Thai Industries, the Free Trade Agreement signed by India and Thailand 'will enhance economic and trade ties'. He was speaking at a seminar organized by FICCI on 17 December 2004. Trade between the two countries was then worth around US$1.4 billion and was expected to cross the $2 billion mark by the end of 2004; by 2008 it could touch $5 billion. He also urged Indian industry to invest in Thailand and emphasized that the country had liberal investment policies. However, Malaysia and Singapore are India's largest trading partners in Southeast Asia. In December 2004 the Malaysian prime minister Seri Abdullah Ahmad Badawi visited India. Malaysia is keen to expand business ties as well as trade with India, and the two countries have decided to set up a joint committee to look at specific areas of co-operation, including education, IT, biotechnology and agricultural research (*The Statesman*, 18, 22 and 23 December 2004).

At the tenth ASEAN Summit that took place in November 2004, India and ASEAN adopted a partnership agreement that will increase trade between them to US$30 billion by 2007 from $13 billion in 2004. India is vigorously promoting its 'Look East Policy' (*The Statesman*, 27 November 2004). By 2011 the pact will lead to a free-trade area with five ASEAN members – Brunei, Indonesia, Malaysia, Thailand and Singapore – and by 2016 with the Philippines, Cambodia, Laos, Myanmar and Vietnam also. The agreement will boost trade, investment, tourism, culture, sports and people-to-people contacts. The leaders of these countries also agreed to intensify efforts to combat international terrorism and other transnational crimes such as drug-trafficking, arms-smuggling, human-trafficking, sea-piracy and money-laundering.[5]

India also wants to improve relations with China, a potential regional superpower. The challenge that India faces *vis-à-vis* China 'is to sustain the steady expansion and strengthening of the relationship in diverse fields even as we attempt to together resolve the border issue' (Sibal, 2003). Since economic liberalization began in India and especially since China joined the WTO, the Indian government has become conscious that the two countries may have to compete in many sectors. As noted elsewhere, the Chinese economy is performing better than the Indian economy, partly because the process of economic liberalization began earlier in China. In the twenty-first century both countries are amongst the fastest growing economies in the world. Bilateral trade between India and China in 2003 was around US$5 billion. In June 2003 Prime Minister Vajpayee visited China. His visit was the first by an Indian prime minister in a decade, although the president, K. R. Narayanan, had visited China in May 2000 and the Chinese premier, Zhu Rongji, had visited India in December 2002. The purpose of Vajpayee's visit was to boost trade and investment ties between the two countries and discuss border disputes and terrorism. Vajpayee declared that India gave high priority to relations with China while the then Chinese premier, Wen Jiabao, stated that Vajpayee's visit would have a positive impact on bilateral relations and regional peace and stability (*People's Daily*, 22 June 2003). India and China hoped that bilateral trade would increase to US$10 billion by 2005. Their hopes have been surpassed and in 2004 the burgeoning trade between these two countries touched $13.6 billion (Kondapalli, 2005). India and China have now agreed to boost bilateral trade to $26 billion by 2008. In the past Chinese made goods were not available in India, however, now consumer items like electric fans are flooding the Indian market. Indian IT products have penetrated the Chinese market and India is also training IT personnel in mainland China.

India also gives considerable importance to maintaining and improving relations with Japan. It should be noted that Japan imposed economic sanctions on India after the nuclear tests of May 1998. Bilateral trade between the countries in 2002 was around US$3.5 billion, and in August 2002, they agreed on a global partnership in the twenty-first century. This was followed by Japanese foreign minister Kawaguchi's visit to India during which she spoke of Japan's strategic partnership with India and India's pivotal role in the vision to create a pan-Asian economic area extending from East to South Asia. India's achievements in the software sector and the East Asian countries' achievements in the hardware sector offer opportunities for mutual benefit. India and Japan would also like to be permanent members of the UN Security Council. On 29 April 2005 Prime Minister Koizumi visited New Delhi and signed a joint statement with Prime Minister Manmohan Singh entitled 'Japan-India Partnership in the new Asian era: strategic orientiation of Japan-India global partnership' and issued an action plan under the title 'Eight-fold initiative for strengthening Japan-India global partnership'. Both governments recognize that there is great potential in Indo-Japanese relations. The total volume of trade between them is valued at $4 billion, but the Indian president, Abdul Kalam, believes that it could expand to $20 or even $30 billion by 2010. India is also the largest recipient of Japanese official development assistance (Japan Ministry of Foreign Affairs, May 2005).[6]

Other countries and regions that are important to India include Russia, Europe and the US. The end of the Cold War and the disintegration of the Soviet Union led to feelings of uncertainty and apprehension about losing a traditional ally in the region. During the Cold War years, trade between India and the Soviet Union had also been brisk, and India valued its trading relations with the Soviets. In the area of defence, too, the Soviets were important, first as strategic partners, but also as suppliers of military/defence equipment and hardware, often at concessional rates. Since the Sino-Indian war of 1962 and India's humiliation, India has adopted relatively high defence budgets. The global arms industry is, therefore, important for India, although it does have an indigenous arms industry. Pant comments that 'the most important element of Indo-Russian bilateral relations is, perhaps, the defence ties between the two countries. Not only is Russia the biggest supplier of defence products to India but the India-Russia defence relationship also encompasses a wide range of activity including joint research, design, development and co-production' (Pant, 2004: 8). Moreover, following India's nuclear tests in May 1998, Russia, unlike other nuclear powers, did not impose economic sanctions on India (Ministry of External Affairs, Government of India, 2001: 281). A regular dialogue has been maintained between New Delhi and Moscow since the creation of the Russian federation. Putin's visits to India in 2000, 2002 and 2004 have further consolidated ties between 'two old friends'. During his October 2000 visit to India, President Putin declared that it was in Russia's interest to 'have a strong, developed, independent India that would be a major player on the world scene' (World Socialist Web Site, 25 November 2000). During his December 2002 visit to New Delhi two important declarations were adopted; the Delhi Declaration on Further Consolidation of Strategic Partnership between the Republic of India and the Russian Federation and the Joint Declaration on Strengthening and Enhancing Economic, Scientific and Technological Co-operation between the Republic of India and the Russian Federation. Co-operation and collaboration between India and Russia is ongoing in many sectors including nuclear energy. The Oil and Natural Gas Corporation (ONCG) of India is investing nearly US$1.7 billion in the Russian oilfield Sakhalin-I. This is the highest ever overseas investment by an Indian company. India has acquired a 20 per cent stake in Sakhalin-I. During Putin's visit to India in November 2004 energy co-operation was given considerable importance. The Indian Union petroleum minister, Mani Shankar Aiyar, wants Russia to ensure India's energy security. Russia has offered several investment opportunities to India in Eastern Siberia, Sakhalin-3 and third country ventures in the Caspian oil fields, including Kurmanghazi of Kazakhstan. India's ONGC and Russia's Gazprom are to enter into a strategic partnership to identify routes for the transportation of Iranian, Burmese, Siberian, Caspian and Central Asian hydrocarbon resources to India (indiainfo.com, 28 November 2004).

Europe is one of India's main trading partners and also an important investor of capital in the Indian economy. The strategic partnership between India and the EU 'is based on shared values such as democracy, pluralism and liberalism – all values of open, inclusive societies' (Sibal, 2003: 6). The political relationship between India and the EU has been institutionalized and there is potential for expanding trade and economic co-operation and collaboration between these entities. At Euro 25 billion in 2003, trade between India and the EU is 'far below its potential' according to the Indian government. Ambitious but realistic targets were set at the third India-EU Business Summit in October 2002 at Copenhagen for raising the current level to Euro 35 billion by 2005 and Euro 50 billion by 2008 (Sibal, 2003).

India also maintains bilateral relations with all the countries of Europe. However, India invests more in Britain than in any other European country. The UK attracts about 60 per cent of Indian investment into Europe. India is the eighth largest investor in the UK and the UK is the third largest investor in India. Bilateral trade between India and the UK was worth around £5 billion in 2001. On 6 January 2002 Indian prime minister Atal Bihari Vajpayee and the British prime minister Tony Blair signed the New Delhi Declaration entitled 'India and United Kingdom: Partnership for a Better and Safer World'. They reaffirmed the strength and depth of the bilateral relationship between the two countries. They also pledged to work together to identify and develop new areas of partnership between the two countries 'to the benefit of our peoples, and to help create a better and safer world'.[7] The declaration specifically addressed three areas: peace and security, development and trade and investment.

On 20 September 2004, the new Indian prime minister, Dr Manmohan Singh, and Tony Blair also signed a joint declaration that built on the New Delhi Declaration. The 2004 declaration addressed foreign and defence policy, security challenges, economic and trade issues, science and technology, development partnership, sustainable development and education and culture. Prime Minister Singh and Prime Minister Blair reaffirmed their commitment to strengthening their 'comprehensive strategic partnership for the benefit of both our peoples and the international community based on universal values of democracy and respect for the rule of law, human rights and fundamental freedoms'.[8]

The United States of America is India's largest trading partner. The value of trade between these two countries in 2002 was around US$23 billion in goods and services. The US is also the main destination of India's IT services exports (worth around $5.7 billion in 2002) and a major source of foreign investments.

India believes that the US and India both have a role to play in shaping a new democratic pluralistic world order and that they are 'natural partners'. India and the US have established over fifteen institutional forums that meet regularly. India's relations with the US had suffered a setback after the nuclear tests of May 1998. However, President Clinton's visit to India in March 2000 was clearly meant to convey a positive message to the Indians; the Americans wanted to do business with India. This strengthened relations between the two countries. Since 9/11, security and defence co-operation between the two has also been given a fillip. Areas for dialogue include energy and environment, science and technology, biotechnology and health, information technology and cyber-security, combating terrorism and missile defence. However, the Indian government fully recognizes that the US administration has its own concerns, priorities and perspectives. 'Our approach seeks to deal with these differences in a transparent, positive manner, according to enduring principles of our foreign policy that sought never to define relations with any one country through the prism of any other country or regional equations or alliance systems' (Sibal, 2003). The US, too, is aware that New Delhi has its own concerns and is prepared to collaborate with Washington only when it serves Indian interests. Pollack comments that the US sees 'a long-term strategic opportunity in enhanced ties with New Delhi' (Pollack, 2004). Prime Minister Vajpayee was keen to diversify and deepen Indo-US economic ties.

As India continues to liberalize and modernize, the US sees it as an opportunity to use India to balance Chinese power in Asia (*The Economist*, 2 April 2005). The partnership between India and the US got another boost when Prime Minister Manmohan Singh visited the US in September 2004 and met President Bush. Since January 2004, the two governments have been working closely together to conclude phase one of the Next Steps in Strategic Partnership between India and the United States (NSSP). It is claimed that it will lead to 'significant economic benefits for both countries and improve regional and global security'.[9]

The need to sustain economic growth has led to an emphasis on economic factors in India's relations with other countries and organizations. Self-reliance will not be enough and with the liberalization of the economy new opportunities for trade and investment must be sought. At the same time India's interests must be protected, for example at WTO negotiations, although even here the identification of common concerns and co-operation and collaboration with other countries that have similar concerns is the key to success. India continues to give national security great importance, but is beginning to define it more broadly. With the end of the Cold War bipolarity has ended and the US has emerged as the world's sole superpower. However, India is opposed to unipolarity as it could become a form of imperialism and in favour of a multipolar order. It is conscious of its size and other assets and aspires to be one of the poles of the multipolar world that it envisages.

Notes

1. The Pandavas and the Kauravas were two rival clans that fought the war in *Mahabharat*, an epic written by Sage Veda Vyasa.
2. Sir Creek is a disputed boundary and Bagliar is a hydroelectric dam that India has decided to build in Kashmir. The decision has led to a water-sharing dispute between Indian and Pakistan.
3. Website of the NAM available at www.nonaligned.org.
4. Available at http://indianembassy.org/policy/Foreign_Policy/2004/AR2004.htm.
5. Available at www.digantik.com/Digantik/ntlaseanmeetdec7.htm.
6. Available at www.mofa.go.jp/region/asia-paci/india/pmv0504/summary.html.
7. Available at www.number-10.gov.uk/output/page3364.asp.
8. Available at www.indianembassy.org/press-release/2004/sep/17.htm.

References

Asthana, V., 1999, *India's Foreign Policy and Subcontinental Politics*, Kanishka Publishers, New Delhi.

Bajpai, K., 2001, 'Through a looking glass: strategic prisms and the Pakistan problem', *IIC Quarterly*, Monsoon, Issue: Relocating Identities.

Bandyopadhyaya, J., 1991 (second edn), *The Making of India's Foreign Policy*, Allied Publishers, New Delhi.

Chellaney, B., 1998–99, 'After the tests: India's options', *Survival*, Winter.

Dixit, J. N., 1998, *Across Borders – Fifty Years of India's Foreign Policy*, Picus Books, New Delhi.

Dubey, M., 1993, 'India's foreign policy in the evolving global order', *International Studies* (New Delhi), 30: 2.

Dutt, S., 2002, 'Indo-Pakistan summit: faltering steps towards peace?', *New Zealand International Review*, January–February.

Dutt, V. P., 1999, *India's Foreign Policy in a Changing World*, Vikas Publishing House, New Delhi.

Gupta, S., 1995, 'India redefines its role', *Adelphi Papers 293*, Oxford University Press for IISS.

Hewitt, V., 1997, *The New International Politics of South Asia*, Manchester University Press, Manchester.

Hill, C., 2003, *The Changing Politics of Foreign Policy*, Palgrave, Basingstoke.

Jha, N. K., 1989, 'Cultural and philosophical roots of India's foreign policy', *International Studies* (New Delhi), 26: 1.

Kapur, H., 1994, *India's Foreign Policy, 1947–92: Shadows and Substance*, Sage, London.

Kapur, H., 2002, *Diplomacy of India – Then and Now*, Manas Publications, New Delhi.

Kegley, C. W. and Wittkopf, E. R., 1999 (seventh edn), *World Politics: Trend and Transformation*, St. Martin's Press, New York.

Kondapalli, S., 2005, 'India and China: seeking common ground, 12 April, available at www.rediff.com/news/2005/apri/12wen2.htm.

Ministry of External Affairs, Government of India, *Foreign Relations of India, Select Statements, January 2000–March 2001*, New Delhi.

Muni, S. D., 1993 'India and its neighbours: persisting dilemmas and new opportunities', *International Studies* (New Delhi), 30: 2.

Nehru, J., 1961, reprinted 1969, *The Discovery of India*, Asia Publishing House, Bombay.

Pant, H. V., 2004, 'Indo-Russian ties', *The Statesman*, 20 December.

Paranjpe, S., 1998, 'India's security policy', *International Studies* (New Delhi), 35: 2.
Pollack, J. D., 2004, 'The United States and Asia in 2003', *Asian Survey*, January/February.
Rajan, M. S., 1993, 'India's foreign policy: the continuing relevance of nonalignment', *International Studies* (New Delhi), 30: 2.
Rajan, M. S., 1998, 'The goals of India's foreign policy', *International Studies* (New Delhi), 35:1.
Saez, L., 2004, 'India in 2003: pre-electoral manoeuvering and the prospects for regional peace', *Asian Survey*, January/February.
Seth, S., 1993, '"Nehruvian socialism," 1927–1937: Nationalism, Marxism, and the Pursuit of modernity', *Alternatives*, 18.
Shivam, R. K., 2001, *India's Foreign Policy: Nehru to Vajpayee*, Commonwealth, New Delhi.
Sibal, K., 2003, 'Indian foreign policy: challenges and prospects', presentation at Geneva Forum, 23 January, available at www.meadev.nic.in/speeches/fs_Geneva.html.
Singh, J., 1999, *Defending India*, Macmillan, Basingstoke.
Singh, J., 2000, 'Dimensions of India's foreign policy in the new millennium', School of International Relations of the St. Petersburg State University, 24 June in Ministry of External Affairs, Government of India, *Foreign Relations of India, Select Statements, January 2000–March 2001*, New Delhi.
Natwar Singh, K., Valedictory address at Petrotech – 2005, Vigyan Bhawan, New Delhi, available at www.meaindia.nic.in/speech/2005/01/19ss01.html.
Singham, A. W., 1977, *The Nonaligned Movement in World Politics*, Lawrence Hill & Co., Westport, Connecticut.
Smith, B. C., 1996, *Understanding Third World Politics*, Macmillan, Basingstoke.
Sondhi, M. L. and Nanda, P., 1999, *Vajpayee's Foreign Policy – Daring the Irreversible*, Har-Anand, New Delhi.
10 Downing Street, 'India-UK: towards a new and dynamic partnership', available at www.number-10.gov.uk/output/page6364.asp.
Thakur, R., 1994, *The Politics and Economics of India's Foreign Policy*, Hurst & Co., London; St. Martin's Press, New York.
Wolpert, S., 1993, *A New History of India*, Oxford University Press, Oxford.

Conclusion: beyond globalization

The history of India began a long time ago. The fertile soil of the Indo-Gangetic plains not only attracted wave upon wave of foreign invaders but also gave birth to several civilizations, each one of which contributed to the cultural diversity that we find in India today. Nehru notes: 'The diversity of India is tremendous; it is obvious; it lies on the surface and anybody can see it ... There is little in common, to outward seeming, between the Pathan of the North-West and the Tamil in the far South. Their racial stocks are not the same, though there may be common strands running through them; they differ in face and figure, food and clothing and of course language' (Nehru, 1969: 61). India also exported its diverse culture to foreign lands from Southeast Asia to the British Isles. The agents exporting Indian culture included traders and migrants. Nevertheless, by the end of the nineteenth century an Indian nation had begun to emerge. The Indian nationalist movement had a key role to play in the growth of Indian nationalism; however, there were many factors, both indigenous and foreign, that led to the growth of national consciousness. As Bose and Jalal assert, 'anti-colonialism can be seen now to have been a much more variegated phenomenon than simply the articulate dissent of educated urban groups imbued with western concepts of liberalism and nationalism' (Bose and Jalal, 1998: 107). Nevertheless, underlying the nationalist movement was an Indian identity that had taken shape faced with colonial rule and exploitation. It formed the basis of a national identity. The British Indian state introduced territorial borders that coincided with the boundaries of this national collectivity and modern institutions. However, the process of modernization did not involve basing the colonial state on the democratic will of the people of India. Bose and Jalal write that 'having imported the notion of unitary sovereignty from post-Enlightenment Europe into colonial India to replace pre-colonial India's view of layered and shared sovereignty, the crown raj made certain it stymied any move towards the acquisition of substantive citizenship rights. In colonial India there were to be no citizens, only subjects of the empire and "traditional" princes' (1998: 103).

Globalization involves the interconnectedness of societies. This book has noted the features of contemporary globalization but also argued that earlier phases of globalization were equally significant and instrumental in bringing about a 'global world'. Earlier phases were associated with foreign invasions, trade, imperialism and missionary activity that took place many centuries ago. Later European colonialism, the emergence of a global economy and India's integration into it, and migration from South Asia all led to, on the one hand, a transnational Indian culture, notwithstanding local identities, and on the other a resistance to the trundling juggernaut of globalization that by the twentieth century was seen as western imperialism. India wanted to be independent and embrace universal values but above all it wanted to be recognized as a sovereign state with the same rights as western developed states.

The enshrinement of universal values in the Indian constitution was perhaps the first step towards achieving the democratization of Indian politics. The preamble to the constitution declared that the people of India had 'solemnly resolved to constitute India into a sovereign, socialist, secular democratic republic' and to secure to all its citizens, justice, liberty and equality. The fact that Ambedkar was the chairman of the Drafting Committee that drafted the constitution was significant as he was born a Dalit. His belief that political democracy was meaningless without economic democracy was not based simply on a preference for socialist principles and ideology, but on first-hand experience of the discrimination against and exploitation of people from the lowest castes in Indian society. The fundamental rights guaranteed by the Indian constitution such as the right to equality and the right to freedom were alien values in a caste-ridden society. Even today the Dalits are asserting themselves as the Bhopal Declaration adopted in 2002 shows. It argues that even after fifty-four years of independence the Dalit community is denied of its basic human rights and that concerted action by society as a whole is necessary for their development. The twenty-one-point action plan that was also adopted even calls for the amendment of Article 21 of the constitution of India that deals with Fundamental Rights. These rights should be expanded to include the right to a standard of living adequate for the health and well-being of women and men equally, including food, safe drinking water, clothing, housing, public health and medical care, social security and social services, the right to a living wage and the right to own five acres of cultivable land or to gainful employment.

The dominance of the Congress and the BJP has been challenged by political parties representing the interests of the lower castes and OBCs at the state level. In the late 1990s the United Front was formed and offered an alternative to the Congress and the BJP. However, within two years it had ceased to exist and the political parties that were part of the alliance had defected to either the Congress or BJP. But most of them retained their identity and remained committed to their agenda and ideology. As a result coalition governments have had to be formed and the dominant party cannot afford to ignore their coalition partners. The UPA government formed in the summer of 2004 is dominated by the Congress but supported from outside by the left parties. The latter's views are a valuable contribution to debate in India about economic liberalization and globalization; for example, the views and suggestions of the left parties were taken into consideration in drafting the new Patents (Amendment) Bill 2005.

But caste and class are not the only basis of identity in India. Religious and ethnic identity are equally strong and the former led to the partition of British India in 1947. However, after India became independent religious identity was not taken into consideration in the reorganization of states. Only linguistic identity could form the basis of a new state. Hence Maharashtra, Gujarat and Haryana came into existence. Regional identities are accommodated by granting statehood to geographically contiguous populations that possess a common cultural/ ethnic identity. The number of states has increased to twenty-eight. The newest of which are Jharkhand, Chhattisgarh and Uttaranchal, created in 2000. However, the Indian federation is 'indestructible' and does not allow secession.

Given the strength of state identities, centre-state relations are not always harmonious. It is an issue that has sometimes caused rancour. The constitution had deliberately made the centre stronger than the states to prevent the disintegration of the Indian state. However, this sometimes led to the abuse of power such as the arbitrary dismissal of state governments. The problem was that the political party that was in power at the national level also wanted to be in power at the state level. Economic liberalization may reduce the financial dependence of the states on the central government and promote economic growth.

There have been different phases of globalization that have affected all countries including India. Trade in ancient and medieval times was global and made many kings and kingdoms in India wealthy. The principal traders included the Chinese, the Arabs, the Romans and later the European nations such as the Portuguese, Dutch, France and English. One of the trading companies, the English East India Company laid the foundations of British rule in India in the eighteenth and nineteenth centuries. They also integrated India into the global capitalist system. India's trade and external relations were in foreign hands for almost two centuries. The roots of *dirigisme* lay in the objectives of colonial rule and impacted on the pattern of investment, industrialization and agricultural production even after India became independent. Industrial enclaves had emerged but the integrated industrialization of India had not taken place. The destruction of Indian cottage industries had led to the peasantization of the Indian economy and widespread poverty. When the country became independent planning was introduced to make the best use of the country's resources. Each five-year plan set certain targets. However, the over-riding concern was retaining economic sovereignty. State-led development succeeded in reducing the level of poverty in the country very gradually, but economic growth was not rapid. However, the process of economic liberalization that began in the early 1990s marks the beginning of a new stage in Indian politics.

The Indian government has to maintain a balance between economic liberalization that involves the removal of government controls and barriers to trade, disinvestment, promoting exports, attracting foreign direct investment and creating a climate that is conducive to private investment and other features of economic liberalization on the one hand, and promoting equity and social justice on the other. Growth rates have been good in the post-reform period and especially since 2003. Some Indian industries, such as the TATA group, are doing very well and may soon become multinationals as they are beginning to acquire foreign businesses. However, the Indian government is being cautious. According to the government, 260 million people still live below its poverty line, while according to a DFID report 350 million live on less than US$1 a day, the international poverty line. The Indian government would like to achieve the Millennium Development Goals and has even welcomed foreign assistance in order to do this. Indian foreign policy is also giving considerable importance to economic relations with other states, especially the developed and oil-producing states. It is also promoting good relations with the Indian diaspora for economic self-interest. On the other hand, the general elections of May 2004 confirm that Indian voters are more interested in local and regional issues than in pan-Indian issues. Regional identities continue to be very strong in India. The proliferation of political parties representing different states and regions as well as classes has led to a decentralization of power. Globalization has only served to increase the competition between the states for investment for economic development and this is likely to strengthen regional identities further.

However, globalization is not just about economic liberalization. Global issues have been identified by the international community and international organizations such as the UN. They range from global warming to HIV/Aids, and many of them affect the Indian people. The Indian government's participation in these organization is, therefore, crucial. At the global level, however, it is not just inter-governmental co-operation that is important. Global governance involves the participation of actors at all levels, the local, national, international, transnational and global. Global social movements are also playing an important role in bringing about change. Alternative Indian approaches to development, such as Gandhi's beliefs and values as well as movements inspired by him, contribute to and draw inspiration from these movements; for example, the environmental, women's and Dalit movements. Globalization should not, therefore, be narrowly defined as economic liberalization only. Moreover, as Higgott points out, global governance should not be seen merely as a response to globalization. He writes that 'the global governance agenda has to be widened to address the "justice agenda" in a more overtly political way than has been the case to date. Failure to do so will ensure that global governance will remain inadequate to the task of redirecting resources from the winners of globalization towards the direction of the world's poorest citizens, and globalization will become more, rather than less, contested' (Higgott, 2000: 153).

References

Bose, S. and Jalal, A., 1998, *Modern South Asia*, Routledge, London.
Higgott, R., 2000, 'Contested globalization', *Review of International Studies*, Vol. 26, special issue, December.
Nehru, J., 1969, *The Discovery of India*, Asia Publishing House, Bombay, New Delhi, London, New York.

Index

References for notes are followed by n

accountability 42, 67
Adivasi movement 163, 168–9
Administrative Reforms Commission 59
Afghanistan 17, 206
Africa 185
agriculture 20, 99–100, 108, 116, 140, 144
Akali Dal 62, 89, 95n
Akbar 31–3, 76
Ambedkar, B. R. 79, 85, 163, 216
  constitution 47, 48, 55, 80
  Dalit movement 165, 166
Andaman and Nicobar Islands 48, 144
Andhra dynasty 25–6
Andhra Pradesh 26, 48, 60, 62, 117, 144, 185
Arthashastra 22–3
Arunachal Pradesh 48
Aryans 16, 19, 40n
  economy 20
  political and social organization 19, 21–2
ASEAN 208–9
Ashoka 23
Asia-Pacific region 186–7
Assam 48, 62, 78, 86, 87, 88–9
Aurangzeb 33, 76
Australia 186
Ayodhya 57–8, 64, 81, 83, 91

Babri Masjid mosque 57–8, 64, 81, 83
Babur 30, 31, 58, 76
Bangladesh 178, 200, 207
Bengal 30, 34, 36, 38
Bharatiya Janata Party (BJP) 1, 62, 64–5, 216
  Bharatvarsha 19
  centre–state relations 61
  diaspora 176
  dress 95n
  Hinduism 17
  in Lok Sabha 89, 90–3
  national identity 72–3
  secularism 57, 58
Bharatvarsha 19
bhoodan movement 170
Bhopal Declaration 166, 167, 216
Bihar 25, 34, 35, 48, 53, 68n, 82, 87, 185
  caste system 84
  economy 118, 120, 121
  population 104
  social movements 171, 172
Bombay 34, 86
British rule
  East India Company 34–6
  freedom struggle 39–40
  Indian Civil Service 59
  Indian constitutional development 44–7
  Indian economy 127–34
  Indian mutiny 36–7
  Indian nationalism and Muslim communalism 77–9
  Morley-Minto reforms 38–9
  see also United Kingdom
Buddhism 17, 22, 24, 27, 163
  spread 23, 25, 28, 177
  Turko-Afghan persecution 29

business processing outsourcing (BPO) 146–8

Calcutta 34
Canada 181
capitalism 11–12, 67, 128
Caribbean 184–5
caste system 19, 21–2, 61, 73, 81, 82
  ethnic groups 74–5
  identities 83–5
  political parties 65, 67
  reservation policy 54
  Tamils 26
  untouchability 158, 163, 164–8
centralization 58, 59–61, 71
Chandigarh 48
Chandragupta Maurya 22, 23
Chhattisgarh 44, 48, 87, 217
chief minister 53
China
  diaspora 188
  economic development 99, 101, 103, 120, 139, 141, 146, 153
  education 149
  FDI 149, 150
  pre-colonial India 25, 27–8, 127
  relations with 201, 209
  trade with 151, 152
  war with 108, 138, 196, 200
Chipko *andolan* 171–2
Cholas 26, 127
communication 5, 9
Congress Party 14n, 62–3, 64, 65, 66–7, 170, 216–17
  BJP government and 91–2
  dress 95n
  economic policy 1, 112
  establishment 37–8, 78, 156
  foreign policy 195, 198
  independence 39, 47
  linguistic states 44, 87
  in Lok Sabha 93
  Muslims 82
  national identity 72, 73
  secularism 57
constituent assembly 47–8
constitution 42, 47, 48, 73, 156, 158, 216, 217
  constituent assembly 47–8
  distribution of powers 49–50
  fundamental rights and directive principles 54–6, 196
  national integration 79–81
  nature of federation 58–9
  secularism 56–8
  state government 52–4
  states and territories 48
  union government 50–2
constitutional development 44–7
cultural imperialism 7, 11, 28, 35–6, 87–8
cultural nationalism 64–5, 72–3
culture 10, 16–17, 32

Dadra and Nagar Haveli 48
Dalits 68n, 84–5, 216
  social movement 61, 163, 164–8
Daman 34, 48
debt 60
defence 108–9, 138, 196, 210
Delhi 37, 48, 118, 119
democracy 42–3, 66–7
development 156–9, 173–4, 218
  Gandhi 159–64
  see also economic development
diaspora 176–91
directive principles 55–6, 84, 196
Diu 34, 48
Dravidians 19, 26, 40n
dual citizenship 176, 188–9
Dubai 182
dyarchy 46–7

East Asia 208–10
East India Company 34–6, 37, 127–30
economic development 1, 98, 217–18
  achievements of planning 115–21
  centrally planned economy 105–7
  five-year plans 107–15
  problems holding India back 98–105
economy
  Aryan age 20
  BJP policy 92
  business processing outsourcing 146–8
  emerging opportunities 142–3
  employment opportunities 148–9
  English East India Company 36
  First World War and Great Depression 132–3
  foreign aid and capital 135–7
  foreign investment and domestic infrastructure 149–50

foreign policy 207, 212
growth 6, 66, 144
Indian investment in UK 148
Maurya dynasty 23–4
patents 140–1
redistribution 152–3
reforms 145–6
Second World War 133–4
see also industrialization; trade
education 35–6, 101, 149
electricity 116–17
emigration *see* migration
employment 148–9, 161
environmental problems 9–10, 171–3
ethnicity 71, 73, 74–5, 94–5, 95n
European Union 211

federalism 49, 58–9
Fiji 187
First World War 132
foreign direct investment (FDI) 112, 113, 118, 119, 136–7, 149–50
foreign policy 194–7
   globalization 205
   mandala theory 23
   national security and regional hegemony 200–3
   nonalignment 197–200
   nonalignment and post-Cold War relations 203–5
   in twenty-first century 205–12
forests 171–2
French 34–5
fundamental rights 54–5, 56, 80, 216

Gandhi, Indira 54, 57, 63, 94, 171, 198–9, 200
Gandhi, Mohundas Karamchand 4, 13, 39, 55, 156, 162–3
   Adivasi movement 168–9
   anti-apartheid movement 173, 185
   Dalit movement 164–6
   development 4, 157–62, 218
   Hindus 169–70
   nonalignment 199
GATT 139–40
gay and lesbian movement 173
global governance 8, 157, 218
globalization 1–3, 43, 70, 93, 95, 124–6, 216
   economic development 217–18

environmental problems 172
foreign policy 205
perspectives 5–13
process 126–7
social movements 164
waves 138–9
Goa 34, 48, 61, 118, 200
Government of India Act, 1919 45, 46–7, 67, 78
Government of India Act, 1935 45, 47, 55, 67, 168
governor 52–3
gramdan movement 170–1
Great Mutiny 37
Gujarat 44, 48, 86, 217
   earthquake 179
   economy 60, 118, 119, 130
   Narmada dam 172
   riots 57
Gulf 181–4, 207
Guptas 27

Harijans 79, 158, 165
Harsha Vardhan 28
Haryana 44, 48, 86, 217
health 101, 102
Himachal Pradesh 48, 64, 84, 118, 171
Hindi 32, 81, 87–8
Hinduism 16, 17, 20–1
   BJP 64, 65, 72–3
   under British rule 36, 37
   dress 95n
   Gandhi 169–70
   identity 82
   nationalism 77
   partition 43
   political system 44
   pre-colonial period 21, 27, 28, 29, 30, 33
   revivalism 12, 77
   secularism 57–8
   see also caste system
HIV/Aids 119
Hong Kong 151, 186–7
human capital 101–2
human rights movement 173
Humayun 31
Hyderabad 43

identities 16, 190, 215
   under British rule 77–9

caste system 83–5
   linguistic 86–8
   national 71–3, 215
   religion 82–3, 217
   tribal 85–6
indenture 177–8
independence 40, 43–4, 79, 94
India Act, 1784 44–5
Indian Councils Act, 1861 45, 46
Indian Councils Act, 1892 45–6
Indian Councils Act, 1909 38–9, 45, 46
Indian National Congress *see* Congress Party
Indo-Greeks 24
industrialization 9, 12, 60, 98, 116, 131, 134
   Gandhi 159, 160, 161
   government policy 105–7, 108, 111
Indus Valley Civilization (IVC) 18
inequality 102–3, 118, 152–3
infrastructure 5, 104, 150
insurgency 88–9, 94
internationalism 195
international relations (IR) 7, 70
Iran 207
Iraq 207
Islam *see* Muslim League; Muslims

Jahangir 33
Jainism 22, 27, 163
Jammu and Kashmir 48, 53, 62, 82
   insurgency 88, 89, 94, 206
   see also Kashmir
Janata Dal 62, 64
Japan 131, 151, 209–10
Jayaprakash Narayan movement 171
Jharkhand 44, 48, 86, 87, 168, 169, 217
judiciary 52, 53–4

Kanishka 25
Kanvayana dynasty 25
Karnataka 48, 53, 60, 117, 119, 171
Kashmir 44, 91, 201–2
Kautilya 22, 23
Kerala 24, 48, 60, 104, 120, 144
   migration 181, 183
khadi 159, 161–2
Khan, Sir Syed Ahmad 78
Kushans 24, 25

Lakshadweep 48, 82

languages 16, 32, 33, 40n, 81, 82
   identity and 44, 86–8, 217
Latin America 184
legislatures
   states 53
   see also parliament
lion emblem 24
Lodhis 30
Lok Sabha 50, 51, 52, 62, 66
   eleventh 89–90
   fourteenth 93
   twelfth 90–3

Madhya Pradesh 25, 48, 53, 64, 104, 118
   tribal groups 85, 168
Magadha 25
   see also Bihar
Maharashtra 44, 48, 53, 62, 86, 87, 165, 217
   economy 118, 119, 130
   tribal groups 85, 168
Malaysia 151, 186, 208
Manipur 44, 48, 87, 88, 89
Maurya dynasty 22–4
media 58, 87–8
Meghalaya 44, 48, 85, 87, 88, 89
migration 6, 42, 142
   from Indian subcontinent 176–87
   rural–urban 160
Millennium Development Goals 119–21, 218
mixed economy 105–7
Mizoram 48, 85, 88, 89
Modi, Narendra 57
Mohammad of Ghur 28–9, 75
Morley-Minto reforms 38–9, 46
Mughals 31–3, 34, 76–7
Mukherjee, Gita 65–6
multiculturalism 190–1
multinational corporations (MNCs) 6, 11, 124, 146–8
Muslim League 38, 39–40, 62, 78, 169
Muslims 12
   communalism 77, 78–9
   identity 82–3
   partition 43
   pre-colonial period 28–30, 32, 33, 75–7
   political parties 91

Nagaland 44, 48, 85, 86, 88, 89

Nagas 86–7, 89
Naramada *bachao andolan* 171, 172
national anthem 74
national identity 71–3, 215
National Integration Council (NIC) 81
nationalism 80–1
    cultural 64–5
    Nehru 195
    pre-independence movement 36, 37–8, 39–40, 73, 77–8, 215
national security 90, 102, 195–6, 200–1, 212
    see also defence
nation-state 2–3, 70–1
Nehru, Jawaharlal 215
    Babur 31
    central and state politics 94
    civil service 59
    Congress Party 66
    constitutional development 46, 47
    foreign policy 5, 194–5, 198
    Hinduism 16–17
    independence 71, 156
    industrialization 98, 136
    National Integration Council 81
    Turko-Afghan invasion 29
nonalignment 194, 197–200, 203–5
nuclear weapons 92, 201, 203–4, 210

Orissa 23, 35, 48, 85, 168
    economy 118, 120, 121
Oudh 34

Pakistan 39, 40, 43, 79, 92
    relations with 201–3, 204
    terrorism and 206
    wars with 108, 196, 200
panchayats 55, 66, 158
Pandyas 26
parliament 51–2
    see also Lok Sabha; Rajya Sabha
parliamentary democracy 66–7
particularism 71
patents 140–1
peace movement 173
Persian 32, 33
pharmaceuticals 140, 141
political culture 61–2
political parties 62–6, 67, 216–17
Pondicherry 35, 48, 144

population
    demographic characteristics 103–4
    growth 100–1, 115
Portuguese 34, 200
poverty 13, 16, 56
    government policy 109–10, 115, 117, 152–3
president 50–1
press 58
prime minister 51, 63
Punjab 48, 60, 78, 79, 84, 117, 118
    Akali Dal 59, 62
    British rule 36
    Hindi speakers 44, 86
    insurgency 64, 88, 94
    pre-colonial period 19, 24, 25, 27, 30–1

Rajasthan 25, 48, 64, 168, 172
Rajput dynasties 29
Rajya Sabha 49, 51, 52
Ram Mohan Roy 36, 37
Rao, Narasimha 1, 90, 111, 112, 204
Regulating Act, 1773 44, 45
religion 12, 32, 54, 82
    identities 82–3, 217
    secularism 56–8
    see also Buddhism; Hinduism; Jainism; Muslims; Sikhs
reservation policy 54
Rig Veda 19, 20
Russia 204, 210–11

Sanskrit 19, 40n
Sarkaria Commission 60–1
satyagraha 39, 162, 163, 166
Sayyid dynasty 30
Second World War 133–4
secularism 56–8, 84
Shah Jahan 33
Shakas 24–5
Shiv Sena 62
Shiva, Vandana 12
Shunga dynasty 25
Sikhs 30–1, 36, 57, 62, 95n
Sikkim 48
Singh, Jaswant 43
Singh, Manmohan 1, 59, 203
    economic development 100, 102, 111
    foreign policy 148, 202, 209, 211, 212

social movements 10–11, 13, 163–4,
    170–4
  Adivasis 168–70
  Dalits 164–8
Southeast Asia 185–6
sovereignty 2–3
Soviet Union 199–200, 210
states 48, 217
  government 52–4, 79–80
  nature of federation 58–9
  political parties 62
  relations with centre 59–61
  see also individual states
supraterritoriality 8
Supreme Court 52, 53
Surinam 184, 185
swadeshi 159

Tamil Nadu 48, 60, 62, 144, 185
  economic development 104, 118, 119
  secessionism 81
Tamils 26–7
technological backwardness 103
television 58, 87–8
Thailand 208
tourist industry 17–18
trade 6, 11, 13, 217
  balance-of-payments crisis 111–12
  with China 209
  discriminating protection 133
  end of company rule 130–1
  First World War and Great Depression
    132, 133
  GATT 139–40, 141
  with Japan 210
  mercantilist period and East India
    Company 127–30
  with Pakistan 202
  post-independence 135–6, 137–9
  pre-colonial period 20, 25, 26, 27–8,
    34, 127
  promoting exports 151–2
  social movements 173
  with Thailand 208
  with US 211
trade-related intellectual property rights
  (TRIPS) 140–1
tribal identities 85–6, 168–70
Trinidad and Tobago 184, 185
Tripura 44, 48, 87, 88, 89
Turko-Afghan invasion 28–30, 75

UN Charter 196–7
unemployment 100–1, 161
United Kingdom
  business processing outsourcing 146–7
  development aid 120–1
  Indian investment in 148, 211
  Indians 178–9, 180, 181, 187, 189
  multiculturalism 190, 191
  trade with 151
  see also British rule
United Liberation Front of Asom
  (ULFA) 88–9
United Progressive Alliance (UPA) 56,
  61, 66, 93, 217
United States of America
  Indians 179–81, 188–9
  relations with 205, 211–12
  trade 151
untouchability 27, 79, 81, 83
  constitution 54, 80
  Dalit movement 164–8
  Gandhi 158, 163
urbanization 10, 160
Urdu 32, 76
Uttaranchal 44, 48, 77, 86, 171, 217
Uttar Pradesh 48, 53, 64, 82, 86, 87, 170,
  185
  Chipko andolan 171
  Dalits 85
  economic development 104, 117, 118,
    121

Vajpayee, A. B. 17, 65, 91, 152–3
  foreign policy 92, 201, 202, 206, 209,
    211, 212
  globalization 1–2
Vedas 19, 20
villages 157–8, 159, 160

welfare state 55, 56
West Asia 181–2
West Bengal 48, 60, 82, 84, 85, 87, 130
westernization 11
women 65–6
  Chipko andolan 172
  migration 181, 182–3, 190–1
World Bank 121

EU authorised representative for GPSR:
Easy Access System Europe, Mustamäe tee 50,
10621 Tallinn, Estonia
gpsr.requests@easproject.com

www.ingramcontent.com/pod-product-compliance
Ingram Content Group UK Ltd.
Pitfield, Milton Keynes, MK11 3LW, UK
UKHW042122200326
4879IPUK00002B/27